A SPITFIRE NAMED
CONNIE

A SPITFIRE NAMED CONNIE

LETTERS FROM A NORTH AFRICA ACE
A TALE OF TRIUMPH AND TRAGEDY

AIR MARSHAL 'BLACK' ROBERTSON

FOREWORD BY FIELD MARSHAL
THE LORD WALKER OF ALDRINGHAM GCB CMG CBE

AIR WORLD

AIR WORLD

A SPITFIRE NAMED CONNIE
Letters from a North Africa Ace – A Tale of Triumph and Tragedy

First published in Great Britain in 2022 by
Air World
An imprint of
Pen & Sword Books Ltd
Yorkshire – Philadelphia

ISBN 978 1 39909 903 5

Typeset by SJmagic DESIGN SERVICES, India.

Printed and bound by CPI Group (UK) Ltd, Croydon, CR0 4YY

Pen & Sword Books Limited incorporates the imprints of Atlas, Archaeology, Aviation, Discovery, Family History, Fiction, History, Maritime, Military, Military Classics, Politics, Select, Transport, True Crime, Air World, Frontline Publishing, Leo Cooper, Remember When, Seaforth Publishing, The Praetorian Press, Wharncliffe Local History, Wharncliffe Transport, Wharncliffe True Crime and White Owl.

For a complete list of Pen & Sword titles please contact

PEN & SWORD BOOKS LIMITED
47 Church Street, Barnsley, South Yorkshire, S70 2AS, England
E-mail: enquiries@pen-and-sword.co.uk
Website: www.pen-and-sword.co.uk

Or
PEN AND SWORD BOOKS
1950 Lawrence Rd, Havertown, PA 19083, USA
E-mail: Uspen-and-sword@casematepublishers.com
Website: www.penandswordbooks.com

MIX
Paper from
responsible sources
FSC® C013604

All letters, methinks, should be as free and easy as one's discourse.
Letter to Sir William Temple, Dorothy Osborne, Lady Temple

Sir, more than kisses, letters mingle souls.
Letter to Sir Henry Wotton, John Donne

For my brothers

Contents

Foreword

by Field Marshal the Lord Walker of Aldringham GCB CMG CBE

Those who join our forces have always sought adventure, roving and the off-chance they may be able to lay down their lives for their country. This characteristic was no more apparent than at the start of the Second World War. The prospect of fighting for King and country, for many, caused them enthusiastically to seek early enlistment. Those who yearned to fly with the Royal Air Force, with the special skills needed, were undoubtedly attracted by the compelling, even glamorous, nature of the of the Service as a whole and not least its iconic Spitfire. The reality of the long war inevitably dampened the initial fervour but was replaced by a powerful determination to defeat the enemy.

As the war dragged on, so too did the need for those involved to know that their home fires were burning brightly. This is the story of one man's war; told through his letters to girlfriend, fiancée and then wife, with the courtship developing and establishing itself over the five or so years of conflict. They are a remarkable and prolific record of the feelings and sentiments, of the highs and lows, of the frustrations and triumphs and of the failures and successes in one couple's survival of wartime conditions both at home and in battle.

The letters themselves bring an authenticity to the narrative which portrays life more widely during the war. Some 77 years after its end, they bring into sharp focus the many events that were peculiar to that war. The strong bonds of friendship developed instantaneously in danger; the sadness at the far too early death of someone close; the absence of things taken for granted in peacetime; the speed at which plans changed and changed again; and the stoic nature that the people of our country demonstrated throughout. They make a powerful story.

Introduction

The genesis of this book was belated realisation that I hadn't done my father full justice in *Fighters in the Blood*, the interwoven stories of our contrasting RAF careers. At the time I thought there 'was no more that need, or indeed that could, be said'. On reflection, and in light of further material that came available, I was wrong. He deserved a story all his own.

No sooner had work begun on setting matters right, on 18 December 2019, than brother John reminded me that it was twenty years to the day since our father died. Not only that, in a couple of days it would be seventy-seven years since he was shot down in Tunisia. A more propitious omen would have been hard to imagine. Within a week there was further encouragement, if not to right a wrong then certainly to compensate for previous omissions. John had finally unearthed Father's flying log book, missing in action for several years. Some seven months later, just as the first draft neared completion, he made a similarly helpful discovery: a small hessian, draw-string bag marked with Father's name and initials. Never before opened, it appeared originally amongst Mother's effects, but had again been temporarily mislaid. Inside were nearly fifty letters brought back from North Africa: a couple from his fiancée, some from his mother and the rest from various friends.

These latest discoveries, together with individual diaries and a compendium of more than 300 of Father's wartime letters that came to light only when his wife of more than half a century died in 2007, helped fill some of the gaps in the story of his short career. The letters themselves had lain untouched, carefully preserved in their original envelopes, for over seventy years. Most of the envelopes were numbered consecutively in date order, some franked with entreaties such as 'GROW MORE FOOD – DIG FOR VICTORY', others – small, brown, flimsy and headed, 'On His Majesty's Service' – misappropriated in what almost certainly amounted

INTRODUCTION

to an abuse of privilege on Father's part. But such things, even if they were noticed, tended to be overlooked in wartime.

This, then, is the background to this prequel to *Fighters in the Blood*. Reference to a wealth of new information makes it possible to paint an intimate and authentic picture of life, love and loss in a bygone era: an age of innocence when language was restrained, when emotions were understated, and when relationships fused in the cauldron of conflict were all too often severed in the brutality of battle.

GAR
Cheltenham
January 2022

Chapter 1

20 December 1942, Souk-el-Khemis, Tunisia

A crashing sound filled the cockpit. It was accompanied by an enormous thump. He'd no idea what happened. All he knew was pain. There was blood everywhere and he could see nothing out of his right eye. Some 1,500 feet above the North African scrub, there was no time for calm evaluation of the situation. *I need to put this thing on the ground – and quickly too.* Lowering the wheels wasn't an option, but that didn't concern him. The Spitfire was a pretty rugged aircraft and the ground looked reasonably level, although it would be tacky after the recent rain. There could be the odd rock around too – the least of his problems in the circumstances. *Just land, will you – this really hurts!*

Fighting immense pain, and with his vision further impaired by a damaged windscreen – he'd been hit by an explosive shell – he saw his speed reducing below 180 knots. *Way too fast – no time to worry though.* But some actions were still automatic: propeller to fine pitch, mixture to rich, flaps . . . *What about flaps? Select down – still much too fast. No matter – anything to relieve the agony.* The ground rushed up to meet him. It was just a blur as his ears filled with the sound of rending metal.

And then it was over. He careened to a halt incredibly quickly, or so it seemed. Then came a further surprise. Pilot Officer 'Robbie' Robertson found himself staring out where the nose of his aircraft should have been – but there was nothing there. It was canted way off to the left. Amazed that he'd survived his crash-landing, the next task was to put distance between himself and what was left of his aircraft. Still racked with pain, he had the presence of mind to check that the magneto switches and fuel cock were turned off – actions that would have become second nature over the eighteen months or so he'd been flying Spitfires – although he'd no recollection whatsoever of performing them.

Releasing the hood and opening the cockpit door, Robbie managed to drag his bruised and battered body out of the wreckage. It proved a difficult exercise but he had a considerable incentive – and not just the risk of fire. He'd heard too many stories about German aircraft strafing downed crews on the ground. Somehow he managed to crawl just a few yards from the wreckage before he finally collapsed. The last thing he remembered before passing out amongst sparse, wispy vegetation at Souk-el-Khemis was glancing at his wristwatch; it showed 1640 – twenty minutes to five.

With no idea how long he'd lain there, he was woken by the sound of an engine. Opening his one good eye he could just make out the shape of an approaching vehicle. His body may have been in poor shape but Robbie's brain was still functioning, at least after a fashion. He knew that he couldn't have been there long because it was still just about light and sunset wasn't until around 1730 that Sunday. This sort of information was second nature to those who flew the evening patrols, a precaution against the Luftwaffe's regular dusk attacks on the airstrip at Souk-el-Arba. Once his vision cleared enough for him to identify the source of the engine noise, he was relieved to see that it was a British army lorry. It came to a halt still some way off. A soldier jumped out and edged cautiously towards him, rifle at the ready. Robbie gave what he hoped was a friendly wave. *That's all I need now – shot by my own side!* Persuaded that the injured pilot was in fact British, a couple of soldiers eased him up onto the back of their truck. It would be the last thing he remembered for some time.

Chapter 2

1 September 1939, Plaistow, East London

In the years before the Second World War Plaistow United Swimming Club, founded in 1920, developed into one of the country's best; in 1936 it supplied five members of the English Olympic water polo team. For the 21-year-old Ron Robertson, a competitive swimmer and water polo player living in nearby Manor Park, the Club's headquarters at the Romford Road Baths was the obvious place to spend his leisure time. Little wonder, then, that what first caught his eye about a raven-haired schoolgirl, Connie Freeman, was her style in the pool, arms moving with the elegance of a ballerina as they brushed the side of her head in a steady backstroke rhythm. It came as no surprise to learn that her ambition was to become a sports mistress – provided she passed her School Certificate Examination.[1]

The extent of any early mutual attraction between the pair was limited, certainly initially, by two factors: a six-year age gap and the few opportunities they had to meet outside the confines of the pool. Their friendship was in its infancy when, like other relationships within that coterie of like-minded youngsters, it was thrown into turmoil by the outbreak of the Second World War. On 1 September 1939 Operation PIED PIPER, the government's evacuation scheme, began in earnest. Its aim was to move civilians out of areas thought to be at greatest risk of involvement in the coming conflict, in particular major cities like London, seen as prime targets for any German bombers. It was an immense undertaking. Over the course of the first three days 1.5 million people were moved. In England alone, 673,000 unaccompanied schoolchildren, 406,000 mothers with young children and 3,000 expectant mothers were relocated to rural areas deemed to be less at risk. For the 15-year old Connie, evacuation meant a move from her parents'

---

1. The School Certificate Examination was usually taken at 16. Performance in each subject was graded as Fail, Pass, Credit or Distinction. Students had to gain six passes, including English and mathematics, to obtain a certificate. A 'matriculation exemption' required at least a Credit in five subjects, including English, mathematics, science and a language.

home, in Woodford, to Brentwood, a dozen or so miles further to the east of London. It would be the first of several temporary homes dictated by these strange new circumstances.

At the time Ron was working for a London insurance company, the Ocean Accident & Guarantee Corporation Ltd, based in Moorgate. And there he remained. Poorly paid he may have been, but he thought himself lucky to have a job at all at a time when both money and employment were in relatively short supply. For him evacuation, although not entirely unexpected, meant the severing of everyday links with a number of close friends, not least the round-faced young swimmer to whom he found himself strangely attracted. Thus began an eight-month period of relative inactivity that became known as the 'phoney war'. It was a period of frustration for a young man whose ambition had long been to join the RAF. Six months earlier he'd applied and been accepted, subject to passing a medical examination. But, despite pestering the RAF recruiters with regular letters, he'd heard nothing more. Apparently there weren't enough doctors available to carry out all the required examinations.

Just how much the resultant irritation contributed to Ron's decision to begin a lengthy correspondence with Connie will never be known. But it's clear, even from those early days, that there was a certain spark in their relationship. This much, and a good deal more, can be gleaned from the evidence that remains. Save for a few notable exceptions – including Connie's 1942 diary, his own for 1943 and 1945, and a brief correspondence with his mother – it's mainly Ron's letters, some sixty transcribed pages of his taped recollections and his log book around which this story unfolds.

His first note to Connie was written a month or so after war began. Together with its immediate successors, it lays the foundations of a romance that was eventually to flourish – initially against the background of his friendship with another young woman! These early letters also hint at the effects of the phoney war and begin to chart Ron's progress towards the eventual realisation of his RAF ambitions.

Save for occasional minor corrections, the edited extracts that follow remain faithful to the original texts; in the interests of brevity, and to avoid repetition, salutations have generally been omitted.

8 October 1939:

I hope this letter reaches you . . . I don't know whether you've heard much about what's happening down here – there's not much to tell but I thought you might like to know we haven't forgotten you . . .

My two brothers have been evacuated to Swindon so we went down to see them two Sundays ago. They're very lucky with their 'digs' – I hope you are . . .

By the way – my romance is all off – my little Betty decided she liked someone else about a month ago – so I'm all alone again. She's written to me since then however, and asked me to have a day off on Friday next & go out with her. I don't know what the idea is but I'm going anyway . . .

I don't think there's anything else I can tell you at the moment but if you'd like to have a letter from me now and again drop me a line & I will forthwith put pen to paper.

And so it begins . . .

15 October 1939:

Your many-paged epistle came last week, for which many thanks. When I think of the short time you have to answer all your fan-mail I think myself doubly lucky to get such a manuscript . . .

By the way – do you get much free time? Only I've got a few days due to me – and can't think of anything to do with them and thought I might come down and take you somewhere or other? Don't think from the sound of this that I'm doing it because I've got nothing else to do – but I'd like to see you again.

I've had a letter from the RAF telling me to enlist at some recruiting office. It will probably be months before anything happens to my application but I'm going to enlist some time next week. I've told you – I'm due to be conscripted in January and I don't fancy peeling potatoes and scrubbing floors as I'm afraid I'll have to if I manage to get dumped in some darn infantry regiment . . . the last thing I want to be is a foot-slogger.

I saw Betty on Friday – but alas! – all is really over this time. We had quite a good time together – but she doesn't like me enough to carry on – so I told her that in that case I thought it would be better if we didn't write to each other anymore. She didn't like the idea but agreed in the end.

22 October 1939:

I suggested coming down because I thought you might get time off in the week . . . I don't want to barge in on anybody else but if you're not having anyone see you next Saturday or Sunday I could easily see you then . . .

By the way – I don't have to enlist after all. I had another letter from the RAF – telling me my application would be dealt with in the usual way and if I was ever conscripted I had to show a letter (they enclosed it) to whoever was in charge of the signing-on business – so I don't get conscripted!

25 October 1939:

I've been making enquiries about coaches etc. . . . so should be at this 'Yorkshire Grey' place about 1.45 – will this be O.K.?

There's a train which leaves Manor Park at 1.30 & arrives at Brentwood at 2.5 – so I can catch that if I miss the coach, I'll make certain about the coach though – so be at the 'Y.G' about 1.45 & I'll alight complete with gas-mask (which, by the way, I'm fed up carrying!) . . .

By the way, tell old Mrs J. you won't be in for your tea. Do you have to get in early?

A few words of explanation are warranted here. 'Mrs J.' was Connie's landlady, the first of many in the early months of the war. Turning to the note below, before she was evacuated to Brentwood, Connie's home wasn't far from where Ron lived with his parents and two younger brothers, Alan and Neil. This explains his familiarity with the Freemans' Woodford home, evident in a letter that reinforces his growing affection.

31 October 1939:

By the way – I saw an awfully nice photo on the mantelpiece – your mother said you had it taken on your own one day – do you know the one I mean? – anyway – have you got another like it? Think how it would cheer me up when I awoke if I had it stuck on my dressing table!

9 November 1939:

I was awfully pleased to get another letter from you – I knew you'd be in rather a flurry what with your moving and dashing about in general. Your billet sounds a lot better than the last one – especially the bath . . .

I can't see why you don't like that photo – I think it's awfully good.

Have you been able to go to the Romford Baths yet? I went to our baths on Wednesday, about 5.30 – there was only one chap in there, Mitchell – we swam about and jawed quite a bit about the war. It's awful the way everybody talks of this bally war – it quite gets on your nerves – still – I suppose we have to put up with it though . . .

I don't know when I shall be able to see you again (that is if it's OK with you) – as I'm rather broke at the moment but if no-one's coming down in about a fortnight's time I'd like to come down again. I thoroughly enjoyed my last visit. If you don't have to go shopping on Saturday mornings now perhaps I could come down for the day . . .

P.S. I've just thought – we could go to Romford Baths if I came on a Sat. morning, couldn't we? Have you got your costume down there?

Three years later, almost to the day, the swimmer Ron mentions here, Plaistow stalwart Bob Mitchell (a past Cambridge captain and English international who later joined the RAF), would play a key role in the pair's story – albeit unwittingly and in absentia.

14 November 1939:

I've got into the habit of looking for your letters so I was awfully pleased to get your latest . . .

You certainly seem to be having a far better time at your new billets or billet than you had at the other . . .

I've worked out that my next Saturday off is the 9th Dec. which seems a long way off – I'll see what can be arranged at the office – which Saturday do you think you could manage? Do many of your relations come down now? It's a pity you can't leave Brentwood – because this means that you can't go swimming – what a pity!

I haven't seen Mr & Mrs Lunn for about 3 wks so I can't tell you much about what's happening here. I did speak to Dorothy for about five minutes on Friday – she & Ron went to see Stanley & Livingstone & apparently they both enjoyed it – I'll try & dig up some news for you before I write again.

I had a letter from Betty the other day – according to that – I could probably go back and everything would be as it was before, but I don't think that would work – besides I've got other ideas, I wrote and told her today.

The Lunns and their daughter Dorothy (aka 'Dolly') mentioned here go on to become a regular feature of this correspondence; they lived close to

Ron's home. He visited them regularly and got on particularly well with Dorothy's father, a Plaistow committee member. However, Mr & Mrs Lunn's attitude towards their daughter's boyfriend, Ron Hawkey (another Plaistow swimmer), could not have been more different. Dorothy's mother in particular could barely disguise her antipathy.

20 November 1939:

As I'm as broke as blazes, (hence the fact that the stamps I said I'd send haven't arrived – although they will in due course) I don't see how I can manage this Saturday – much as I'd like to . . .

It's been decided that in order to keep the club [Plaistow] together a supper is to be held each month . . . I don't think I'll go – as neither you nor young Dorothy will be there – & I'm not awfully impressed with the remaining club members . . .

I had a letter from Betty today – we're supposed to be meeting on Friday week to have tea & so forth. I don't know whether the old business is going to start all over again – I can't make up my mind whether I want to start all over again – very worrying for me – you've no idea!

I think – if you're not having anyone else down – that I'd like to come down on the 9th Dec. It's my Saturday off . . . Of course – if you've anything you'd rather do let me know – I don't know how the idea strikes you? Have you thought of getting a job yet? Half the girls in our place are getting married and then coming back to work at the Ocean. They'll only remain until after the war's over though.

P.S. Just found <u>one</u> stamp which I attach.
P.P.S. It's an 'Ocean' stamp.

26 November 1939:

I hope you didn't think that stamp was the only one you're going to get. It just happened that I had an odd one so I attached it to my letter.

Tomorrow is the great day! For the first time this month we shall be paid. What a glorious sensation! Tinkling silver and crisp crinkling notes. I'll send some stamps as soon as I see some real money again.

By the way, I had to change my plans re Betty rather rapidly the other day. I went round to have lunch with my uncle and he told me that they'd arranged to see the Crazy Gang on Friday and had bought me a ticket. I had to rush off and phone Betty & arrange to see her on Thursday.

Are you doing anything this Saturday? It's not my Saturday off but I expect I could leave pretty early, then we could tootle about in the afternoon.

Let me know if this is OK & also whether you want anything brought down.

Is the Maylands Golf Course the one next to an aerodrome? If it is, I know it quite well – I've been to the 'drome with a friend of mine. From what I gather, the pilots have to be very careful not to decapitate golfers & horse-riders who seem to infest the edge of the landing-field . . .

30 November 1939:

This is just a note to let you know that I understand about Saturday . . . I expect I'll see you next Friday at club – I told Dorothy you'd be coming up so she'll be able to talk to you. I can just imagine what a noise there's going to be when you meet. I don't suppose anyone else will be able to get a word in edgeways.

3 December 1939:

There seems to be quite a lot to tell you since my last short note.

To begin with – on Thursday I met Betty at Ealing and we started off by having tea – then went to see Dodge City which I'd already seen so as soon as we saw that we came out and left the other picture. We happened (quite accidentally believe it or not) to reach a park which was open, although it was pitch dark and about 8 o'clock. Anyway we entered the park and began what turned out to be a great discussion. Apparently she thought it would be a good idea if we started to go out together again. Well – much to my amazement I found myself telling her that she was about as stable as a jellyfish and couldn't be trusted etc. etc. I wasn't really annoyed but I thought I'd better tell her how I felt about things. Anyway, she agreed with all I said about her and after that we parted quite good friends – I'm rather glad it's over though . . .

I've got to go and sign on on Saturday afternoon between 4-5 so it looks as if I shall be in the Air Force soon – I hope.

At last, three months after the outbreak of war, there are signs that Ron's transition from City worker to aspiring RAF pilot is about to begin. However, things don't go quite according to plan.

Chapter 3

20 December 1942, No. 1 CCS (Casualty Clearing Station), Tunisia

C oaxing his dusty vehicle carefully away from the Spitfire's wreckage, initially there were no tracks to guide the army driver but he sensed he was heading in the right direction. He knew it wasn't far to the nearest field medical facility. He needed to get his unexpected passenger there just as soon as he could; he didn't like the look of his injuries.

Night had fallen by the time the lorry arrived at No. 1 CCS. It mattered not. Medical support was available round the clock; like war, it was a twenty-four-hour operation. Cleaning up the mess that was the pilot's face – matted blood, numerous cuts and scratches plus the beginnings of severe bruising – the receiving team decided on an immediate operation. After stitching up a deep gash across Robbie's forehead, the duty surgeon did his best to dig out the shrapnel embedded in the right side of his temple and around his eye; however, he made no attempt to remove the pieces embedded in the eye itself. Once he woke up, and with a somewhat macabre sense of humour, Robbie asked if he could keep the metalwork as a souvenir. More than happy to oblige, the doctor returned soon afterwards with an envelope containing nine or ten fragments, evidence of a head-on encounter with a German fighter, assumed at the time to be a Messerschmitt (Me) 109.[2]

In considerable pain, heavily sedated and barely able to see, Robbie was only vaguely aware of the passage of time. All he knew was that at some stage during the day following his accident he was bundled into another lorry. There he spent the next several hours in considerable discomfort, inwardly cursing the driver. *Bloody ambulance drivers ought to be shot – they drive like it's the North Circular!* Not only was he still in severe pain,

---

2. Consistent with Robbie's log book and wartime terminology, the 'Me' prefix is used for the Me 109 and Me 110 throughout. Latterly 'Me' became less common for Messerschmitt aircraft and was replaced by 'Bf', the official Luftwaffe designation that reflected the aircraft's Bayerische Flugzeugwerke (BFW) origins.

with each lurching movement of the rattling chassis he found himself wondering whether he was about to experience another crash. Like him, such roads as there were needed the sort of tender loving care that was notable only by its absence.

Eventually he was manhandled into what appeared to be a slightly better-equipped casualty station, No. 19 CCS. Here, after having his right eye bathed in what was to become a daily ritual, he spent an uncomfortable night drifting in and out of consciousness. Later the next day he was sufficiently aware to realise it was Connie's birthday. His fiancée would be 19 on 22 December. How on earth was he going to tell her about all this? For the moment, though, it didn't matter. Even had he the wherewithal, he couldn't see well enough to write. Everything around him seemed blurred, an impression that extended to the sounds of activity in what appeared to be some kind of ward. All he could think of was Connie, how much he missed her, and how he wished he were with her once again rather than . . . *rather than what?* He wasn't quite sure what was happening, in part because there was more than a whiff of disorganisation about the environment in which he found himself. His only consolation was that things seemed to be worse for the 'other ranks'. For a moment he counted himself lucky to be an officer. It was an unworthy thought, he knew. But he excused himself on the grounds that he was still in colossal pain.

As his mind wandered, Robbie began to develop another thought. Irrational it may have been, but it didn't seem so at the time: he'd let people down, most of all his fiancée. It was an idea that refused to budge, even when, together with a number of other bed-bound patients, he was transferred next morning to an ambulance train. His destination was the 84th General Hospital at Souk Ahras, in north-east Algeria, close to the Tunisian border.

Chapter 4

5 December 1939, Manor Park, East London

on's hopes of an early call-up are proving increasingly forlorn, or so it seems. Meanwhile, for a man clearly developing an increasing fondness for the schoolgirl with whom he's now corresponding regularly, it remains something of a mystery why he refers so often to his dealings with any number of other young ladies. It's no surprise that Connie eventually reacts, albeit not until well into the new year.

5 December 1939:

I'm awfully sorry I missed you when you came up. It will be quite some time before I get another chance, I'm afraid, especially with Christmas coming . . .

Apparently the Betty business wasn't as successful as I imagined. After I told her just what I thought about her she rang me up yesterday & said 'had I forgotten I was going to take her out before I went abroad?' Well – I said 'No' – but as I probably won't go till about March I said she wouldn't see me for some time. She then said that wasn't soon enough & was going to write to me. I haven't had a letter yet but what can I do about it? . . .

11 December 1939:

I only imagined that I'd be away by March, but as they don't seem to be in any hurry to call people up for the RAF I may not go until much later. In any case, if I'm accepted as a pilot I should be in training for four months before I was sent anywhere. Under the new scheme I should spend part of that time in Canada, which seems rather a pleasant thought at the moment.

I'm glad you're able to get home for Christmas – it will certainly make a change for you. Have you thought anymore about getting a job? . . .

I hope I'm able to see you when you come up – I may have an extra day at Christmas.

By the way – I won't need your assistance with Betty after all. I wrote, after she wrote on Saturday, telling her that what I said on that Thursday still goes & I didn't want anything else to do with her. She sounded quite peeved when she rang me up today – still, I expect she'll get over it. It's only her pride that's hurt a bit . . .

. . . Mum & I had quite a long talk before I went to sign on on Saturday . . . I said I was going to join the infantry & try and get a commission if I failed the medical exam for a pilot.

It was finally decided that I should try & get into the RAF in any capacity, with the hope of transferring to a pilot if the occasion arose. I shall feel awful if I'm not a pilot in the end. By this time I suppose you're rather fed up with the war & the talk about it, so I'll say cheerio for the time being.

17 December 1939:

I was only playing about when I asked whether you were going to knit for me – but I'd be awfully pleased if you did manage to. Since when has your mother evinced a desire to knit for me? It's a nice thought, though, you can tell her when you write again.

I went down to the club on Friday for the first time for months . . . Dorothy was doing her little paddle up & down – she can do back crawl better than front crawl at the moment. It's easy to see she's terribly pleased to get back to it again . . .

My uncles & I were going out on the Friday before Christmas but I don't think we are now – so I'll be down at club to see you. In any case I expect I'll see you once or twice before you go back.

3 January 1940:

I went round to see the Lunn family on Saturday & was staggered to hear that Dorothy contemplates getting engaged to Ron before he has to join up. Mr and Mrs aren't at all pleased about it – but don't for Heaven's sake mention it . . . In any case I doubt very much if anything will happen before Ron goes.

This conscription is getting quite a business, isn't it? It was pretty obvious, though, that everyone would have to be called up sooner or later and this method saves time . . .

I went out with Betty last Monday but I'm afraid I wasn't very thrilled. We went to the Regal, Marble Arch and saw James Stewart & Jean Arthur in Mr Smith Goes to Washington or something like that. I'm not sure whether the title is correct but it was quite good anyway . . .

7 January 1940:

Little Betty thinks she's got a crush on me again and asked to me to go to Sadler's Wells on Jan 13th to see Madam Butterfly, but as I've already seen it and think my uncles are coming over that week-end I politely declined. She sounded rather peeved on the 'phone but I expect she'll get over it.

I took Joyce out again on Saturday & we had quite a time.

Our Public Liability dept. or rather, some members of it, are arranging a supper & dance on Feb 8th & I've been asked to go. On the off-chance I asked a girl in another dept. on the same floor as mine, to go with me. I was very surprised when she agreed, as she's been engaged for about a year. She's awfully nice though, blonde and all that sort of thing. I'll bet there won't half be some dirty linen washed in public after that night out . . .

I know it's a long way ahead but my next Saturday off but one (the next one is Jan 20th & I'm broke) is on Feb 10th. If you haven't anything special on I thought perhaps I might come down & you could flood my ears with Brentwood propaganda. Still – we can talk of this nearer the day.

I'm glad you enjoyed yourself on Wednesday – I did – immensely.

11 January 1940:

First of all, let me thank you for all the knitting you did on my behalf . . .

I shall be quite sorry to leave the office now. Ever since the war started people have been getting much more together & everyone seems to want to help the other. I suppose it's because no-one knows how long we'll all be together on such terms & so wants to make the best of their time. It seems a pity that it took a war to bring things to such a pitch.

5 DECEMBER 1939, MANOR PARK, EAST LONDON

I still haven't heard a word from the Air Ministry about being called up, although the two chaps who had to sign up with me (not for the RAF) have been asked to go pretty soon – I don't want to stay if everyone else goes. Don't send me my mittens – keep them until I go – I'll be sure to come and see you before I actually leave . . .

16 January 1940:

I had an awfully good weekend, as I told you, my uncles came over, so on Saturday we all went for a swim in the afternoon. The pool was nearly empty – we thoroughly enjoyed it. At night we all popped to a local pub to gather in some bottles & then proceeded home to empty them. We just sat around the fire & talked, which as you know, is one of my favourite pastimes . . .

I managed to listen to Madam Butterfly before we went swimming on Saturday. It brought back old memories of Sadler's Wells – so much that I feel I must go as soon as we're paid again. . . .

Alan went back to Swindon on Monday – he wasn't very keen on it, poor kid . . .

22 January 1940:

I still haven't heard anything re the RAF but that little blonde girl I told you about said that if I'm called up before that supper-dance on Feb the 8th she'll come out with me before, so things aren't so bad, after all.

28 January 1940:

You seem to be having quite a cushy time lately don't you? What with coming home at odd week-ends. Do you think you'll be able to come to the next Plaistow supper? . . .

Are you still bound to keep within the confines of Brentwood on Saturdays – only as I've told you – I've got the 10th Feb off – which is Saturday week & I thought if you weren't coming home or going anywhere I could possibly help you spend an hour or two somewhere. Although don't say you'll come if there's anything else you're likely to be doing . . .

9 February 1940:

I'll catch the 1.30 from Manor Park which arrives at Brentwood at 2.6 pm so if you're there about then all will be well.

By the way, do you have to get home as early as you used to? . . .

P.S. I had a marvellous time last night!

12 February 1940:

Staggering news! I popped into Mrs Lunn's on Saturday evening & was told that Dorothy and Ron contemplate getting engaged. They'd got as far as looking for a ring & although D. has told Mr & Mrs, Ron hasn't said a word. I don't know what's going to happen when he asks for parental consent – although they seem to have given up trying to convince Dorothy that he's not the one for her. I can't actually make out whether they're engaged now or when they get the ring, so please don't congratulate Dorothy until I tell you.

Having got that off my chest there's nothing else of any great interest, except I enjoyed seeing you again . . .

I'm enclosing those snaps you asked for. Take any you please because I can always get copies done.

19 February 1940:

I hear you carried on a running conversation with Mr Lunn on Saturday. I thought he'd tell you, but as he didn't, the great glory devolves up to me. Miss Dorothy Lunn became engaged to Mr R. Hawkey on Wednesday 14th Feb., so you can congratulate her with impunity . . .

I'm afraid that, although they reluctantly gave their consent to Dorothy's engagement, both Mr & Mrs hope that nothing comes of it.

When Ron brought D. home on Saturday Mrs Lunn actually spoke to him but she breathed a great sigh of relief when he left, so you can imagine that things aren't as pleasant as they might be.

25 February 1940:

Now that the engagement worries are over & Ron has more or less (mostly 'less') been accepted as one of the Lunn family there's no news worth telling. I hope to let you have something next week though, because we get paid next Tuesday & so I'm going to ask Yvonne to come out again. I hope she's not doing anything on Saturday. If she does come out I'm afraid it will have to be the last time. If I took her out again I'm sure I'd fall for her & that certainly wouldn't get me anywhere – it would be like loving a typhoon. I don't know whether I told you but a friend of mine joined the RAFVR [Royal Air Force Volunteer Reserve] *just before me, (the one who showed me over Maylands Aerodrome) has just been told he's got to report at Uxbridge RAF Station on Friday, so I hope that I shall go in a couple of months' time, or sooner if I can manage it . . .*

I forgot to tell you that the chap who has to report to Uxbridge has fallen violently in love with some girl (I've seen the photo & I must say I don't blame him) and now doesn't want to go, although he was terribly keen at first. He'll probably get engaged before he goes – but I hope that nothing like that happens to me, for various reasons.

3 March 1940:

As we were paid last week (I'm nearly broke again, already), I made up my mind to go out with Yvonne on Saturday . . .Well – it so happened that Yvonne and various girls from the office were going out that Saturday – so it was arranged that next Saturday would suit our purpose just as well – so I popped off and got seats for Shephard's Pie, so all's OK.

But, having made up my mind to go out I wasn't going to be put off by little things like this so I rang up a girl I know – a friend of Betty's, who's been evacuated to Harrow – (she's an Ocean girl) & we went to see Bing Crosby in Mississippi at the Plaza . . .

Afterwards – it was a beautiful day – albeit somewhat windy, we went for a walk through St James's Park, Green Park, & Hyde Park – finishing up at the Corner House at Marble Arch. We managed to get a snappy little table for two – quite near the band – which, by the way, played the whole time. We left the Corner House about 7.45 and then went for a walk. It was a really good day from my point of view & I certainly didn't hear her complain, so everything's OK. She's a very attractive girl, her name's Madge . . . but she's an awful flirt – or at least she's supposed to be.

Ron's going to try & join the Navy . . . he said he was going to Romford recruiting office last Saturday to see about it. I know I said that the Lunn family had finally taken him to their bosoms but I'm afraid they've cast him out again – It was like old times again last Friday, Mrs L didn't have a good word to say for him.

I'm going to see Die Fledermaus on Wednesday at Sadler's Wells. I'm going with a chap at our office, so I'm rather looking forward to it. I've made up my mind to enjoy myself as much as I can before I'm called up – if I'm <u>ever</u> called up, as you no doubt gather – still – it's a great life at present . . .

10 March 1940:

Yesterday I went with Yvonne Riley to see Shephard's Pie. It's a smashing show . . . As I told you last week – once more out with Yvonne & I shall fall – in fact I'm a little that way inclined now – so I think I'll have to leave her alone for some time. She's awfully good company though – Ah me! . . .

I've been so long on the RAF list that I'm wondering whether I shall have time to get my summer holidays in this year . . .

7 April 1940:

The Lunn romance isn't going very well as regards the opinions of Mr & Mrs. They still don't like the idea of Ron as a son-in-law, in fact if he manages to marry her after all – I should think he might get a medal . . .

My romances haven't been going too well lately. I arranged to see Madge on the Thursday before Good Friday but her mother rang to say she had 'flu & couldn't come. I was a bit dubious at first but as she's still away from the office, I hope she's back Monday, I suppose she must have been ill that Thursday & not undesirous of coming out with me. I'd like to see her again . . .

18 April 1940:

I'm so sorry I haven't written before, but as nothing has happened I thought I'd wait until something did. Well – alack – it has now! I knew Madge was coming back to work on Monday so I waited patiently for a letter, which, as I said, alack!, came today. It appears that whilst she was away some chap started to pay great attention to her, I can't say I blame him, and she fell. So here I am, broken-hearted again. You know, I won't have any heart left if everyone goes around breaking it, don't you go and do it will you? . . .

Neither Ron nor I have heard any more about being called. I presume, by the time they're taking to call him up, that he's been accepted for the Navy. If the army wanted him he'd have been popped off much earlier . . .

24 April 1940:

I'm afraid, by the sound of your letter, that I laid it on a bit too thick about being broken-hearted. I'm not as bad as all that – just a bit peeved . . .

My young brother's had a rotten billet given him now. The people don't even feed him & he has to get his meals at a British Home Stores. Mum wrote to the billeting officer & Alan went round to see him; but we don't know what's going to be done as yet.

Dorothy & Ron are going to Shanklin for a week commencing 4th May, so that they manage to get a holiday before Ron's called up. So far he hasn't heard a word about being conscripted.

Yvonne & I are going out on the 4th May, I think. I don't know where we're going although I'd rather like to see the new Leslie Henson show . . .

I keep hearing tales of chaps being asked questions on trigonometry at RAF interviews and it certainly doesn't cheer me up. I shall have to stop reading other books and concentrate on my little trig. book.

5 May 1940:

I was awfully pleased to see you on Friday – quite an unexpected pleasure . . .

Well – to begin from the beginning – I met Yvonne at 6.45 on Saturday evening & as she didn't feel like eating much we went to a place called the Silver Bar. It's just by the Strand Corner House – all soft divans, chairs & secluded tables – (very romantic). It's an awfully nice place – maybe I'll take you there one day. Well – we stayed there until about eight & then strolled to the Savoy Theatre . . . the show is very good . . . Evelyn Laye got a tremendous reception. As I said before, Yvonne is marvellous company – but she doesn't seem to want to settle – although as she's only eighteen that's quite understandable – but I still think she's very nice . . .

Mum, Neil & I went to Upminster & saw my grandmother, aunt & uncles. I do hope nothing stops our holiday. The old car's going like clockwork & I'm itching to drive it again.

Dorothy & Ron are at Ventnor by this time, they left on Saturday morning. Things are still very bad in the Lunn household. Mrs L says some pretty awful things about Ron but I think Dorothy is getting more used to it by this time, at least she doesn't go up in the air so much.

Have you seen any of the shows in London at the present? As I told you – if I'm still here I'd like to take you to see one about the first weekend in June. What do you think?

I'm going to a wedding next Saturday. Do you remember that girl I almost went to the dance with? Well – she's going – only she's married now. Still I expect we'll have a good time.

12 May 1940:

This is about the only letter you're likely to get for a fortnight I'm afraid. You see – I go away either on Friday night or Saturday morning . . . although I'll drop you a card to let you know what it's like to be on holiday – I haven't been away for nearly a year.

By the way, I think my chances of getting to be a pilot in the RAF are pretty small. A friend of mine at the office had to go to Uxbridge on Tuesday for what he thought would be a medical exam but when he arrived they told him that it was impossible to become even a gunner because so many people had applied they had enough air-crews for this war and the next. This chap had matric[ulation], also got distinction in maths so as I said before – my chances appear to be very slim. He's going as a wireless-operator on the ground in about a month's time.

I went to a wedding yesterday at Wood Green. The bride is a girl at the office – I've been quite friendly with her since she arrived two years ago. She'd also invited that little blonde girl – so everything was OK.

After the ceremony we went to the hall where the reception was being held & danced and sang – eating the while. We left at five o'clock – just before the business finished & went to the Piccadilly Brasserie. It was quite empty so we got an awfully decent table – not too conspicuous – & not too near the orchestra. (You have to bear in mind that the little blonde is married.) We asked the conductor to play a couple of tunes for us. He came over and chatted for a bit & smiled sweetly at us when he was playing – all very tasty. I think he thought I was married to her. She is nice though.

Well – we then went for a walk & saw General Ironside(s)[3] just going into some building near Admiralty Arch. I think it's the War Office. He inspected a few chaps drawn up on guard. After this we walked some more & then I took her home to Chingford, at least as far as the [trolley]*'bus. It was stretching Providence too far to take her right to her door-step.*

4 June 1940:

Just a short note to let you know I've booked up for Up & Doing *Sat 15th June. I could only get the upper circle but as it's the first row it should be alright. There's not much to talk about so I'll wait until I see you & then we can talk for hours in the Corner House.*

16 June 1940:

Your father phoned me on Friday morning & told me the bad news . . . Well, young lady – I'm awfully sorry you were unable to come because I was looking forward to taking you out again & I suppose you're pretty peeved at having your week-end messed up. Still, these things can't be helped . . . In the end I went with my three uncles & changed my two seats for four together. It was a real good show & what with one thing and another we managed to enjoy ourselves pretty well. I do hope you're not worrying too much over this business as I know what you're like for worrying about little things. I'd still like to take you out before I go, though, which time shouldn't be so far off because I've got to go to Uxbridge on Wednesday to appear before another selection committee & possibly have another medical. This is the last of this selection business & I imagine I'll go in about a month or sooner.

26 June 1940:

I thought I'd just drop you a line to wish you all the best in matric. It's not half as bad as you imagine – you'll realise that once you start. Besides – If I can get 'General Schools'[4] without swotting – surely you can beat that.

---

3. General Sir Edmund Ironside was Chief of the Imperial General Staff at the time. In a series of unusual moves, on 27 May 1940 he became Commander-in-Chief Home Forces then retired less than two months later.
4. The School Certificate Examination; see Footnote 1 above.

14 July 1940:

I suppose by this time you will have finished matric. & will be awaiting the results with some trepidation. My brother wrote the other day & said he thinks he's just about got through General Schools but as the result won't come out until about August we can only hope for the best . . .

I'm going to the South West Essex Tech. each Tuesday & Thursday to take a course on Maths & Mechanics. The Trig. fair gives the jitters to little me! . . .

If you're still in the mood would you like to try another night out when you come home for good? I don't mind at all what you choose – a picture, a show – a day out somewhere – anything you like – it doesn't matter a bit to me – I just like taking you out.

I hope I don't get called up before I finish my maths course – but as soon as I do – they can call me as soon as possible. By the way, my uncle has been accepted as an observer in the RAF – he'll be home for about four months, though. It's quite possible that we may get stuck at the same training school.

16 July 1940:

If, as you say, you'll be home in a fortnight don't bother to write anymore. I'm surprised at the remarks re matric – but wait until the results come out – it's quite likely you've done pretty well . . . I had a pretty good time last night. The younger of my uncles has to report to Aldershot in the REs [Royal Engineers] *on Thursday so we went to the Regent Palace Hotel to do a spot of celebrating. It's an awfully nice place – if you haven't been to it, it's worth trying.*

This is Ron's last note for some time. Nearly eight months after he told Connie he expected to 'be in the Air Force soon', through no fault of his own he finds himself still in London, still working in the insurance business. But as the tenor of his most recent missives suggest, things are about to change. A day or two later an official envelope arrives containing his RAF joining instructions. In a few short weeks he's due to take the first significant step towards fulfilling his flying ambitions.

Before he leaves for No. 1 Aircrew Reception Centre, Babbacombe, Ron manages to see Connie once or twice. From his perspective her brief return home could hardly have been better timed. They even manage a day in

5 DECEMBER 1939, MANOR PARK, EAST LONDON

London and a stroll along the Embankment by way of a romantic farewell. He also finds time to say goodbye to his Ocean colleagues, when he's delighted to learn that a position will be held open pending his return from military service, whenever that might be. Reassuring though the thought is, it's relegated to the back of his mind as he boards his train at Paddington. All he can think about is realising his dream of becoming a pilot. It's an exciting prospect – if only he knew just how . . .

Chapter 5

23 December 1942, 84th General Hospital, Souk Ahras, Algeria

For the first time since his accident, the night he arrived at the hospital in Souk Ahras Robbie slept peacefully, albeit heavily sedated. Next morning he woke up feeling relatively refreshed, if still depressed by the unexpected turn of events. *Accidents happen to other people, not to me.* For a moment he was tempted to believe the good fortune that had been his constant companion since he first began flying had finally deserted him. On reflection, he realised that far from abandoning him, it was Lady Luck who'd in fact ensured his survival. By rights he should be dead by now, like so many of his erstwhile colleagues. *Just count your blessings, Robertson!*

From what little he could see, there was activity all around him. But it was activity that reinforced a previous impression of mild chaos in the medical world. Common sense then prevailed. *It's wartime – a foreign country. People are under pressure but they're doing their best. What more can you expect? Just be grateful you're still in one piece.* As he gradually absorbed his new surroundings, the inchoate thoughts of the previous day took firmer hold. He felt increasingly uneasy. If he were honest with himself, he was slightly ashamed. It seemed to him that wounded officers were treated, if not better than the other ranks, then certainly differently. It was an impression that subsequent events would reinforce. He found it hard to forget that only seven months earlier he'd been just such an individual, a relatively lowly sergeant. But if the newly-commissioned pilot officer found it difficult to avoid a mild sense of guilt, in the circumstances it was guilt he was prepared to live with.

Time passed slowly in his new surroundings. Lying quietly, barely able to move, there was plenty of opportunity to mull over the events that led to his present predicament. He could recall with absolute clarity the circumstances leading up to his accident, but not the precise cause. Those details would emerge later. All he knew for now was that he wanted this current episode, this deeply uncomfortable experience, to be over as quickly as possible. Desperate to climb back into a Spitfire cockpit, he passed the next couple of days fitfully, in and out of sleep. Then, on 24 December, the stitches in his forehead were removed – not that it was much of a Christmas present. He was still suffering from constant headaches and the after effects of severe bruising.

Christmas Day itself passed with little celebration, just the thought that his mother, a devout Christian, would be up early attending communion. (Her letter of 28 December, once it eventually arrived, confirmed as much: 'Dad & I went to Communion on Xmas Day & it was marvellous – I think we both came away with that feeling of the "Peace of God which passeth understanding"'). At last able to move around a little, this thought spurred him to attend a hospital communion service the following day. If the effect of hauling himself out of bed for the simple ceremony was to improve his overall demeanour, there was a downside too. It accentuated the homesickness he felt.

On 27 December he managed to get a message off to his 72 Squadron colleagues requesting various items of personal kit, which made him feel a little better. His mood further improved the next day when a doctor stopped by his bed and expressed a degree of guarded optimism. In his view Robbie's eye would eventually recover and he'd be able to see again. Despite this boost to his spirits, largely confined to bed and unable even to read, the days continued to pass incredibly slowly. The frustrations he felt were compounded by the constant babble of conversation all around him, a cacophony of sound dominated much of the time by the 'very affected voice' emanating from the next bed. Robbie soon developed a deeply unfavourable view of its owner. *Chap seems like an upper-class twit!* It was an impression he would soon be forced to revise.

His change of heart occurred when the individual concerned, a Coldstream Guards officer, was visited by his colonel and Robbie, eavesdropping, learned the reason for his hospitalisation. When his unit's position had been overrun, he'd apparently managed to escape from his slit trench and plant explosives under a number of German tanks, risking his life while sowing chaos and confusion amongst the enemy. Ashamed now of pre-judging this individual on the basis of scant evidence – prejudice in fact – Robbie made a promise to himself. *Never again will I judge someone on first impressions, least of all the sound of his voice.* Not one to suffer fools gladly, this may not have been his epiphany but the latter-day Robbie certainly developed a more benign, less critical mien. That said, events tend to suggest that this was at best only a marginal character adjustment – and some time in coming too. Meanwhile, he learned that the next stage of his recovery would involve another transfer, this time to a larger, better-equipped hospital. First, though, he needed to rest and gather more strength. It would be an exhausting journey.

Chapter 6

19 August 1940, No. 1 Aircrew Reception Centre, Babbacombe

From the late summer of 1940 Ron's letters take on a different form and content. Previously they'd been written neatly, usually in fountain pen, sometimes on quality notepaper but occasionally scribbled hastily on office memo pads. They now reflect his changed circumstances. He uses anything that comes to hand. Usually it's scraps of paper torn from exercise books or notepads but very occasionally he manages to borrow headed RAF stationery. Sometimes he's even forced to write in pencil. The pressures to which he's subjected as a raw RAF recruit, working literally from dawn until dusk – weekends, too – are such that he snatches any and every opportunity to pen Connie just a few lines, sometimes even during lectures. The results are often composite notes put together over several days. They go on to trace the progress through initial training of an aspirant pilot, one three or four years older than the majority of his colleagues – a factor that will later turn out to be significant. He may be posted to Babbacombe but he finds himself billeted in Torquay.

As they describe his progress, Ron's letters serve as Connie's introduction to the RAF. He resumes his correspondence with her at a critical time – some seven weeks into the Battle of Britain, which began officially on 10 July 1940.

19 August 1940:

So far so good – I've met two chaps I saw at Uxbridge and we're sharing a room in an hotel. It's got running hot and cold water & everything's very good – so far. I'm writing this on top of the cliffs overlooking a marvellous bay.

Can you let me have a photo of your little self – the other chaps have one each & are proudly displaying them in our room whereas I haven't one.

20 August 1940:

We've just come back from a talk by our CO. He's awfully decent, as are all the other officers and NCOs [Non-Commissioned Officers] *down here. We've been given permission to go out until 9.30 but as there's a raid in progress we are now sitting in our little room, hence the fact that I'm starting a letter to you which I'll continue when your letter arrives, which I know it will.*

It was rather funny coming back from the lecture tonight. We were walking along the road when we heard a couple of bangs & just afterwards a German bomber came over so low we could almost have touched it. Of course, we all stopped & star-gazed but the corporal shouted 'Haven't you ever seen an aeroplane before? – keep marching' – actually the rear-gunner could have knocked spots off us in the road and here we are sitting in our room because someone's discovered there's a raid.

By the way – if your letter comes tomorrow I shall just have been vaccinated & injected with all sorts of junk so probably won't feel like writing much more – If I do feel rotten I'll just finish this letter rather hurriedly. I never thought I'd look forward to letters so much – we haven't a wireless & can't get (or rather forget to get) newspapers.
21/8/40

Just come from the tailor's – my uniform fits like a sack – everything's got to be altered and we're not allowed to wear it until the tailor thinks it fits. We've got a large notice stuck up in the hall saying 'No leave will be granted during this course' – this particular course lasts a fortnight & then we're pushed off somewhere else for eight weeks' ground work – I don't know whether we'll get any leave in that course . . .

Let me know all that's happened to you since I've been away – it seems years since we walked along the Embankment, actually it's only a week tomorrow. I haven't managed a swim yet although I'm still hoping . . .
23/8/40

We had our vaccinations and injections on Wednesday – so far my vaccination hasn't troubled me – but the two injections on my right arm gave me quite a bit of trouble – some chaps were as sick as blazes so I'm really pretty lucky . . .

I've now heard that we work like blazes at the Initial Training Wing[5] & won't get any leave until it's over – in which case I won't get any leave until

---

5. 5 ITW (Initial Training Wing), Torquay.

the end of October. Still – as long as I get through I don't mind – although I must admit I'd like to take you out before then.

We had our blood tested today so that its classification can be put on our identity discs. If at any time we need a transfusion it will be easy to get someone with the same type of blood.

At the moment, what with being vaccinated – injected & having my blood tested as well as spending half the day cleaning buttons & buckles on my equipment, I feel more like a cross between a guinea pig and a char-lady than a budding airman.

The places round us are being bombed often & well – but so far, as you can see, nothing has hit us.

24/8/40

I was so pleased to hear from you – it's just like old times to get a letter from you. I'll let you have a photo as soon as I can but our uniforms won't be back from the tailor until Monday or Tuesday – they ain't 'arf particular! . . .

Well young lady – I'm writing this on my bed at 1.45 Saturday – just before going to see Northwest Passage at Torquay. We had PT for an hour this morning – the sun was glorious – I feel as fit as anything.

I'll have tons to tell you when I come home – things which you can't really write about because each item is so small & insignificant in itself – such as the view from various places – the officers and NCOs' manners towards us & all sorts of things. One thing I do know & that is I'm jolly proud of being in the RAF . . .

30 August 1940:

Yesterday (Thursday) we were inspected by the CO of the whole Training Wing & unfortunately, as he was so pleased he's asked Lord Trenchard[6] to come down and see us. This means that we go on parade at 2.45, have a short address, get inoculated again at 4 pm, and then march to Paignton at 6.30. Personally I can see half the squad falling by the wayside & only hope I'm not one of them . . .

By the way, don't worry about writing 'interesting' letters – as long as I get a letter of some description that's all I want. You see it's not actually the news that is so interesting it is the fact that it's very 'lifting' to hear

---

6. With no official role, 67-year-old Marshal of the Royal Air Force the Lord Trenchard of Wolfeton acted as unofficial Inspector-General of the Service he effectively fathered.

from folks at home. No doubt your father will enlarge on the subject as he probably experienced the same feeling in the last war . . . I'll endeavour to write at least once a week to let you know my progress . . .

I had a pretty good time yesterday – in the evening we went for a swim in Babbacombe Bay & then went off to a local pub. At 9.20 just as we were about to come home (in by 9.30) the warning went and we stayed in the pub until 11.45 & then thought we'd better try & get home . . .

Well young lady – I hope you miss me just a bit every now & again. I find there's quite a few things I miss but then we're all the same so I mustn't grumble.

It must be pretty rotten up in London now – I don't like to think of people I know having to walk about the streets expecting an air raid every minute . . .

9.30 AM. Sunday.   Quite a lot has happened since I last wrote . . . We paraded at 3 pm on Friday, & after an address by Trenchard had tea. At 4.45 we were inoculated and at 6.30 were marched to Torquay & not Paignton as I thought. Anyway, the walk didn't do us much good & so far we've got 3 chaps in hospital and 8 had to go to Torquay by lorry . . . I didn't feel as bad as I expected & apart from my arm being a bit stiff I was alright.

We've had it drummed into us that we get thrown out for the first mistake and unless we get 60% in some subjects and 80% in others we don't continue the course but are remustered as air gunners. We work from 6 am to 5 pm or 6.30 – including Saturdays . . . The whole point is that they're cutting down the course as much as possible and are putting people through at a terrific rate.

5 September 1940:

Mum wrote & told me that they were having air raids most nights from dusk till dawn . . . I only hope that no one I know gets hurt in all the 'dust-up'. I'm writing this at 1.30 on Thursday just before going to a 2 hrs lecture on gas. It's a rotten subject and the time to learn about it has been cut . . . We are certainly working like blazes now and it appears that we shall have to work even harder . . . our 8 wks course is going to be cut down a bit . . .

It's now Sunday morning and I haven't been able to touch this letter since Thursday. Sometimes we scarcely get time to have our meals.

We're all rather peeved at the moment as church parade has finished but instead of getting the rest of the day off as usual we've been confined to quarters and told to 'Stand By'. . . It appears there's an air raid in progress in Scotland somewhere & we're to stay here until the possibility of <u>our</u> being bombed has passed away! What a war!!

I met a chap on Thursday I hadn't seen since I left school. He was just off to Leicester for flying training. I'm looking forward to getting my wings like anything – I only wish I could be taking an active part in this war.

I do hope you're not letting the raids get on your nerves too much – I know what a little worry you are. If you start to wonder how much damage the raiders are causing remember how little they achieve compared with the losses they suffer. It won't be long before they lose heart & stop this attacking. If you could only see the chaps down here and the whole team spirit of the RAF you'd realise that <u>nothing</u> can beat them . . .

P.S. Have you a photo yet?

11 September 1940:

I've just had a letter from Mum (it took 3 days to reach me) which says that the docks and ferry as well as East Ham have been well and truly bombed. I still can't imagine what it must be like up there but hope and trust that you'll be alright. The feeling down here is very high and whereas, when we came here everybody wanted to go to fighters, most people are praying they'll get sent on bombers so that we can give Germany a taste of her own medicine . . .

How are your mother & father keeping during all this trouble? Wasn't there some talk of you & your mother evacuating somewhere when this war first started? I may be wrong but I thought I'd had a talk about it with Mrs Freeman, but forget the ultimate result . . .

I've played two games of polo since I've been here and we won both matches. The competition isn't great and I managed to score 2 each time, despite the fact that the idea is 'Stop a man at all costs'. It's rather reminiscent of the practice matches we had at Romford Rd when no referee was present.

I was on guard on Monday night from 8.30 - 10.30 & 2.30 am - 4.30 am. The second period was the worst – no one to talk to – nothing to see & as cold as blazes. It's amazing the things you think of though, I suppose it's the quietness which helps you. Did you ever do Travels with a Donkey by R.L. Stevenson when you were at school? There's a part in it where Stevenson puts his sleeping bag down in the shade of a great forest and stares at the stars half the night – I couldn't help wishing all this were over & we could gaze up at night without the drone of a bomber. It's surprising how your ideas change when you undergo something like this – I never thought that I should ever want to go out and bomb people but at the moment there's nothing I'd rather do. It's easy to look back now on things you've done at home which, at the time, appeared trivial and not worth mentioning and realise that they form part of something that can never really be replaced. I think I'm getting morbid, which is a bad sign, so I'll turn to other things.

I can see that if I do get any leave, when I come to see you we'll spend a pleasant evening in an air-raid shelter. You know, this 'Leave' business is becoming a large part of my daily thoughts, as is the case with most of the chaps here. It doesn't say much for our self-control as we've been here less than a month. Still – I expect that everyone's the same.

You'll no doubt be pleased to hear that my young brother Alan has got matric and six credits. Mum & all are very pleased about it and are trying to get him into the Ocean. I hope they succeed – although at present I doubt if anyone else is being taken on as things are so unsettled.

We have our maths exam a week on Friday – if I fail I get turfed out straight away – you've no idea what that would mean to me . . . Actually, navigation is the most important thing we do whilst down here but we don't start that for a week or two . . .

Sunday.[7] 5.15 pm or RAF time 1715 hours.

We've moved to a far better room . . . big enough for twelve but there's only six of us in it . . . It's simply marvellous here [the Elfordleigh Hotel, Torquay] *. . . I can't help going into raptures over the place . . .*

Monday evening – I've just got your letter and can't really describe how I feel about it all. It seems all wrong somehow – I wish I could do something for you – actually all I can do at the moment is swot like mad & pass through as soon as possible. The quicker I get into action the happier I'll be. Thank God you're still fit though – I should feel very bad if anything – even the slightest injury came to you or your people. I hope the shock of all this hasn't had any ill effects on you. If you'd rather not write for a time – please don't hesitate – or imagine that I'm thinking you've forgotten me – I understand. I'm so glad you got matric – all that work wasn't in vain . . .

---

7. Ron began this letter four days earlier, on the Wednesday.

A SPITFIRE NAMED CONNIE

If you let me know which nights you stay in I'll try & phone you later on – although the chaps here seem to have a certain amount of difficulty in getting through to London. It may not be so bad to Watford,[8] though.

To put Ron's recent letters into context, they're written at the heart of the Battle of Britain. As a recruit of less than a month's standing, his pride in 'the whole team spirit of the RAF' would eventually be justified by the outcome of a battle that ended officially on 31 October 1940. While 'The Few' are justifiably credited with securing a hard-fought victory, as Ron's prescient observation suggests, it was essentially a team effort. Dowding[9] and Park,[10] leaders of Fighter Command and 11 Group respectively, may have been the architects but their triumph would have been impossible without the contributions of largely unheralded teams of telephonists, plotters, controllers and engineers. Civilian recovery teams, aircraft factory workers and 30,000 or so members of the Observer Corps manning some fifty observation posts played a notable part too. Indeed, as a result of its contribution, in April 1941 King George VI granted the Observer Corps its 'Royal' title.

When Ron says 'I can't really describe how I feel about it all,' he's referring to the 'Blitz'. It began just four days before this latest letter. Such was the initial intensity that from 7 September raids on London continued for fifty-seven consecutive nights. It concluded on the night of 10/11 May 1941 with the Luftwaffe's heaviest raid yet. Over 500 aircraft dropped more than 700 tons of bombs across London, killing nearly 1,500 and destroying some 11,000 homes. Vere Hodgson, a charity worker who lived and worked in Notting Hill, kept a diary throughout the Blitz. Written at her 'desk in the evenings when [she] came down on fire watch',[11] it provides a contemporaneous account of one Londoner's experiences and in many ways exemplifies the spirit of the time. On Sunday 11 May she wrote: 'Just trying to recover from last night! . . . heard the terrible news that Westminster Hall was hit . . . Also the Abbey and the Houses of Parliament. They saved the roof to a large extent . . . At first they thought Big Ben had crashed!'[12]

---

8. In early September Connie was moved from Brentford to yet another evacuation billet, twenty or so miles north-west of London.
9. At the time, Air Chief Marshal Sir Hugh Dowding, later the Lord Dowding of Bentley Priory GCB GCVO CMG.
10. At the time, Air Vice-Marshal K.R. Park, later Air Chief Marshal Sir Keith Park GCB KBE MC* DFC.
11. Vere Hodgson, *Few Eggs and No Oranges: the Diaries of Vere Hodgson 1940-45* (Persephone Books Ltd, London, 1999), p.xxii.
12. Ibid., pp.169-71.

Following this bombardment London wasn't given a total respite. Luftwaffe activity continued sporadically thereafter, with a notably intense raid on 27 July. According to Vere Hodgson's diary of the following day:

> Last night the Germans sprang an air raid on us – much to our surprise. I was asleep . . . once again Wailing Winny set up. They buzzed over us for about two hours. Our guns cracked up all around, and as I lay in bed I watched the shells bursting in the sky. Several times I put my head out of the window, but the police were chatting away on the step nonchalantly. I could hear no bombs.[13]

Ron's concerns about the effects of the Blitz are well-founded. Barely four miles north of the hardest hit areas, Docklands and the East End, his home was relatively vulnerable. Connie's parents lived a further half-dozen miles away, but crucially to the north, further from the main axis of the German attacks. Although both families' homes survived unscathed, many of their friends and acquaintances were less fortunate.

18 September 1940:

We've just had a raid warning – the first for about a fortnight . . . the 'all clear' went – after just half an hour . . .

Have you been successful in landing a job in Watford yet – it would be very convenient for you if you did manage it.

I've sent a card & a letter to Mrs Lunn but haven't had a reply yet. I hope they arrived O.K. – although Mr & Mrs L. may have moved owing to the raids.

Mum says that the raids haven't eased off a bit – they come with monotonous regularity. I wish my folks could get down here – it would do them an awful lot of good – besides taking them out of London.

I managed to scramble through my maths exam with my usual luck – although I made a mess of the first two sums. I got 66% – a pass is 60% – so I'm O.K. until the navigation exam.

I've just been to the canteen next door – they've got a marvellous selection . . . You'd be surprised at the cost of all this . . . the loss they make

---

13. Ibid., p.196.

must be enormous. Actually all the wealthy old dears of Torquay, who have a misguided conception that we're all going to be heroes, give contributions towards our stuff. I can tell you, that if I go to another place for training, I'm going to miss the extreme kindheartednesses of all Torquay-ites.

1 October 1940:

I'm as peeved as you are that I didn't get through on Saturday, in fact more so – as I'd been looking forward to a chat all the week . . .

I hear from Dorothy that Ron's house has had the roof blown off . . . I can't understand why Ron hasn't been called up yet. They must want people or they wouldn't be rushing our training like this & yet chaps like him are still in civvies.

Do you remember that house I told you about when I saw you last – the one we intended taking in Aldersbrook Rd[14] with tennis court etc. etc.? Well – Mum wrote & said that a bomb on the corner of the road – one in the garden & one next door hadn't improved it much – in fact only the walls are standing so we're <u>not</u> moving after all. It's a good job we didn't move in (we were due in in 3 wks' time) or we should have lost everything. Mum's now thinking of moving to Upminster to live with my aunt while the war's on . . . So far, things are OK at home but the continual night after night bombing is rather getting on Mum's nerves now – especially as the only sleep they get – if any – is down in the cellar. Still, I expect things are going to turn for the better soon. I hope you get that job you're after – it certainly sounds pretty good.

7 October 1940:

We had our armaments exam on Saturday & although our marks haven't yet been published I think I got through OK. As soon as that was over we were marched off to get our flying kit. It's marvellous stuff – supposed to cost about £30 & I can believe it. We get silk gloves, woollen gloves & soft leather gauntlets – the whole lot are worn one on top of the other. Then we get great 'teddy bear' inner suits, all zip fasteners etc. then an outer suit with a great soft woollen collar. The flying boots are lovely – I'd like to use them as house slippers – they're all fleecy wool inside. We haven't our helmets yet as they're still at the tailors. We finish the course next Saturday & may leave

---

14. In East London's Manor Park district.

any time after that although we still don't know where we're going. The only thing that is pretty definite is that we're not getting any leave. Still – we're bound to get some at some time or other and I'll certainly come and see you as many times as possible during my leave – that's something I promised myself for a long time.

We had a marvellous time on Saturday night. Four of us were invited out to dinner & dance at the Palm Court Hotel by two old, or rather, elderly ladies who happened to know one of our chaps. They are fairly rolling in money & we had anything & everything to eat & drink . . . The people at the hotel are making up a party to go & see Clarkson Rose's show Twinkle on Tuesday & have asked us to go along with them as well as attend another dinner & dance on Saturday. The only snag is that our navigation exam is on Friday & I must swot like blazes this week, as if I fail I don't go to the Flying School – that's why I'm writing this in one of our lectures so that I can work tonight . . .

I heard from Mum the other day & she's decided not to go to Upminster but stay at home. Dad would have an awful ride to work . . . so for the time being the family Robertson is staying put . . .

The only reason I don't mention air raids is because we don't have any – we had one the other day when I wrote to you but no bombs were dropped. The 'All Clear' usually goes about ¾ hrs after the warning.

I'm glad you got that job – I'll bet you enjoy yourself now. If you like a job it makes it much easier to learn . . .

15 October 1940:

I'm awfully sorry you weren't in when I phoned . . . I'll try again on Saturday about 8 pm – if I don't get through at once I expect the call will come to you about 10 pm. Well . . . we've finished all our exams – or at least – the ones that matter – and are now on a fortnight's (?) course of Link trainer. It's a gadget made like a small aeroplane. It has a full-sized cockpit but very small tail and wings – it's fixed to the floor but can rotate & dive & do all sorts of queer things. Every movement is recorded by the instructor who sits outside the room and communicates with you by telephone. It's meant to help you when you first start flying . . .

We all thought we'd be going this week & so miss exams on Recognition of Aircraft and Law & Administration but unfortunately as we're here we're getting both these exams . . . We don't have to pass the exams but if you're after a commission it's as well to do as well as possible. I don't give a hang whether I get a commission or not so long as I get my wings.

Mum says the raids are continuing as usual – from what I can see it seems even more certain that if I ever get any leave I shall speak my little piece in an air raid shelter.

Just think – even if I get through all the Elementary Flying & Advanced Flying schools I won't get into action until about next February – it seems years.

Well – young lady – I'm glad you enjoy working at or rather near Watford . . .

It's now 6.45 pm & I'm afraid I must leave this and try & learn something of aircraft recognition. When we get to EFTS [Elementary Flying Training School] *this is a most important subject as they get rather peeved if we shoot down one of ours in mistake for a Jerry . . .*

Ron's concern that he 'won't get into action until about next February' is more than justified. After a summer in limbo awaiting joining instructions, a swimming injury at the end of his initial training looks set to delay further the realisation of his ambitions. His next letter comes from Torbay Hospital.

27 October 1940:

Your parcel reached me on Tuesday just after I was brought in here. The gloves are really superb . . . I don't know how you guessed my size. I would have answered your two enclosures before but it took me two days before I was even able to read them. You see we were playing polo on Tuesday afternoon when I got a smack in the eye which seems to have cracked up quite a few things. My sight is OK I'm glad to say but the eyeball has been cut as well as the lid & so is rather painful to move . . . I wasn't even allowed to sit up until Saturday. I can sit up and wear dark glasses now and also walk to the bathroom and shave myself so things can't be too bad. I must get out by Wednesday because there's a draft being sent to a flying school and I think I'm in it . . . The nurses are awfully decent here & I manage to get a lot of titbits I really shouldn't have. One consolation is as this is an eye ward & not a medical we're allowed to smoke – so I sit and suck my pipe . . . much to the annoyance of the sister & joy of the nurses.

Excuse the writing but it's rather a job looking through one bleary eye & dark glasses . . . I do wish I could get leave before going to the EFTS – otherwise it may be more than five weeks before we get any . . .

On leaving hospital Ron is given a period of sick leave; his injury is more serious than his letter suggests. In addition to burst blood vessels, the muscles surrounding his eye are so badly damaged that he can hardly move it; he's suffering from double vision too. Once he returns to Torquay, his training inevitably delayed, he's transferred from A Flight to Z flight, effectively a holding element at 5 ITW. For once he has time on his hands and subsequent letters develop a familiar theme: dalliances with other young ladies. How he – or Connie for that matter – rationalises these situations remains something of a mystery.

11 November 1940:

I saw our MO [medical officer] *& he told me to go to the hospital on Tuesday & then see him on Wednesday . . . You've no idea how good it was to see you again – It reminds me of one of Bing's songs – 'So easy to remember but so hard to forget' . . . You'll probably think I'm cracked but just to see you for a while & remember all the things we used to do is a great help & they're the sort of things which make all this business here worthwhile. I'm not the only one who thinks of these things in the same way, because most of the chaps here feel the same. After all – that is what we're fighting for – to clear up things in general so that we can get back to normal & begin enjoying ourselves again. I could talk about this for hours so I'd better stop before I get too far.*

If only my leave had been longer! – still – I'm jolly glad I managed to get those few days . . .

1 December 1940:

I've had quite a good time since I came back. To begin with, no one knows much about us & consequently no one cares . . .

This morning I got up too late for breakfast & so went down to the Palm Court Hotel & had some there. I had so much that I had to leave off before the last course. I then read a paper & smoked until half past eleven & then came back to lunch. This all sounds very nice & easy I know but I'd change it any day if only I could come home again. I enjoyed my last leave much more than the first. I wasn't so rushed everywhere – even so it seemed that I'd been home scarcely any time at all. My eye's a little better but not quite O.K. just yet. I do hope that it won't be too long before it finally clears up.

I went to the nurses' dance on Friday night and had to crawl through a window to get back into our hotel again – I'm not sure it was worth it because I had a row with my little nurse. I, so she said, paid too much attention to another of the nurses & she, according to me, paid too much attention to another RAF chap. Hence – we are parted but I'm taking the other nurse out at 3 pm today so I'm not really heartbroken. The latest one is rather nice – I'll tell you more about her later – that is, if we go out again much more . . . I'm glad I managed to catch you before you left on Thursday morning. I was awfully sorry I didn't phone on Wednesday & hope that you didn't wait in for the call. As I tried to explain my uncle had the day off as he's joining the RAF (yesterday actually) and we all sat around talking 19 to the dozen all night. What with answering various queries & telling him this & that about the RAF I forgot about my phone call until too late.

10 December 1940:

We're still doing nothing apart from attending signals classes now & again just so that our morse doesn't get forgotten . . .

As regards my little nurse – she's got brown hair – but alack! – I don't think all is going as well as it might. To begin with she's engaged to some chap in Somerset (I knew this when I was in hospital). I rang her the other day & she said she was working the rest of the week and couldn't get out. It didn't sound very convincing – in any case I've not phoned her since as I've got no money but I may do after Friday (pay day).

I had a letter from Mum today – she says they're moving to 75 Windsor Rd.[15] at the end of this month. I hope you'll be able to come home with me one day & see the place – it's awfully nice. Mum also says she'll go to Newquay to see Neil at Christmas if I don't manage to get any leave. I'm rather doubtful as to whether I shall get any now as we've got a new CO & he seems very hot on discipline & takes a very poor view of chaps dodging lectures to go to the pictures & the like. We'll certainly have to watch our step now . . .

By the way – (I have to put this bulletin in all my letters) my eye is <u>gradually</u> getting better but it seems to improve slower & slower – still – I'll just have to wait and hope for the best . . .

(Just remembered – I've forgotten to answer your question re Dolly.)

I enjoyed myself very much when I paid my last visit to the Lunn abode – I didn't say anything about our talk but I really couldn't see that Mrs L was trying to push Dolly off on me . . . Anyway – I got there about 10 am & Dorothy & I went for a walk to see the new house . . . came away & walked down to some pub . . . We sat on a settee & talked of this & that & then

---

15. In Forest Gate, some three miles east of their current home.

ambled home. We sat in the Lunn abode until about 5 pm & then popped off – Dolly to work – & I to Wembley.

I'm afraid young Dolly doesn't realise how near I came to kissing her goodbye – I don't know why I felt like it but I did. Now, don't go getting odd ideas, young lady – there's nothing like that about it – I'm just giving you an account of what happened.

19 December 1940:

Quite a few things have been happening since I last wrote to you. To begin with the new CO put all the chaps who were just waiting posting to a flying school all in one flight & so we do an awful lot of work again. Still – it passes the time & I don't spend as much . . . I had a letter from Dorothy yesterday . . . I hear that Mrs Lunn censors all the letters D. writes to me – I don't know why.

I see from today's papers that the Strand Palace had a lot of windows broken in a recent air raid although nobody was injured.

I was on guard last night (complete with gloves) for the first time for about three months – it came as an awful blow – but as we had tons to eat I didn't mind so much. We also have the pleasure (?) of mounting guard on Christmas Day – so that's all the celebrating I'm likely to do. Still – I don't care a great deal – as long as my eye hurries up & gets better (it's still taking its time) I don't mind much else.

We manage to get quite a bit of fun out of life even when we're supposed to be working. For instance – the other afternoon we were sent out for a route march with an NCO but all the marching we did was down to the front to the Palm Court Hotel & there we sat for the afternoon . . .

I'm all off the young females of Torquay – I'm a disappointed man (more or less). I've had a long letter from Yvonne, though, & also from Joan Clarke. Do you remember her? She used to go to your school & now works at the Royal London with my brother.

I'm not going to apply for any leave until my eye has healed properly & I've passed my last exam . . .

6 January 1941:

I expect you were 'all peculiar' when you were told that I phoned & you were asleep – but there was really no necessity to wake you up . . . I only had *three minutes anyway & you couldn't have got to the phone by that time. I only wanted to wish you a happy birthday & Christmas.*

I expect you did feel a bit out of place at Christmas without the usual gang & all the socials etc. – but then so did a good many other people – it certainly didn't seem like Christmas to me although I had quite a good time. I spent the day with a friend of mine & his wife. We ate & drank (very moderately) then sat around the fire . . .

On Wednesday night I felt pretty homesick. You see – I went down to the Spa Baths & there were only two other chaps in. We swam up and down undisturbed – just as we did in the winter at Romford Rd . . .

The old eye showed great promise last week & I thought I might be able to see the MO this week & ask for a Medical Board Exam but it seems to have come to a standstill now & so I don't suppose I'll be OK for a bit.

15 January 1941:

*I'm afraid my last letter was badly worded. I didn't mean to say that you ought to be ashamed of yourself for thinking you had a rather uninteresting time at Christmas. All I meant to do was point out that ** it was a pretty awful Christmas all over this year as everyone was, in nine cases out of ten, parted from all their friends.*

*Now a spot of news. I'd just written up to ** in navigation when the officer said 'Did you chaps know that you're having an exam on supplementary navigation on Friday – that's the 17th of Jan?' You can imagine how we feel at the moment! As a rule we dodge navigation altogether & go to breakfast or tea – depending on the time of the lesson. When we do go in we write letters. All this afternoon we've been working like slaves. We've only got tomorrow to finish the whole course in. Still, they can't do much to us if we fail (I hope). Having got that off my chest I'll continue with a spot of good news. My eye is OK now & I saw the MO on Sunday. He said he can't do anything until I've seen the eye specialist. They're trying to arrange for me to see him this week but I doubt whether it will be as soon as that – the machinery of the RAF works in a slow and peculiar way.*

Mum says that they're very pleased with the house in Windsor Rd. I'd like to see how it looks now that it's furnished.

As for my muses – they don't exist anymore – I'm all alone now and have been for quite a while – although I don't feel any ill-effects.

2 February 1941:

I'm still in Torquay. The posting was postponed for about a fortnight & we're due to go (or be postponed) on the 12th. I'm not so eager to go at the moment as it has been decided to have a swimming gala between 5 & 3 Wings on the 12th Feb . . . Still – I'll bet we're posted on the very day that the gala takes place – but I'll be very pleased whichever way it turns out.

I'm glad you are going to work in London again.[16] There's no place like it is there? I only hope things will remain pretty quiet there for you.

We've got an observer to teach us navigation now. He's only about 25 but he got the DFM [Distinguished Flying Medal] *for photographing the first Kiel raid. He's on a sort of rest cure at the moment.*

As regards my 'correspondent' she's 17½, blonde & fair haired. She likes swimming and swam for her school for three years. She's fond of most games & likes Bing Crosby. That's about all she told me but I've asked for her photo just to see what she's really like – I'll bet she's pretty awful . . .

I hadn't heard from Dorothy for some time so I wrote to Mr & Mrs Lunn. I had a letter from D. a few days later saying I was 'a naughty boy for not writing to her before'. I ask you – what do you do with a girl like that – it was her turn to write anyway . . .

Apparently Ron has finished his course & will soon be going on some ship or other so that he can do his three months at sea before trying for his commission . . .

It would be jolly good if you could get a home in Wanstead or Woodford – even if I only had a short leave I could come & see you – apart from a selfish point of view I know you'd be a lot happier if you could see your old crowd again.

20 February 1941:

The posting was postponed again and it's more than likely to be postponed on Tuesday again. We're not doing so badly really as we're doing advanced navigation – stuff we're not supposed to do until we get to Service flying school. It's very interesting, we plot courses, work out wind velocity,

---

16. Connie has joined her father's firm, Appleton, Machin and Smiles, London tea merchants with offices in Cannon Street, London.

*drift etc. When we don't do navi, signals or arms we go for route marches &
do gym work. Altogether we could be a lot worse off.*

*I had a marvellous time that weekend I was home . . . I'm glad you were
in when I phoned – I liked speaking to you again – it seems years since
I last saw you. By the way – where's that Polyphoto you promised me? I was
looking forward to having another photo of you. Be a good girl & let me
have it.*

*I had a letter from my girl-correspondent the other day – enclosing a
photo of herself – she seems awfully nice. I'll show you the photo if I ever
get back to civilisation again . . .*

*I turned up at Torquay Club night last Monday and they were one short
so I got a game of polo. It wasn't a bad game but their opponents weren't so
hot & we won about 7-nil . . .*

I'll be able to tell you more when and if I ever get to EFTS . . .

23 February 1941:

*I don't know whether I've told you before but we've got a corporal
here who plays for Penguin IIs[17] – so we play together on the squadron
team & go swimming together most nights of the week. On Wednesday the
instructor – a chap by the name of Nicholls or Nicholl – who was the News
Chronicle swimming coach & columnist gave me about a quarter of an
hour's coaching – it was quite like old times . . .*

*Yesterday I was told I was being sent to a flying school at Brough but ten
minutes later I was told I couldn't go as I was still under the MO. Anyway
the CO is trying to get me an eye test before next Wednesday & if I pass
OK – I'll be sent off. Actually I don't think I'll get the test in time so you
can address your next letter here. If I go I'll let you know by telegram – just
saying 'Posted' & you'll know what's happened. In any case, all my letters
will be forwarded . . .*

*One of the girls at the Ocean has a friend who wanted to write to a chap
in the RAF & so she got her to write to me – I've never had such a letter!
It was about five pages long & contained enough questions to last me for
six months. I'll be a week before I can get down to answer it. She's 17½, has*

---

17. Penguin Swimming Club (SC), founded in 1916, was a notable presence in the pre-war
    years, fielding a number of water polo teams. It merged with Hammersmith Ladies SC
    in 1976 and was subsequently renamed the West London Penguin Swimming and Water
    Polo Club.

blonde hair and blue eyes – I think I'll ask for a photo before I get let in to answer all her questions.

If I get my eye test after the draft has gone on Wednesday I'll put in for some leave – in which case I'll certainly come over & see you again & we can maybe go out one Saturday.

This is the last letter Connie receives for ten days or so. The explanation is contained in a succinct telegram of 25 February: 'POSTED = RON.' After what seems an almost interminable delay, he's about to begin his flying training proper – in a cockpit at last, rather than behind a desk.

Chapter 7

30 December 1942, 84th General Hospital, Souk Ahras, Algeria

As Robbie continued his gradual recovery, a brief incident lifted his spirits. In response to his request for a care package three days before, on 30 December he received an unexpected visit from 72 Squadron's duty sergeant. He'd been despatched with a parcel put together by Robbie's closest friend, a South African, Pilot Officer Francis 'George' Malan, a younger brother (there were three more siblings) of one of the first Battle of Britain aces, the revered 'Sailor' Malan.[18]

The package was accompanied by a brief note in which George apologised for being unable to visit due to pressure of work – a typically understated euphemism for the business of war. It concluded, 'Hope I've put in all you want,' followed by a P.S.: 'Have put in a pair of my socks in case you're short.' It hurt to do so but Robbie couldn't help but smile. More than that, he was deeply touched by this thoughtful gesture from a man to whom he'd become even more closely attached during their short time together in North Africa.

Thoughts of his colleague took him back to a time earlier in the year and their concerted efforts to side-step 72 Squadron's anticipated move overseas. The rumour became rife during a period of relative inactivity when relocated to Ayr in August; there was simply too much time for contemplation in Scotland. The last thing either George or Robbie wanted was to be separated from the ladies in their lives, particularly if the chances of action were slim, as they assumed would be the case if 'shunted off to the Far East or wherever'. On the other hand, the prospect of a second front excited them: 'there'd be so much fun flying over the Channel with lots to do and lots of chances to fire the old guns.'

---

18. Group Captain A.G. Malan DSO* DFC*; see also Chapter 24 comments after Ron's letter of 30 August 1942. Like his sibling, Sailor was never known by his Christian name, Adolph.

The pair were ready to do almost anything to avoid an overseas deployment, including seeking transfers to another squadron. Their efforts to escape the inevitable culminated in George's unavailing appeal for help from his famous brother. At the time Squadron Leader Sailor Malan was running the RAF's Central Gunnery School at RAF Sutton Bridge. After commanding 74 Squadron and then leading the Biggin Hill Wing, he'd been withdrawn from operations in the late summer of 1941. The RAF's highest scoring fighter pilot at the time, with more than twenty-seven confirmed 'kills' (the vast majority Luftwaffe fighters), he was simply too valuable an asset to be risked further in the combat arena. But with Sailor absent when George conducted what was quite literally a flying visit to his Lincolnshire base, all he could do was leave a message. In the event, this may have been a blessing in disguise. It's hard to believe that a disciplinarian like Sailor Malan would have had any truck with special pleading, least of all on the part his own flesh and blood.

Returning to the relationship between Robbie and George, there was an equally close bond between their respective fiancées, Connie and Vickie. A measure of the pair's closeness is evident in a letter from Connie on 5 December. Responding to Robbie's mention that George would be joining him soon, she writes that, 'Vickie hasn't heard a word since he went. I do hope he joins you as both Vickie & I should like to feel that you were together.' Two days later she reiterates these same sentiments: 'I do hope George has joined you by now – I'd like you to be together again.' There's a similar theme in her note of 11 December: 'I had a letter yesterday from Vickie & she has just received her first letter from George in which he says he is with you. We are both so happy about you being together again.' Vickie then writes to Connie saying – "Apparently Frank[19] & I are coming to London for your wedding so now you know!" What have you two been planning out there? Still it will be rather marvellous won't it darling!'

The mutual respect the two pilots developed during the months they'd flown together, with George as Robbie's regular number two, was in evidence again once George eventually arrived at Souk-el-Arba. (After marrying Vickie on Friday 16 October, just days before his colleagues set sail, his departure was delayed by their honeymoon.) But these were difficult times. The pressures of combat, combined with a hostile ground environment, had begun to wreak changes and affect the behaviour of some individuals. It was a process that led one 72 Squadron colleague to enter a diary note on

---

19. It seems that, unlike George's squadron colleagues, his wife referred to him by a form of his first name, in the same way that Robbie was Ron to Connie.

8 December: 'Altering judgement of certain people now in respect of flying, leadership and companionship on the ground.' Pilot Officer William James 'Jimmy' Corbin, who'd taken part in the latter days of the Battle of Britain and would later earn a DFC (Distinguished Flying Cross), wasn't alone in making such contemporaneous judgements. Robbie himself had at times expressed exasperation at the lack of airborne leadership demonstrated by a couple of the more senior pilots; he expected more from them. It was, therefore, with a vicarious sense of vindication, pleasure accompanied by a tinge of sympathy, that he noted the 'removal' of one such individual, a decorated flight commander to boot, a few days before he was shot down. If the departure in 'a funny do' of an individual described in Corbin's diary as a 'nervous wreck' caused few tears, his replacement by David Cox[20] met with universal approval.

Unlike Jimmy Corbin, others left recording their misgivings until years afterwards. One who did so wrote privately to Robbie, decrying a particular character best left unnamed who was 'determined he was going to be the great man of 72 and went to every length to make sure all competition, conjured up in his imagination by jealousy I believe, was eliminated.' In his letter of 7 January 1985, New Zealander Owen Hardy[21] also cast doubt on the 'kill' claims of another pilot Robbie didn't rate highly. Intriguingly, Hardy's letter, more than forty years after the events in question, corroborated the wartime view of another erstwhile colleague. Speaking of this same pilot in a letter of 6 October 1944, Warrant Officer Jim Norton wrote that he eventually 'found out how selfish he was. He really disgusted me. My! Did his head get swollen. I was not sorry when he went. He began to get me down with his moans about not being able to get any more [enemy] a/c. I can't stand that sort of thing.'

These latter comments take on greater significance much later when the circumstances of Robbie's final sortie with Sergeant Roy Hussey[22] are revealed. For now, suffice it to say that they cast a somewhat different light on the camaraderie traditionally associated with wartime fighter squadrons. They tend to suggest that war highlights, and possibly even exacerbates,

---

20. Wing Commander D.G.S.R. Cox DFC* retired in 1946 with seven confirmed victories to his name.
21. Wing Commander O.L. Hardy DFC* retired from the RAF in 1969. After wartime service as a member of the Royal New Zealand Air Force he went home to university before returning to the UK and rejoining the RAF. His tally was three confirmed and three shared destroyed, a probable, five damaged and one destroyed on the ground.
22. Flight Lieutenant R.J.H. Hussey DFC DFM was killed in February 1945 in a P-51 Mustang accident; he was credited with ten confirmed 'kills'.

individual character flaws. But it's equally possible to argue that conflict can also bring out the very best in people – as was undoubtedly the case during the Battle of Britain – if not altogether eliminating, then certainly ameliorating previously perceived shortcomings. War, though, is a wearing process, the more so a lengthy struggle. This much is abundantly clear in Hardy's later recollections. In December 1996 he wrote:

> Those of us privileged to fly Spitfires were at least employed in a variety of roles and not permanently on ground attack. Not so the rocket firing Typhoon crews who worked the battle area in close support of the army. Most of those pilots began operations during the latter stages of the war and no doubt during their initial flying training they had been fired up by youthful ideas of becoming fighter aces. Alas, there was no glory in store for them. If they survived two months on operations they were exceptionally lucky. On one occasion in France we shared the same airfield with Typhoon squadrons and the difference between the squadron crews was most noticeable. Their faces, silence, and lonely withdrawn behaviour reflected the mental stress they were undergoing, which caused us to admire all the more the determination with which they faced up to the demands of each day, day after day. And I suppose, in a way, we also felt humility. Shamefully, their courage and sacrifices and the contribution they made to winning the ground battle has never been properly recognised. I have a sneaking suspicion that they were much braver than most of us fighter pilots, including some of the aces. I salute them.

For the record, both Owen Hardy and Robbie himself could count themselves worthy of this last accolade, each having accounted for more than five enemy aircraft.

Chapter 8

27 February 1941, No. 4 EFTS (Elementary Flying Training School), RAF Brough

Together with what little he possessed – most importantly his precious flying gear – at 9 pm on Wednesday 26 February Ron finally left behind the delights of the South Devon coast. After a seventeen-hour journey by train and a less than comfortable coach, he and some forty others eventually arrived at RAF Brough on the northern banks of the Humber, a dozen or so miles from Hull.

After months of induction training, when he arrived at No. 4 EFTS it seemed that Ron had entered an entirely different world. It wasn't just the excitement of being on an airfield at last, seeing and hearing the Tiger Moths he was soon to fly, it was the intoxicating atmosphere that so enthused him. Before being requisitioned for RAF use, Brough had been home to a private flying club. In relative terms everything smacked of luxury, not least the food and sleeping accommodation. But the most noticeable difference was the discipline – or rather the lack of it. After the tight control to which he'd previously been accustomed, standards at Brough appeared extraordinarily lax. Organisation lay in the hands of a flight sergeant, sergeant and corporal whose singular aim seemed to be to sit out the war without bothering – or being bothered by – anybody at all. Their objective seemed to be to do as little work as possible. The result was a state of what might be termed peaceful co-existence between staff and students, certainly until the flying element of the course began. Things then seemed to tighten up somewhat.

For Ron, and indeed for almost all the trainees, bizarrely nothing contributed more to this initial sense of relaxation – the sense of release from a prior straitjacket – than the fact that they were finally allowed to wear shoes. For the preceding months they'd struggled with the heavy boots they were required to wear almost constantly. The result was a series of expeditions that did much for the local shoe trade. After all the delays he'd experienced, and concerns about his damaged eye, the sense of relief Ron felt with his arrival at Brough transcended the physical; it was an almost other-worldly pleasure. His head was quite literally in the clouds as he prepared to embark on the next, critically important stage of his training.

Once he begins flying, Ron's letters become relatively few and far between. And because he finds himself so busy they continue occasionally to comprise elements written days apart. His next is forwarded from Watford to Connie's home; her peripatetic evacuation existence has come to a welcome end.

2 March 1941:

I hope my telegram reached you before you sent off your next letter. Anyway – here I am at last . . . We were given a marvellous lunch in the mess, which, by the way, is more like the dining room of some hotel. The food is excellent . . . I'm sure this will spoil me for civilian life again. We do arms, signals, navigation, airmanship, rigging, engines, and the final exams are on 31st March! We remain here for a week or two after that to complete our flying but I can see I'll have to work like blazes to get through – so if my letters are somewhat shorter than before, please forgive me. With luck we'll get a week's leave after this course – so I hope I'll be able to see you again.

It's been very windy up here & so we've not been able to fly, but yesterday we managed to get up for a short while . . . you've no idea what it's like to be miles up in the air, gazing down on roads, rivers, and tiny fields and trees. I'm looking forward to my next flip – I do hope I get through OK.

16 March 1941:

I'm glad you managed to get on your own again – I expect your mother & father are pleased – it makes a lot of difference to be independent. I'm glad, as well, that you've got nearer home again – besides being much nearer all your friends it means that I can see you even if I only get a short leave.

There's not much news up in this part of the world – I've done 5 hrs 55 minutes flying now and enjoy it more every time I go up. We've got our half-term exams next week – I can scarcely believe I'm half way through this course. I'll be glad of a rest after I do finish – we're doing quite a bit of work really.

I don't know whether Dorothy has written & told you but she's broken her engagement with Ron. I'm not very surprised & can imagine how pleased her people are.

As regards entertainments – these are non-existent at Brough – there's only three pubs. In any case I'm too damn busy to go out & so I don't miss anything.

I went to Harrogate last Saturday to see a girl I used to know at school. I caught the last train home by the skin of my teeth but I had a jolly good time when I was there. I'm going again next Saturday.
<u>*Monday.*</u>
I have to write this in bits – I'm afraid. The raid warning went just as I got to the 'Saturday' & and so we all shot out in case we had to go down to the shelters. I'm now out at our other sleeping place and as I've got an arms exam tomorrow I'm afraid I'll have to leave this now & do a spot of swotting . . .

30 March 1941:

I see from your letter that when I last wrote I'd done nearly 6 hrs flying – well – it's up to 11½ hrs now. I went solo just before I'd done 8½ hrs & since then I've managed to do 1¼ hrs on my own. It's far more fun without an instructor – you can go up to about 3000' (we very rarely go above that) and just do whatever we like. I like flying more and more these days.

The old senior flight has gone and we're the seniors now. Quite a lot of us have been given rooms instead of having to sleep in the dormitory & somehow or other I managed to get one. I've central heating, cupboards, a light specially fitted over the wash basin, a divan bed with a feather pillow – & curtains!
<u>*31/3/41.*</u> *I had to leave this letter as we all toddled to the shelters – I had a grand day today – I got 2 hrs 5 mins in. It would have been longer but as I was going solo my engine cut out just as I was taking off & I just managed to get the old machine back into the field. I had it tested & took off again but just as I was about 100' up the engine conked again & once more I had to shove it down in a hurry or I'd have to swim for it – the Humber runs by one side of our field. Anyway – everything's OK – I've done 13.35 hrs now.*

You sound awfully happy now that you're living at Woodford . . .

I feel as pleased as blazes at the moment – I can't think of any particular reason apart from the fact that I had a glorious time with my instructor this morning – he let me do spins, climbing turns, & sharp turns as well as a spot of low flying (hedge hopping) & then he did some loops with me – I wish I could take you up with me one day – I'm sure you'd like it.

I'm sorry if there's little in this letter apart from flying but we do little else nowadays. They've cut our lectures to 2 hrs a day & we fly the rest of the time so you can see my outlook is becoming rather restricted.

We were at Brough the night they bombed Hull[23] – we went to the shelters at 9 pm & came back at 4.30 am – quite a night – most of us were OK as we took blankets down there and just went to sleep.

14 April 1941:

We finished our exams on Friday – I must say that either the exams were fairly easy or else I must have done more work than I thought – but in any case I think I've done fairly well – It's a great relief – as you probably know – when exams are over & you don't have to do any more work for a while. We're supposed to be leaving at the end of this week but today it's raining like blazes so if it continues like this I can see us getting stuck here another week. Whenever we get out of here I hope we get a spot of leave – I feel as though I could do with a spot. Dorothy phoned me the other night – she's got a week's leave[24] from the 20th so I may be able to go and see her.[25] I'll be able to see you as easily as anything now that you're so near – good work!

I've spent the last 1½ hours doing aerobatics – most of them are pretty easy to do – but a slow roll is really awful – so many things can go wrong. When I first tried to do one on my own I got stuck sideways & the darned plane just refused to roll over – I got tired of it after a while & then just let it drop into a spin – I like spinning. By the way – I've been recommended for fighters – I'm terribly pleased about it – I've always wanted to fly a fighter. There's only 12 of us out of about 54 but most of them are pals of mine – including my particular pal so everything in the garden's lovely.

---

23. Hull was subjected to large-scale night bombing throughout March 1941; over 200 were killed.
24. Dorothy had joined the WAAF, the RAF's female auxiliary.
25. The Lunns' new house was no more than a few hundred yards from Ron's parents' home.

I still wear your gloves when I fly – I much prefer them to the gauntlets we're issued with. I've only got another 10 hrs 35 mns to get in this week and I've finished the course here – I do wish the weather would buck up & clear up – then there'd be more chance of getting leave . . .

We haven't any idea where we're going when we get shifted but I hope it's nearer home this time.

We've got a ten weeks course at SFTS (Service Flying Training School) and then – if we pass – we get those very elusive wings. If all goes well – I'll be in action about August, by that time it will have taken me just a year to get through all these courses.

Well, young lady, if I remember rightly you were going to send me one of those little Polyphotos some time ago, but it hasn't arrived yet – do you look as bad as that?

There's not much else to say so I'll just pack up for a bit & hope that I'm very shortly knocking at your door.

In this, Ron's last letter for some time, he's re-adjusted his sights. Thoughts about when he might get to grips with the enemy have been delayed from February until 'about August'; but even this aspiration is destined to move further into the future. His thirst for action has been encouraged by his instructor, Sergeant Tommy Ellis, credited with two 'confirmed' victories with 92 Squadron during the Battle of Britain. Indeed, it was Ellis who recommended him for fighters. Meanwhile, for the first time in his nascent flying career he experiences mortality. It was a sobering sight for those who witnessed the accident. On 7 April a fellow-student,[26] flying in the airfield circuit, collided in mid-air with the Chief Flying Instructor (CFI). While the latter managed to land his damaged aircraft safely, the student entered a spin and crashed; severely injured, he died the following day. There are further, less dramatic losses: a number of Ron's friends fail to make the grade and depart almost overnight.

For the record, he completes his basic flying course on 25 April and leaves Brough as an 'average' student with 50 hrs 05 mins in his log book. A step closer to the award of the coveted RAF flying badge, a short period of leave follows when he's able to catch up with various members of his relatively large family and see Connie occasionally. In her case, travel is the issue. Although she lives relatively nearby, the tube journey involves a change and takes a disproportionate amount of the limited time Ron has available. Then he's off to Kidlington for the next stage of his training.

---

26. LAC Joseph W. Savage.

Chapter 9

1 January 1943, 94th General Hospital, Algiers

There would be no New Year's Eve celebrations for Robbie. On 31 December, together with others including the Coldstream Guards officer he'd so misjudged, he was loaded on board another ambulance train, this time destined for Algiers. Less than 300 miles to the west as the crow flies, the journey would take almost twenty-four hours. There was plenty of time to reflect once again on his relatively fortunate lot as a commissioned officer. What he was coming to see as a considerable gulf between the way officers and men were treated was exemplified by their respective travel arrangements. Finding himself sharing a compartment with just one other officer, he was able to stretch out lengthwise across the seats on one side while his companion did the same on the other. By contrast, other ranks seemed to be treated more like cattle, crammed indiscriminately into their allotted carriages. This still gnawed at his conscience. *After all, we're all in the same war, fighting the same enemy, getting shot at by the same people. Surely we should be treated the same?*

After dozing for a few hours, Robbie levered himself up from the bench seat and set off for the nearest lavatory. It proved a difficult journey. Walking still wasn't easy for him. The swaying motion of the train led to the occasional stumble which left him resting on his hands and knees. If this was a shock to the system, he was soon in for a bigger one. For the first time since his accident he was able to examine himself closely in a mirror. He was taken aback. The image in front of him was unrecognisable. Unable to shave for eleven days, a partial beard was the least of his concerns. The face that squinted back at him seemed to comprise a single massive bruise, painted in vivid purple – evidence of the gentian violet with which his face had been daubed as a post-operative precaution against infection. Once the initial shock had worn off, he was left with a single overriding concern: would he *really* be able to recover the sight in his right eye?

He took this residual anxiety back with him to his compartment, a journey which meant edging past a couple of Arabs squatting in the corridor. He didn't recall them being there when he passed by earlier in the opposite direction and wondered idly how they'd got there. The answer came when the train next slowed almost to a walking pace – a relatively regular occurrence it seemed. A number of Arabs clambered aboard and immediately established themselves with their colleagues in the corridor. However, their tenure lasted only until they were discovered by a couple of the French Army officers who were accompanying the train. Without waiting for it to come to another virtual halt, these Beau Geste lookalikes had no compunction about ejecting their ticketless fellow-travellers. The train's part-time guards simply opened a door and levered the unfortunate Arabs out onto the trackside using brute force, speeding them on their way with a judicious boot.

The train finally arrived in Algiers on New Year's Day. Once transferred to hospital, Robbie settled gratefully into a proper bed once again, still suffering from severe pain around his eye. Unable to raise his head from the pillow, there was simply no relief from the incessant throbbing. It wasn't long before he had a visitor in the shape of a Major Fergus, an Edinburgh-born Harley Street eye specialist he would later describe as 'one of the finest people I've ever met'. Unceremoniously, Fergus delivered the news Robbie had been dreading. He would never see out of his right eye again. Worse than that, it would have to be removed straight away. Adamant in his refusal to accept what the medical profession saw as the only possible solution, Robbie prevaricated, pleading for a less drastic solution. *Couldn't they just remove the remaining shrapnel around his eye and leave it in place? That way he'd still look relatively normal and, who knows, he might even be able to wangle his way back onto flying again.* His dogged persistence paid off and the surgeon agreed to this alternative approach. An operation on 9 January worked to the extent that yet more detritus was removed from around his eye; but it left him still in excruciating pain, unable to sleep. It didn't help matters that a small amount of shrapnel remained embedded in the lower part of his eye. Shortly afterwards he received another visit from Major Fergus. There was nothing else for it, he explained; they had to revert to the original plan and remove his eye. *No way!* Robbie still refused to budge.

But after twenty-four hours without sleep, and unable to stand the pain any longer, on 10 January 1943 Robbie finally bowed to the inevitable and agreed to the removal of his eye. Major Fergus carried out the operation next day, leaving the patient feeling markedly better. A few days later he conducted another procedure to remove the remaining pieces of shrapnel embedded in Robbie's lower eyelid. Soon afterwards the invalid learned, through an unusual route, just how right he'd been finally to accept his surgeon's advice. Strangely, the story came not from a doctor but from the padre who was a regular ward visitor. On this occasion he stopped by Robbie's bed to reveal that had he not agreed to the operation there was a very real danger that he would have lost the sight in his other eye too. Septicaemia had set in.

The patient was now considerably improved. The constant pain, the agony at times, that he'd lived with for some three weeks had gone at last. It was thus a very relieved individual who apologised to Major Fergus for the trouble he felt he'd probably caused with his persistent refusal to accept the loss of his eye. The surgeon, however, would have none of it: 'That's alright my boy – we're here to help, not to criticise your actions.' Fergus also reassured the patient that he'd be fixed up with an artificial eye once he returned to the UK, 'and no one will know the difference'. Robbie wasn't so sure. *I'll still feel that things aren't normal – but then again what options do I have?*

Chapter 10

3 May 1941, No. 15 SFTS (Service Flying Training School), RAF Kidlington

O n 3 May Ron arrived at RAF Kidlington, home to No. 15 SFTS. The pressures of learning about a new aircraft type, the Airspeed Oxford, and the pattern of work that previously led to the odd composite missive is set to continue – as are the recreational activities he's always enjoyed, not least swimming.

6 May 1941:

Here's a letter at last but I'm afraid that it won't get posted for a day or so as I can't get hold of any stamps & it's a job to get out and post a letter if you do get them.

This isn't a bad place really, although it was pretty awful when I arrived. We're confined to camp on Mondays, Tuesdays & Thursdays in order to swot up all our notes on lectures etc. Oxford is only a short bus ride away & we had a look at it on Sunday. We fly alternate half days – viz. morning one day, afternoon the next. The crates we fly are, much to my disgust, twin-engined – the idea being that we'll probably go on to twin-engined night fighters – although if I have anything to do with it I'll get on to something else. They're amazingly complicated & you spend most of your time twiddling levers, wheels, switches, etc. etc. – so far I'm completely bewildered by the stuff you're supposed to know on the awful things but I'm hoping light will dawn on it in the near future.

Before we came, pupils were allowed one half day a week & one whole day a fortnight with a sleeping out pass for the preceding day, so I could get home easily – unfortunately that's been cut out entirely and we work from 7.30 am to all sorts of hours at night seven days a week. I think they're trying to cram as much as possible during our ten weeks here . . .

At any rate – I had a marvellous time on leave – especially Monday & Friday – I'm glad I was able to see quite a lot of you – it makes all this job seem much more worthwhile. There'd be very little to fight for if it weren't for the fact that after it's all over we can get back & enjoy ourselves in our old haunts with good company.

16 May 1941:

I'm sorry to hear that your firm's place has gone west but I'm awfully glad it happened while you were both at home. I've just had a letter from Mum telling me more news of the raid – it must have been one of the worst London has had.[27] Will it affect your father's job at all – will the firm be able to carry on with the same amount of staff or will some of them have to be fired to bring expenses down? Whatever happens, I hope neither of you loses by it.

I'm glad that we were able to get out a couple of times before they started raiding again – & if you enjoyed it then that's half my pleasure, too.

I've quite got used to this place now – it's not half as bad as I first imagined . . . Next week I've got Saturday off & I think I can get a sleeping out pass for Friday night – if so – I shall get out as early as I can and pop home on Friday night.

I didn't get up till about 8 am this morning then had a shower and walked into Kidlington village for breakfast about 9.30. After that I walked through some of the lanes & found an awfully ancient church[28] – it dates back to 1250 I think. I had a look over it & also some old houses nearby. They're all built of grey stone with tiny little stained glass windows. It's awfully pretty round here – there's miles of country & dotted about are these old grey stone houses. I had a grand time . . .

My roommate has just been kicked out as his flying's not so hot – after about 60 hrs flying that seems a bit silly but there it is. He's awfully cut up about it – so would I be too! He's going to be an observer now.

Apart from feeling something like a bus driver I'm getting to like these twin-engined kites. They go like old Nick when you want them to & they're

---

27. Ron is referring to the London raids of 10/11 May 1941; see Chapter 6 above and comments following his letter of 11 September 1940.
28. St Mary's Kidlington dates back to 1220; its tall spire is a local landmark known as 'Our Lady's Needle'.

awfully comfortable. You can fly without flying kit, helmet, goggles or anything – it's just like sitting in a summer house.

27 May 1941:

I did manage to get home for Friday night & Saturday but there was very little time to see anybody . . .

On Sunday we had quite a 'do'! – They held a church parade & the whole station turned out complete with band . . .

I'm afraid I've seen the last of my home for about 6½ weeks now as they've altered our day off & instead of getting a full day, we get from lunch time on one day to lunch time the next. It's pretty good getting anything off but it's smashed all my chances of getting home each week. Anyway – we're almost sure to get some leave after we finish here & that should be in about another 6-odd weeks' time.

I felt as miserable as anything yesterday – I made a hopeless mess of an instrument flying test & my instructor got most peeved with me. What with that & having our day off altered I could have wept – but everything's OK now. I had another IF [Instrument Flying] *test today and did the best I've ever done under the hood. (Did I tell you – we have a collapsible hood which is put over us & fixed to the instrument panel.) Anyway – I had to fly 8 minutes on one course – 12 on the next & 11½ on the last – after that time we should have got somewhere near our own 'drome again. When I finished the last course I lifted the hood & lo & behold! We were just over the boundary of the aerodrome. I was as pleased as Punch after the mess I made of it the day before. Even the instructor said it was quite good.*

I've been up tonight from 6.10 – 7.30. I should have been back at 7.10 but I got lost. It was glorious up there – the sun had just managed to break through and there were a few puffy clouds dotted here and there. It was while I was doing steep turns round these clouds that I lost myself. I came down pretty low but couldn't recognise a thing & so got the old map out & flew to where I thought I ought to see a town of some description. I did find a small village with a single track railway running through it & so I spent five minutes flying round & round it at an acute angle until I eventually found it on the map – was I glad!

I had a letter from Dolly today – she's still very smitten by this Nils chap – she had a letter & cablegram from him recently & is all-of-a dither over it . . .

I'm glad they were able to salvage some of your firm's records. I should have thought, though, that for a big concern like yours that they would have had duplicate books at their bank . . . still, as long as both your jobs are OK that's all that matters.

5 June 1941:

<u>8.00 am.</u>

I've just had breakfast & I'm going to try & write part of a letter now & the rest when I get time. Now that we've started night flying we get even less time to ourselves than before – anyway – it's good fun – passes the time. I feel all OK again now – as our flying hours were well up our flight commander said we needn't fly on Sunday so we all rushed home for a while . . .

Unfortunately I just missed seeing my uncle in the RAF – he'd been posted abroad for training . . .

Our exams are in three weeks' time & I feel as though I scarcely know a thing – it's awfully difficult to swot up anything at night here. When we're not flying late we finish anything up to 7 pm & then usually go to our mess for a spot of supper & then to bed . . .

<u>12.30 pm.</u> *I still get regular letters from Kathleen – although I'm afraid the answers she gets are only about a third as long as hers. As for Yvonne, she only writes (as a rule) once every blue moon, but she amazed me recently by writing a long letter to me almost as soon as I got back & also sending me a postcard from Blackpool. I've only just answered them.*

I had a nice trip up to Lincolnshire on Monday – it was supposed to be my navigation test & I'm glad to say that I managed it OK. The last 10 miles or so were off the map & so my instructor, who knew the district, took over & landed the plane. I'm just as glad he did as a tyre burst when we were taxying over the 'drome & if I'd have landed the plane I expect he'd have thought I'd have been the cause of it all. Anyway, we stayed for lunch & had a smashing feed & then left about 4.20 after they'd put a whole new wheel on.

We were all asked where we wanted to go on to from here, the other day. I've been put down for <u>day</u> fighters – that's OK as long as there's still a demand for day fighters when our course is finished. Otherwise if there's a shortage of bomber or coastal command pilots we'll all get slung on those. What you actually finish up on depends on the circumstances at the time you've finished – but it gives you a bit of a kick to know you stand a chance of getting what you want – even though that chance may be very slender.

16 June 1941:

Excuse paper & pencil – but this is all the paper I've got & as I have to write in dribs & drabs a pencil is much more convenient . . .

We've been pretty busy lately – flying late most nights to make up for that week of bad weather. Actually there's not much more to do – I've finished all my cross countries & most of my exercises . . . apart from formation flying & I did some of that today. I also managed to scramble through a Flight Commander's 'progress test' OK so I feel pretty bucked with life altogether.

I meant to answer some of my letters last night but after we finished flying at 5 pm I felt so hot I just wanted to go to bed and collapse. Luckily two chaps were going to Oxford on a motor bike to have a swim in the river & asked me to go with them. It was really glorious – we had a great piece of the river all to ourselves with cubicles to change in, boards etc. – there were fields all around – in fact it was 'truly rural' – the only snag was that the water was like ice but after you got used to it was marvellous – we stayed for about a quarter of an hour & then sunbathed on the grass – if all goes well – weather permitting – we're going again on Sunday afternoon. That's the first swim I've had since February.

I've had a letter from Dolly today – she's very upset because she hasn't heard from Nils for six weeks . . .

I've got to do some night flying tonight – I hope I'm on early – I want to get back & have some sleep.

I'm getting lots of hints chucked at me that I ought to become an instructor. I hope nothing comes of it – I haven't the slightest desire to try & teach other people to fly – I want to have a smack at the Jerries on my own. The only snag is that if the CO says I'm to be an instructor, that finishes it & nothing I or my own instructor can say will alter matters – however – I'll find out in due course – & I'll just have to wait & see what happens . . .

Although he doesn't mention it, one of the factors steering Ron towards an unwanted instructor posting is his relative maturity. At a time when CinC Fighter Command has decreed that squadron commanders should be no older than 26, Ron is already 23. His flight commander regards him as 'far too old for fighters'. However, there's something else, ultimately of greater import, that Ron does mention. For the first time in sixty-four letters this one concludes 'Love . . . '. It's taken him long enough but it's a precedent he now follows regularly. Clearly, his romance with Connie is beginning to blossom.

24 June 1941:

I wrote to Mum yesterday & said I'd be home over the weekend but we've just heard that there's a compulsory church service on Sunday morning . . . consequently no passes are to be issued. I don't want Mum to worry if I'm not home & I can't get out to phone her before Saturday – so could you phone her . . . just say you're Connie – she'll know who you are – she knows almost as much about you as I do – having listened to me talking about you for years . . .

I don't like the idea of you wandering about fire watching in the early hours of the morning – that's certainly no job for a girl – I think the local authorities are taking this 'Do your bit to win the war' stuff a bit too far.

I've done 3 of my 9 solo landings at night so far – I hope to do the rest tomorrow night. I do hope I get some leave after this course – it seems to be such a heck of a rush – we're scarcely still for 5 minutes.

Are there any open air baths such as the one at Chingford – I can't remember its name. If they are open, maybe we could have a swim one afternoon before going somewhere at night – if I get leave. Anyway – here's hoping I see you soon . . .

5 July 1941:

We've had our exam results & I did about as well as I did at EFTS. Top mark was 86.4% & I came 29th with 78.7% – I got through which is the main point. Unfortunately, & much to my disgust, I'm going to be an instructor. As soon as I heard I applied to see the Flight Commander – he seemed to agree with me that I'd be a pretty awful instructor & gave me permission to see the Squadron Ldr. The S/Ldr was also very nice and I eventually reached the Wing Commander. He was the stumbling block – he ramped & roared for quite a while – he said he was 'amazed & disgusted that I should question his authority & did I presume to know better than he did what the RAF required?' Never, according to him, had anyone been audacious enough to say they didn't want to be an instructor. I should consider it an honour that I had been chosen as an instructor at my age – & so on & so on. I'm as fed up as blazes about it . . .

We go swimming in the river nearly every night now – it's marvellous. I've finished all my flying now apart from a Wing Commander's test – so I had yesterday afternoon off with some of my pals. We were in the river from 2.30 to 6.45 & just dived in the water and lazed on the bank alternately . . .

Another snag about this instructor lark is that it's very unlikely that I'll get much leave – the normal period is 2-3 days – if lucky.

I've just had a letter from Dolly from which it would appear that the romance is still going pretty well – she gets these airgraph[29] letters from him at odd times – all protesting the great love he bears her – at least that's what I imagine.

P.S. Even if I only get a day or so leave I'll pop up & see you – I think we leave on Friday sometime.

This is Ron's last letter from Kidlington. His final course sortie, on 9 July, amounts to forty minutes' night flying and brings the sum total of his experience to 139 hours and 15 minutes. The next page in his log book sees the entry, in red ink, that he's long striven for: 'FLYING BADGE AWARDED W.E.F. 11th July 1941.' The facing page shows that his 'Proficiency as pilot on type', the Oxford, was assessed as 'Average'. More encouraging were the accompanying remarks: 'Very good average. Steady and reliable. Should make a useful night fighter pilot.'

After avoiding an instructor appointment for reasons yet to emerge, and as one of the top four on his course, all of whom earned fighter postings, it was with a spring in his step that Ron left Kidlington. Pending arrival of the telegram containing joining instructions for their new units, he and a close friend from the course, Jack Ranger, spent a number of evenings together in London. (An ex-member of Highgate Diving Club,[30] Ranger regularly accompanied Ron on swimming trips – excursions where he was happy to demonstrate his prowess, courtesy of the Oxford river bridges.) Usually they'd meet with another with whom Ron had developed a close bond, Derek Olver, who'd moved to Kensington with his wife, Kay, immediately after the course. With all three pilots effectively in a state of limbo, after their

---

29. The airgraph service was a way of sending airmail messages to Servicemen. Messages were written on a special form with an identification number and photographed onto microfilm. The microfilm was then flown to its destination, developed into a full size print, and posted to the recipient. In terms of freight, 160 airgraphs weighed the same as the average letter. Copies of microfilms were retained so that if they were lost en route messages could be re-sent.

30. Founded in 1928 and based at Highgate Ponds, by the time it was forced into temporary closure in 1939 the Club dominated British diving, providing members of Olympic, European and Commonwealth Games teams. Originally a bastion of male privilege, women were finally admitted in 1990, although they had long been coached there.

evenings out together, Ron and Jack would either return home or spend the night at the Olvers' flat.

Thanks largely to these regular expeditions to London, Ron spent little time at his Forest Gate home. It was pure luck that he was there on 19 July when his joining instructions arrived, requiring him to report to RAF Hawarden, in North Wales. Immediately he rang Jack, who'd also been assigned to night fighters, expecting to hear he'd be joining him there. Surprised to learn that he wouldn't – he'd been posted to a Beaufighter Operational Training Unit at a different base – Ron's immediate confusion turned to delight when his friend continued: 'They fly Spitfires at Hawarden. My brother was up there.' For a moment he simply couldn't believe his luck. His long-held ambition to fly day fighters was about to be realised – provided he passed the course! Once the news had sunk in, he penned a quick note to Connie and persuaded his brother to deliver it by hand – such was the urgency.

Saturday. 4.30 pm.

In great haste – I've been recalled & am due to report tomorrow (Sunday) – the point is I'd like to see you before I go – could you phone me tomorrow morning & maybe I could see you at Liverpool St on the way to my next station – it's not a very good rendezvous – but I'll be packing all the morning & I'm just going out for the last time with Jack & Derek – I'm posted on my own. So far as I can gather I'm going on to 'Spits' – not night fighters. Alan can maybe give you more news if he finds you in.

Connie wasn't in but she called first thing next morning. After a rendezvous at Liverpool Street station mid-afternoon, the pair travelled together the short distance to Euston, chatting animatedly. Ron's excitement was palpable and infectious. It all but overcame Connie's obvious concerns – not just about the risks he faced, but also about when they might see each other again. For the moment, though, Ron was able to put any such worries out of his mind. *Spitfires!*

Chapter 11

15 January 1943, 94th General Hospital, Algiers

With his eye removed, and the constant pain of the previous three weeks virtually gone, Robbie had plenty of time to think. In fact he did little else. The days seemed endless – endlessly frustrating too. He spent almost every waking hour contemplating an uncertain future. Inevitably it would be devoid of the flying he'd come to love so much. Of this he was sure. He was less certain, though, whether it would involve his other great love, his fiancée Connie. Indeed, the question of their future together became his overriding preoccupation as he lay recovering in hospital. Still barely able to read with his one good eye, let alone write, he'd sent his last letter just a day before his accident. But the time was fast approaching when he'd at last be able to put pen to paper. Never normally at a loss when it came to compiling his regular missives, he was increasingly concerned about how best to impart his devastating news. Less worried about what he should say – he'd already made a major decision about that – he was more concerned about how he should say it.

After turning these issues over and over in his mind during the five days that followed the removal of his eye, Robbie was finally ready to begin what he knew would be the most important letter he'd ever write. He'd already convinced himself that the only honourable thing to do would be to release Connie from their engagement. To put no finer point on it, he considered himself physically diminished – no longer the hale and hearty individual to whom she'd originally been betrothed. He felt that in these new circumstances she had every right to opt out of their marriage commitment. Having come to this difficult decision, on a day that would be forever etched in his memory, he set about the task of putting his thoughts on paper.

In one respect nothing had changed. More than anything, he still wanted to marry the woman with whom he was so deeply in love. The strength of his feelings rendered him simply incapable of breaking off their engagement of his own volition; the decision must lie with Connie. In the end there was no question of choosing his words carefully; there was too much emotion involved. He simply wrote to her as he always did, spontaneously – from the heart. It was as short, and certainly as heartfelt, as any letter he'd ever written:

15 January 1943:

My dearest darling,

I'm afraid I've got rather bad news for you – I've had to have my right eye taken out. It was the only thing to do in the circumstances.

This is going to be a shock to you I know, but keep your chin up dear. I don't feel too badly now it's more or less over – I'll be coming home in a month or so – we can decide what's best to be done about us then. It seems a bad handicap to start our married life on sweet but that is entirely up to you. Do speak to your people and mine and decide what's best to be done. It's not that I've thought better of marrying you – I love you more than anything else in the world and always will – but it doesn't seem very fair to you and I don't want you to do something you might regret in years to come. I must leave this now – I got Else's[31] letter OK – thank her very much.

All my love to you, my dear

Your devoted
Ron xxxxxx

I haven't written before because I couldn't see very well with my other eye and feel pretty bad anyway.

I got shot down on 20th Dec.

Later that same day Robbie underwent a minor procedure, an incision under his damaged eye to allow a build-up of puss to escape. Although this produced a mild improvement, he couldn't bring himself to write to Connie again for days. After all, what more was there to say? He did, however,

---

31. Connie's mother, Mrs Freeman, known as 'Else'.

manage a lengthy letter to his mother; they'd corresponded regularly throughout his time in the Service.

Time now seemed to stand still. Having passed on the news of his accident and his resulting disability, effectively placing his future in Connie's hands, he became increasingly desperate to receive her reply. It was too much to ask, he knew. So a week later he put pen to paper once again:

22 January 1943:

I've just written Mum a long letter giving her all the details of my accident right from start to finish & asked her to tell you all about it – she'll probably show you the letter anyway. I'm not going to tell you all over again because I just want to tell you how much I love and miss you. I've been unable to read or write or even sit up so I've just spent my time lying awake and thinking of you.

I love you so much, dear – if I hadn't had all those lovely memories of times at home I don't know what I'd have done.

This business has worried me a lot though – it's going to be a big decision for you to make whether we get married as arranged or not now.

Please, darling, don't think I'm harping on the subject but I'd rather never see you again than cause you one regret. I can never stop loving you Tubs – but this business does seem to have messed things up for us doesn't it.

I scarcely know what I'm writing – I'm so anxious to get back to you & actually see you & yet I want to stay here long enough to get a reply to my last letter.

Personally I'm not too worried over my lack of an eye. I think I'm lucky to get off as lightly as that but I really am worried about all my friends & relations at home – it's always ten times as bad for them.

Oh darling – I do wish I could see you just for a few minutes & straighten everything out.

I only hope that you're not worrying too much about me – I'm doing fine now & really feel a lot better.

I feel I've let everyone down rather badly – especially you & the idea makes me rather fed up at times but all I can do is just wait until I come home – so many things will have to be straightened out.

This is an awful gloomy letter sweet, but I've always written to you exactly how I feel & I feel a lot better having got all this off my chest . . .

Robbie's gloom was lifted, at least in part, by the news that he was to return home soon. (Little did he know that, frustratingly, his departure from Algiers would be delayed any number of times.) Still not knowing whether news of his predicament had reached Connie, in a reflective, slightly more positive frame of mind, he began another letter:

26 January 1943:

It's ages since I actually addressed you as 'Tubby' isn't it? Anyway – I love you – in fact it's a thousand times stronger than just loving you but at least you'll get what I mean from that. Darl, if only you knew how much I miss you just lying here, reading occasionally, smoking (quite a lot) – I've got all the time in the world to think about you.

The other day I started right from the Embankment before I joined up & thought of all that had happened up to now. I thought of all the times I'd kissed you at 6 o'clock in the morning before I went to catch the 6.50 to Debden – then March 10th when we went to the 'Queens' & I first put the ring on your finger – you looked awfully pretty that night – I had a really nice time just dreaming of all those things.

Tubby darl – don't be too annoyed at anything I may have put in my last two letters – I felt I just had to say all those things.

I'll be in hospital in England for some time when I get back – my one & only consolation is that in that event I won't spend much money so I should have quite a bit when I come home . . .

I expect the Air Ministry sent a note to say that I was in hospital – I've been hoping that it didn't arrive before Christmas and so spoil things for you.

I hope you're buying an odd Bing record here and there – I'd give anything to sit in your drawing room in front of the fire and listen to our favourites again . . .

I hope it won't be long before I'm writing to you from an English address . . .

Chapter 12

20 July 1941, No. 57 OTU (Operational Training Unit), RAF Hawarden

So how did the change from potential instructor to tyro Spitfire pilot come about? Quite simply, Lady Luck intervened on Ron's behalf. Not long after his contretemps with Kidlington's Wing Commander Flying, he was somewhat surprised to find his instructor, Flight Lieutenant Gayner, rushing up to him: 'There you are, Robbie! Would you like to be a night fighter pilot?' There was no doubt in his mind. 'Yes, too true,' he replied, 'Anything to avoid being an instructor.' Apparently another member of his course who'd been posted to night fighters had requested an instructor posting in lieu, giving rise to the opportunity for a swap. (It's entirely possible that this was Derek Olver, one of the few married members of the course.) Had it not been for the fuss Ron made about his mooted instructor assignment, this serendipitous turn of events might never have occurred. His first significant brush with authority thus worked out better than he dared hope; it also taught him a valuable lesson. While there were pitfalls in speaking one's mind, as he was wont to do, there could be benefits too.

Meanwhile, his budding romance seems to be progressing well. Two days after arriving in North Wales he begins writing once again:

22 July 1941:

I've been thinking about you ever since I left – it was awfully nice of you to come & see me off – I felt pretty blue leaving you though – I do hope you're not still worrying yourself about anything – if you hadn't left before the train went I'm sure I couldn't have gone – I hate saying goodbye just as the train leaves – it seems much harder saying goodbye then.

Well, after that rather complicated paragraph I'll tell you what's happened since I left. We arrived after 9 pm & I phoned up Hawarden for a truck. We got to the camp about 10.15 pm & dumped our kit & then a Rhodesian and I went into the sergt's mess where everyone made us feel absolutely at home. Everyone here is easy-going & no one rushes about telling us to do this or that – we're more or less left on our own. We don't do any flying until tomorrow & I don't suppose I'll touch a Spit until next week sometime – we're supposed to do advanced flying, formation and other odd things on other single engined aircraft before we're allowed to go near one of these precious Spits – you can't blame them really – after all – once you get in a Spit it's entirely up to you & and there's no one to help you.

Our quarters are very nice & the grub in the mess is excellent. We've got one of the latest Marconi radios & bags of easy chairs.

Chester's our nearest town but I don't think much of it . . . It's pretty dismal – no buses after 9.10 & so you can't stay unless you want to hitch back & that's not very easy round here . . .

So far as I can see I won't be going into Chester very often – We work from 7 am to 7 pm – by which time everything is closed. In any case, everything here is awfully comfortable & I've no real desire to go outside . . .

If all goes well we should get a week's leave after our six weeks here – so I'll soon be able to take you out again. If you like to pick a pair of 'wings' out I'll buy them for you – otherwise we'll go & get a pair together when I see you again – then you can wear them for good luck.

28 July 1941:

You've no idea how pleased I was to get your letter – I scarcely know how to go on – you know I've always wanted to have things like this, but they seemed never to turn out my way & now they have – well – I'm rather staggered but tremendously happy – I do hope that you never have cause to change your mind – if you <u>do</u> – let me know – it won't make us bad friends or anything like that, but on the other hand it might save you a lot of unhappiness & that's the last thing I want to happen. All I think of now is finishing this course & getting a spot more leave so that we can go out and poodle around . . . there seem to be so many things I want to say to you – I can't just write them here.

We have bags of lectures on tactics, guns, & airmanship & apart from that I've done 4-5 hrs on these kites & I'm waiting to go on the real job this week sometime. It's awfully good here – everything is just OK.

You seem to be having quite a good time at home – I hope old Jerry stays away from your part of the world (unless I get posted there eventually) . . .

Don't start worrying over what <u>might</u> happen to me – it's not half as dangerous as most people think – in any case I've made up my mind to come out on top – otherwise I wouldn't be able to see <u>you</u> again – would I?

This latest letter touches on two significant but unrelated issues. First, there's the unbounded affection that Ron expresses initially. It's a response to 'the first time [Connie] ever said that [she] cared about' him[32] and has unexpected results. He seems to have crossed an emotional boundary of which he's blissfully unaware. For her part Connie appears to have been taken aback by the strength of his feelings, and perhaps even by his longer term aspirations – his hints ultimately at marriage perhaps?

The second noteworthy point is Ron's mention of the 'kites' used in readying pilots for the Spitfire. The Miles Master, a low-wing advanced trainer with tandem seating, played an important preparatory role at Hawarden because there were no two-seat Spitfires. To supplement their theoretical training novice crews sat in a Spitfire raised on jacks in a hangar where they could get used to operating the undercarriage, flaps and other control surfaces. When the time came for his first Spitfire flight, after a preparatory briefing the neophyte would strap himself in then listen with mild apprehension to a few final words from his instructor as he leaned over into the cramped cockpit. There would be a cheery 'Good luck' as the instructor jumped down off the rear of the port wing, and then the nervous young man really was on his own. This was exactly how it was for Ron on the morning of Friday 1 August 1941, a day he'd never forget.

Back now to the fallout from Ron's previous impassioned opening . . .

3 August 1941:

You seem to be in a bit of a mess, don't you? – anyway – for Heaven's sake stop worrying over this particular spot of bother. Anyone would think I was going to ramp & roar & write you rude letters, or something like that – you see (or do you?) I hadn't any bright ideas such as becoming engaged at once – I thought that if you felt the same way as I imagined you did then we might get engaged at some later date, when you were about 19 or something like that. You know that you're pretty young & all sorts of things can happen in a year or so – hence my idea of waiting for a while.

---

32. Ron's letters of 18 February 1942 (see Chapter 16) and 18 March 1944 (see Chapter 27) refer.

This is a very badly expressed letter & I can only hope that you don't get too muddled when reading it. I used to think I was pretty good at writing letters but this is a pretty awful affair, (the <u>letter</u> I mean).

I only hope this letter isn't delayed in the post – I'm sure you're worrying about this affair far too much. If I do get some leave later on I'll pop over & see you & listen to your tale of woe. Just in case I haven't made it clear – if you change your mind & think you can put up with me – well – all you have to do is say the word.

Before I forget, there <u>is</u> one thing that would annoy me more than anything – & that is if you think this has made any difference between us – we're still good pals & so far as I'm concerned – always will be.

P.S. I've done 2½ hrs on 'Spits' – they're beautiful!

7 August 1941:

I'm glad you're not so worried as you were – but if you still have any doubts as to whether I'll see you when (or if) I get leave you can forget them now – even if I only get a weekend – in which case I'll most likely get home on a Friday – I'll see you on the Saturday. Believe me – if it can possibly be arranged I'll see you, if I don't see anyone else . . .

I've done 7.40 hrs on 'Spits' now – I'm absolutely crazy about them. There's just nothing like them – to fully understand what I mean you'd have to fly certain kites & then transfer onto 'Spits' – it's like driving a Rolls-Royce after training on an Austin 7.

I was up with a F/Sgt [Flight Sergeant] *doing a spot of formation the other day when he decided to do a roll – I followed suit but got stuck up on the top – the kite just wouldn't come over – I must have brought the stick back to neutral without knowing it – anyway – the only thing to do was pull the stick hard back and pray. I pulled out OK but old 'Flight' thought I'd gone and spun into the deck and spent a quarter of an hour searching for my remains – while I was up aloft searching for him – he heaved a great sigh of relief when I finally landed back at the 'drome with him . . .*

The other afternoon the weather was awful and flying was washed out so the CO had us all taken to Chester to see Target for Tonight. It's a marvellous film – although for an 'ops' [operational] *station there's miles too much saluting – we all thought the actual film was very good but the bombing looks pretty dangerous – I'd much prefer fighters.*

We still have to do cross-countries while I'm here & I'm hoping to get in trips to my old SFTS . . . I think I know most of England pretty well now –

our sector here is about the only area I hadn't covered until recently. It's jolly funny trying to map read in a 'Spit' – before you've finished finding yourself you're about ten miles past your original point.

Well, darling, I think I've covered about everything this time. Do stop worrying about everything – there's really no need to.

The closure of this latest letter marks another small but significant development. Now that Ron's cleared up any concerns Connie may have had about the direction in which their relationship is heading, in his final paragraph he uses the word 'darling' for the first time.

11 August 1941:

As you probably realise, your letter is one of 'The' events of the week – you've no idea how I look forward to it.

As to seeming out of sorts – why should I be? I'm doing something I've always wanted to do – I'm amongst a crowd of darn good chaps – in fact there's nothing to grumble at at all. If I weren't so very lucky I'd probably be as miserable as sin . . .

. . . I was told to do some air to ground firing the other day but apart from spraying the landscape with .303 I did no damage to the target at all. However, I managed to do better with a camera gun today – I find it easier to chase another aircraft than fire at some little dot on the ground . . .

I'd heard that all the old haunts up west had become rather crowded lately – but you can still get into the Queens Brasserie about 7.30. – we'll have to try & pop up to a show & then to the 'QB' . . .

It seems funny that in a few weeks I'll probably be chasing or being chased by a Jerry instead of fooling around with a ciné camera and another Spit – I'm rather looking forward to it . . .

As for looking after myself – well – I have done so far & my luck seems to be holding – anyway – if I'm due to go I'll go & that's all there is to it – but don't go worrying about it. It's a risk we all take in this war – civilians as well as forces – you just have to make the best of things whilst you can.

Well, darling, don't let's get all morbid about what <u>might</u> happen . . .

17 August 1941:

I'm starting this at 9.30 am – I got up too late for church parade & so I'm keeping clear until it's over & then I'll pop down to the flight & try &

get a flip. We had a formation of 24 aircraft yesterday – half our flight & half the other. Three of our instructors lead the sections and nine pupils make up the rest. It's the first time I've been up with so many planes – it's a wonderful sight but you have to stick to your position like glue or else you'll be bumping into someone else.

My pal & I have just bought a wireless set – I don't know who's going to have it when we leave.

Can you get days off when you like or must you give bags of notice before taking them? If I get some leave (the other course didn't get any at all) maybe we could have a day out somewhere or other . . .

Did I ever tell you of my pal Jack [Ranger] *who went onto night fighters? Anyway – I had a letter from him the other day – there was bags of news in it but one point in particular made me laugh. It appears that he has to do a few hours on 'Moths' again at night before getting transferred to bigger stuff. He was up solo the other day & when coming in to land he turned in at 1000' & then had a fit – you see – on the kites we've been flying for the past 100 hrs there's bags of things to do just before you land – you have to turn wheels – pull levers – & altogether have a pretty busy time before you start to drop in. Anyway – on a 'Moth' you don't do a thing but just throttle back and let it drop in – that's all there is to it, but old Jack was racking his brains to find out whether he'd forgotten anything & looking frantically round the cockpit for something to pull – he got in OK though.*

I've just heard I'm leading a formation in about an hour. Whoopee!

20 August 1941:

That formation flight I told you about was OK but the one the following day wasn't. After it was over I came in to land & the kite started to swing – when it does that there's not much you can do about it but hope. Anyway, the kite smashed itself up but I was absolutely OK and did another 1½ hrs on Spits the same day, so don't start worrying about anything. There's another thing – I'm probably staying here for another three weeks after our course finishes in order to act as an instructor to our junior course & also get extra hours in. I'm probably coming straight down to the south instead of doing the usual few months up north. The only snag is that I'm almost certain not to get any leave but I'll try & get 48 hrs off. I've never wanted leave so much as I do this time.

You're quite right – I've been in the RAF a year & a day now. On 19th August I went to Babbacombe.

A SPITFIRE NAMED CONNIE

Do you remember that Thursday night we had out before I left – I <u>did</u> enjoy that. I always seem to see you just before I go anyway – that's what makes leaving much nicer than it would be otherwise.

Yes – I've (a) had a letter from Derek & (b) we two chaps share a room between us – it's a nice little room too! . . .

From the latter part of your letter it sounds as though you've got something on your mind. Have you started worrying about something again!

Ron isn't entirely truthful about the immediate consequences of the accident he describes here – understandably so. As his final sentence implies, Connie is a born worrier. He's anxious that she shouldn't be overly concerned about him, or doubt his ability in any way, so he paints a rosier picture than was actually the case.

His log book entry for 18 August shows that he 'crashed on landing' after a 1 hour 20 minute formation sortie. Opposite these details is a comment signed off by Squadron Leader F.P.R. Dunworth, CFI 57 OTU: 'INEXPERIENCE 81G/C.6201/163/TRG'. Like so many Ron was to encounter in the months ahead, Dunworth had an interesting tale to tell. By the time he took command of 54 Squadron at the height of the Battle of Britain, he'd already survived wounding and a crash-landing. As if that weren't enough, immediately beforehand he'd experienced a torrid time as a flight commander on 66 Squadron at Kenley where, in early September 1940, 'casualties had been alarming'.[33] To reinforce the point, according to one of Ron's future squadron commanders, Bob Oxspring, a junior pilot at the time, the squadron 'lost eight aircraft and six pilots in just two days'.[34] Also serving on 66 at the same time was another future colleague, Jimmy Corbin, who later recalled that 'Many of those killed were sprogs just like me. Some of them were killed on their very first mission without ever firing a shot.'[35]

Dunworth's entry in Ron's log book followed an interview with Hawarden's Wing Commander Flying, 'a very nice chap', 'Hilly' Brown.[36] With a DFC and Bar and more than fifteen confirmed victories in his Hurricane, initially during the battle of France, Brown had effectively seen it all. He explained to Ron that while it may have been forgiving in the air, the Spitfire's narrow-track undercarriage, powerful engine and nose-heavy configuration

---

33. Group Captain Bobby Oxspring DFC** AFC, *Spitfire Command* (William Kimber, London, 1984), p.54.
34. Ibid.
35. Jimmy Corbin, *Last of the Ten Fighter Boys* (The History Press, Stroud, Gloucestershire, 2010), p.193. Corbin retired in 1945 as a flight lieutenant.
36. A Canadian, Brown was kia on 11 November 1942 flying from Malta.

made handling on the ground an entirely different proposition. This was particularly so for those, like Ron, with limited experience; he'd flown just eighteen sorties and some twenty-one hours at the time. The upshot of this particular misadventure – it wouldn't be the only time his aircraft ended up on its nose – was a twenty-five-minute 'check dual' with an instructor in a Master the following day. Safely accomplished, Flight Lieutenant J.C. Freeborn cleared him for a Spitfire 'dog fighting' sortie later that same day.

Johnny Freeborn, a 74 Squadron Battle of Britain ace, like Brown with a DFC and Bar to his name, was another with an interesting history. Together with Flying Officer Vincent 'Paddy' Byrne, he was court martialled for shooting down a pair of 56 Squadron Hurricanes over the Thames estuary only three days after war was declared. Two contrasting characters, the occasionally blunt northerner and the jovial Irishman were cleared of any blame for a tragic incident in which Pilot Officer Montague 'John' Hulton-Harrop was killed. Fighter Command's first operational fatality, his aircraft crashed at Hintlesham, near Ipswich. (Strangely, Hulton-Harrop, whose engagement had been announced just a week earlier, had survived a mid-air collision with another Hurricane barely two months before.) Hushed up at the time, what later became known as the 'Battle of Barking Creek' was deemed to have resulted from a misdirected interception. Ironically, Freeborn went on to be shot down twice himself, the first time in May 1940 over Dunkirk. Forced to crash-land, he was picked up later in Calais by a Blenheim crew and returned safely to England. The second occasion was in August of the same year; again he survived unhurt.

Byrne was a genuine character: 'short, dark and stocky, the archetypal version of an Irishman . . . with a lilting brogue and irrepressible humour'.[37] Serving with 92 Squadron, he too was shot down over Dunkirk. Once captured, he found himself incarcerated in Stalag Luft III in company with his erstwhile boss, Squadron Leader Roger Bushell, who'd been shot down near Calais earlier in May. By a strange quirk of fate, in his capacity as a barrister, Bushell had assisted in defending Freeborn and Byrne at their October 1939 court martial. However, he's better remembered for masterminding 'The Great Escape' of March 1944 and for his callous murder by the Gestapo after recapture. Byrne was repatriated that same year, the outcome of a lengthy and ultimately successful campaign to feign insanity.

Returning now to Ron's efforts to downplay his landing incident, he's only partially successful.

---

37. Brian Kingcome, *A Willingness to Die* (Tempus Publishing Ltd, Stroud, 1999), p.81.

25 August 1941:

Just to put your mind at rest I'll start by telling you that I'm perfectly alright & have over ten hours more on Spits since then. I'm afraid it <u>was</u> a Spit though . . .

It's <u>almost</u> certain that I'll be staying here for another three weeks as an instructor and so as soon as I've finished this particular piece of the course I'm going to put in for 48 hrs. If it comes off I hope to get home on Saturday or a day or so after . . .

I've only just come down – I was up until 7.25 pm. It was lovely up tonight, although it had been pretty awful all day. I felt awfully happy tonight for some unknown reason & threw the kite about all over the place – much to the annoyance of a chap up with me who was trying to use me as a target for his camera-gun . . .

You know – the more I think of it, the more I'm convinced that I've been awfully lucky in my postings to stations. Wherever I've been I've had a very easy time & met a great crowd of extremely decent chaps – instructors & pupils . . .

I'm hoping like blazes to see you for a short time in a few days.

7 September 1941:

As you can see – I arrived [back] here eventually . . . I did nothing all morning but collect all my belongings & transfer them to another flight. As I expected – my wireless was 'dud' when I came back – my pal had been using it & had used all the accumulator – so I had to get another this afternoon. The new flight seems to be OK & the F/Cdr [Flight Commander] is very nice. I did just 2 hrs flying this afternoon before the weather came down . . .

At the moment I'm ensconced on a pile of blankets in my room trying to forget I ever had any leave & concentrate on the job in hand. I can't keep my mind from wandering though – I had such a grand time I keep thinking about it & going over all I did from last Sunday. I can't remember when I last had such a good time – I hope it won't be too long before I can get down south & see you again . . .

By the way, all low flying over the 'drome has been cancelled – needless to say it was due to Sika – he nearly took a coat of paint off the Group Captain's kite as he went over it – Groupie took a poor view of this & the result is that we have to be careful (more or less) what we do nowadays.

'Sika' was an immensely experienced Czech sergeant who'd served previously on 72 Squadron (a connection that meant nothing to Ron at the time) and was now an instructor. Admired for his spirited flying, it was his habit to end every instructional sortie by beating up the airfield – hurtling along the perimeter track almost at ground level then pulling up into a loop, rolling wings level at the top before beginning a curving descent to land. He encouraged his pupils to follow him in this 'roll off the top' manoeuvre. On this particular occasion, while he may well have taken things a little far, he was unlucky to have been caught by, of all people, the Station Commander. However, the latter's strictures do little to discourage Ron's own airborne exuberance, as is shortly to be revealed.

11 September 1941:

Apparently Dorothy phoned home to see how I was getting on just after I left. Mum told her I'd only been home for the weekend & I'd already written to Mrs Lunn telling her I had three days off . . .

I got off at 5 pm yesterday & not wishing to stay in camp & compare matters with last Wednesday, I buzzed off to Chester and saw a flick. I think you've seen it – Pimpernel Smith with Leslie Howard – have you? Anyway, it's an awfully good film & I thoroughly enjoyed it. Being an instructor you don't get much time off – so far as I can see I was lucky to get off yesterday . . .

I may be here a bit longer than I originally expected – the weather's not so hot & I can't seem to get my hours in . . .

15 September 1941:

I feel pretty pleased with life – I've just come back from flying, I've filled my log-book in, had a wash & am now firmly implanted on my bed starting this letter to you . . .

It's been glorious here today – I was battle flight again so had to be ready to fly at 6 am. When I got down to the flight it was still pretty dark but I took off on a weather test just as the sun came up. Everything looks amazingly clear in the early morning and I felt marvellous – not having a formation to look after I amused myself by doing some aerobatics for the ground crews . . . I finished up by beating up the flight hut at nought feet – the chaps enjoyed it & no one else was more than half awake & so I got away with it.

It's now 8.15 or 20.15 hrs – I've finished my supper & can now continue uninterrupted. As I've told you before – there are two things I look forward to in the week – your letter, and the time when I can sit down and answer it.

Even though there's very little fresh news, as I write I keep thinking of the times we've spent together, and also of what we can do in the future when I get some more leave, so you can imagine that at the moment I feel pretty pleased with life . . .

There's nothing left for me to say but 'Goodnight' – now don't go & get a lavish affair for my birthday – just anything to hold all the junk I carry about with me will do very nicely – it's just the fact that it's from you that makes all the difference.

20 September 1941:

I received both your letter & card OK – for which many thanks – that's an awfully stilted way of opening a letter to you but I've got so many things on my mind at the present time that if I don't put them down in some sort of plain order, I'll get myself in a bit of a mess.

To begin with, I'm <u>almost</u> certain to get posted on Tuesday or Wednesday but whether I'll get anymore leave is a question which has yet to be answered. The fact that I had some about a fortnight ago weighs heavily against me. Anyway – I can only wait and hope now. If what I've heard is correct the two places mentioned in my posting are very near home & with luck I'll be home in about an hour from either of them. I hope I get sent to one of them – it would suit me down to the ground – I could have tea with you & be back inside half an hour . . . I had quite a good birthday – I got tons of tobacco from nearly everyone I know – two of the instructors here took me out to the flicks & then to dinner in an hotel here. It was quite good but I'd swap it all just to be able to take you to supper somewhere . . .

This is all for now – don't bother to answer this – I'm in a heck of a state – the fact is that I <u>may</u> get a couple of days at home with you is driving everything else from my mind & I'm having an awful time trying to calm down & answer all my letters . . .

The concluding part of this, his final letter from Hawarden, contains the first hint of a problem that eventually comes to dominate Ron's very existence, that of managing two occasionally conflicting priorities: his passion for flying and his love for the young Connie. There's more on this to come. For now, though, he gets both his wishes: a few days' leave and a posting to 111 Squadron at RAF North Weald, not far from Connie's home. There's further good news in that he leaves Hawarden with an 'Above the Average' assessment – a rare feat for a U/T (under training) Spitfire pilot.

Chapter 13

3 February 1943, 94th General Hospital, Algiers

L ying in bed contemplating an uncertain future but buoyed by the prospect of an imminent return to the UK, Robbie's spirits were lifted further by a visit from George Malan. He'd managed to arrange a flight back to Algiers. The hour or so they spent together chatting was as pleasant as any Robbie could remember since his hospitalisation. Inevitably, he was keen to catch up with news of his colleagues back at base.

The tale that interested him most was that of Harry 'Chas' Charnock, one of 72 Squadron's most experienced pilots; 'as a natural aviator he ranked with the best,'[38] according to his squadron commander. An ace whose first 'confirmed' came just after the Battle of Britain, Chas was another of those with whom Robbie had a genuine affinity. It was similar, although not as close, to that he enjoyed with George Malan; both relationships were forged in the air and reinforced on the ground. He'd been reported missing on 18 December, two days before Robbie's own accident. News that he was safe arrived the following day but it was all that was known at the time. Now the full story came out.

After shooting down two German fighters, an Me 109 and an Fw (Focke-Wulf) 190, his last recorded victories, Chas was bounced by four more as he headed for home, alone and out of ammunition. With his aircraft riddled with bullet holes and his engine on fire, he was forced to crash-land in enemy territory and escaped from the wreckage only seconds before his aircraft exploded. Wounded in the head and arm, and with burns to his wrist and face, he then traipsed nearly a dozen miles to the safety of the British lines, led by an Arab who overcame his initial reluctance to assist after Chas shot his dog; it had unwisely attacked him. Here he was dragged into the safety of a trench, somewhat dishevelled, and greeted by an Army officer who observed laconically, 'I see you're a member of the rival establishment.' It took a moment for Chas to realise that the old Etonian who greeted him had

---

38. Oxspring, op. cit., p.134.

80

recognised his navy and silver Old Harrovian scarf. He never flew without it. After initial treatment at a dressing station he was driven to the hospital at Bône,[39] from where he eventually sent a cryptic message, 'Please credit squadron with two certainly destroyed.' When news of his escapade finally emerged it prompted a heartfelt tribute from a colleague: 'has that guy got guts – he's shit-hot.' *Amen to that!* would have been George and Robbie's reaction had they been aware of this latest entry in Jimmy Corbin's diary.

Short, wiry and at 37 considerably older than his colleagues, Charnock was a remarkable character. He joined the RAF College Cranwell straight from school and was commissioned in 1925. Five years later his first career came to a premature end when he was court martialled for a low-flying offence and cashiered. At the time he was flying Siskins with No. 1 Squadron, based at Tangmere. Given the relatively relaxed attitude to flying discipline (indiscipline?) in those early days, whatever he did to warrant such drastic punishment must have been quite something. It's a measure of the man – and the RAF's need for experienced aircrew – that immediately war was declared he rejoined as a sergeant pilot. A warrant officer at the time of this latest incident, he was eventually commissioned for a second time and ended the war as a flight lieutenant.

Immediately after his hospital visit, George sent a short cable to his wife, Vickie: 'TELL CONNIE ROBBIE OK & HOME SOON.' In one of the few of Connie's letters that remain, on 21 February 1943 she wrote, 'I thought it was awfully sweet of him.' It was a typically considerate gesture from a man whose friendship Robbie valued above that of any other. Ironically, by the time he finally read Connie's letter, in November (it was redirected and forwarded numerous times), George had been dead for seven months, a victim of our own flak on 26 April 1943.

If Robbie was devastated when he finally heard this news, he was almost equally upset more than forty years later by the manner in which George's loss was dealt with in Bobby Oxspring's book, *Spitfire Command*:

> Although 72 mostly dished out punishment, occasions arose when we had to take it. One offensive sweep[40] east of Medjez saw the squadron encounter a mixed gaggle of bomb carrying Ju (Junkers) 88s and Me 110s escorted by Me 109s and Fw 190s bent on attacking army dispositions in the area. The enemy

---

39. Renamed Annaba in 1962, the year of Algerian independence.
40. An offensive mission where crews sought out the enemy in the air or on the ground in the specific area allocated to them.

dived on their targets through a hail of British flak as 72 engaged. Pryth Prytherch belted a 110 while George Malan and Tom Hughes chased another. Drawing close to his target George was severely hit by our own ground fire and though badly wounded managed to pull off a rough crash-landing. Nearby Tommies whisked him off to a local field hospital, where the army surgeons were shocked at the bitterness with which George died cursing all 'pongos'.[41] [42]

The loss soon afterwards of one of the squadron's most respected pilots and section leaders goes strangely unremarked. Sailor Malan's sibling deserved much better than this from the man who was his boss at the time.

Connie and Vickie continued to exchange correspondence after George's sad demise. Like the aforementioned much travelled letter, one of the most poignant of Vickie's languished amongst the box of letters Connie had faithfully preserved. Dated 14 March 1944 and written from her home in Birmingham, it included this moving extract:

> I had an invitation from a friend of mine to go to her wedding at Brompton Oratory, London, on the 22nd March, and was looking forward to going but on Friday last I had a letter from her saying that her husband to be was reported 'missing' – he is a Squadron Leader. Well Connie I tried to write a letter but found it very hard for I know only too well just how she is feeling. How I wish this war would end!

41. Pongos: slang for Army personnel.
42. Oxspring, op. cit., p.156.

Chapter 14

30 September 1941, 111 Squadron, RAF North Weald

Much to his delight, Ron didn't have to report for duty at 111 Squadron until Tuesday 30 September; it gave him the chance to spend plenty of time with Connie. One particular evening at the Queen's Brasserie would stay long in their memories. They'd arranged to meet a couple of Australians there who'd been on Ron's flight at Hawarden, one of whom caused a good deal of amusement – a possible insight, too, into national character. As the group made to leave at the end of the evening, he passed a final handful of cash to the waiter who'd served them all evening. Given that he'd also been tipped for each round he'd delivered, the man's reaction came as a surprise: 'Do you think that is sufficient, Sir?' to which the Australian replied, 'Well, how much did I just give you?' The waiter opened his palm, showing a handful of coins – recompense the burly Antipodean promptly retrieved and pocketed. Then, picking him up bodily and with his face pressed close, he explained to the startled individual that he was lucky still to be in one piece. And with that the three uniformed airmen, accompanied by a mildly disconcerted young Connie, promptly departed.

After a few days' leave, Ron headed for North Weald not knowing when he'd see Connie again. He needn't have worried; his introduction to the front line proved remarkably relaxed. At the end of his first day on the squadron he was taken to the Sergeants' Mess, where he enjoyed a meal and a couple of beers getting to know his new colleagues. There it emerged that because he wasn't operational, i.e. qualified to take on the enemy, he didn't have to spend the night on base. Without further ado he left the mess, hitch-hiked back to Woodford and spent the night at Connie's home. Next morning he was up bright and early. He strolled the mile or so uphill to Woodford High Road and promptly secured a lift in a builder's lorry to Epping. From there he hitched another lift to North Weald, arriving around 8.30.

Later that same morning came his arrival interview with the boss, Squadron Leader G.F. Brotchie, 'a little tiny man but very, very pleasant' – another who'd earned his spurs in the late summer of 1940. After a short, good-humoured chat with a leader of whom Ron had heard good things, he left the CO's office with his first squadron task: funeral escort next day for a pilot who'd been wounded in the air and killed in the subsequent crash-landing. *Some welcome to operations!*

Given that it was so easy to get back to Woodford, barely a dozen miles away, and there was also a relatively good telephone connection, Ron's letters dried up completely for a few weeks. He finally flew his first squadron sortie on 4 October, a gentle amble around the local area to familiarise himself with various landmarks. Exactly a week later he flew his first operational mission, a convoy patrol just off the east coast. For an uneventful hour or so he followed his experienced leader, cruising up and down the North Sea keeping a number of ships in sight. Sitting in a fully-armed aircraft, guns at the ready, at last he felt he 'was getting somewhere, and it was quite a nice sensation'. If this suggests that Ron was confident and relaxed, nothing could be further from the truth. Deeply conscious of his inexperience, by the end of the sortie his neck positively ached from the almost constant swivelling around he'd been doing in search of intruders.

The first time he went across to France was another landmark. The 1 hour 50 minute sweep over Dunkirk entered in his log book on 20 October (equalling his longest Spitfire sortie thus far) is followed by a comment: 'No flak no 109s'. There may have been no enemy activity that day, but it was marked firmly in Ron's mind as another stage in his education. Flying over enemy territory at last, he felt a twinge of apprehension. *What if I'm shot down? How do I get back – that's assuming I manage to avoid capture? Just trust that the Frogs are friendly!* But he didn't waste much time on such thoughts. He had his work cut out following his leader, one of the squadron's half dozen or so vastly experienced Czech pilots – characters to a man. He was told simply to stick like glue to his leader and keep an eye out for enemy aircraft. *Easier said than done!* When they finally headed back for North Weald, the English coastline had never looked so welcoming.

On the evening of Friday 31 October Ron managed his now familiar trick of hitch-hiking back to Connie's home. This time, though, it was a journey tinged with sadness. It would be his last for some time. After a month when he'd flown twenty-one sorties in as many hours,

Ron's father, Edinburgh Scot and putative sportsman James Fair Robertson. The author's brother inherited his middle name (see Epilogue).

Mabel Robertson, Ron's mother, with Connie (see Chapter 24).

Except where noted, all pictures are from the author's private collection.

'Ferdie' Freeman, Connie's father
(see Chapters 15, 16, 23 and 24).

Connie's mother, 'Else' Freeman
(see Chapter 11).

Ron pre-war, aged 21; the pipe would become almost ever-present (see Chapter 2).

Plaistow United swimmers at a pre-war outdoor event; Ron is back row, third left (see Chapters 2 and 18).

Ron, third left, with close friend Dicky Huband, far left, at 5 ITW, October 1940 (see Chapters 16, 18, 23 and 27).

AC2 Robertson at home on leave, late 1940 – one of the first pictures he sent Connie during initial training at Torquay (see Chapter 6).

Connie Freeman, right, summer 1940, aged 16. Her correspondence with Ron began earlier, in October 1939 (see Chapter 2).

Just some of the more than 300 letters that Ron wrote to Connie.

Connie
in March
1941,
aged 17.

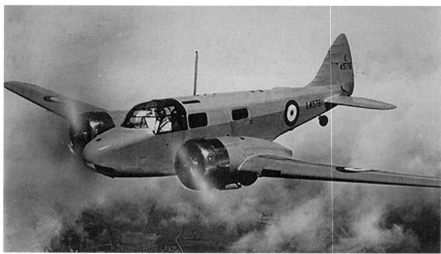

The Airspeed AS 10 Oxford on which Robbie earned his RAF 'wings' at Kidlington
(see Chapters 9, 10 and 16). (A *Flight* photo reproduced on a Valentine & Sons
postcard)

St Mary's, the 'awfully ancient church' Ron found in Kidlington village (see Chapter 10).

The Trout at Godstow, a favourite haunt during the Kidlington course (see Chapter 16).

The Bear at Woodstock, another Kidlington favourite – when beer was available (see Chapter 16).

SUMMARY of FLYING and ASSESSMENTS FOR ~~YEAR~~ Course COMMENCING 1st......11...... 8...... *19.4.1.

[* For Officer, insert "JUNE"; For Airman Pilot, insert "AUGUST."]

	S.E. AIRCRAFT		M.E. AIRCRAFT		TOTAL for year Course	GRAND TOTAL All Service Flying
	Day	Night	Day	Night		
DUAL	3·35	—	—	—	3·35	
PILOT	66·15	—	—	—	66·15	
PASSENGER	—	—	—	—	—	

ASSESSMENT of ABILITY

(To be assessed as :—Exceptional, Above the Average, Average, or Below the Average)

(i) AS A........F........† PILOT........u/T.......Above the Average

(ii) AS PILOT–NAVIGATOR/NAVIGATOR ....

(iii) IN BOMBING ....

(iv) IN AIR GUNNERY...............................

†Insert :—"F.", "L.B.", "G.R.", "F.B.", etc

ANY POINTS IN FLYING OR AIRMANSHIP WHICH SHOULD BE WATCHED.

Has to watch altitdl as a Pilot Navigator ?: YES

Signature........................Mr Brown   Wing Cmdr

Date........23.9.41........   Officer Commanding Training Wing   No: 57 0.T.U.

The logbook summary of Robbie's Spitfire course; it took his total flying to some 209 hours (see Chapter 12).

Sgt Robertson, shortly after joining 72 Sqn. On the back he wrote, *'All my love, darling, Ron. Dec '41'* (see Chapter 16).

Robbie flouted regulations and flew with this picture in his tunic. On the back it reads: *'Ron darling, With all my love, Connie Dec. 1941.'*

Sgt Robertson at Connie's home, top button undone in the Fighter Command manner. On the back he wrote: *'All my love, always, darling. Ron. Mch '42.'* The mirror and clock in the background now reside with Connie's granddaughter and the author respectively.

Groundcrew (A and B Flight 'erks') at Gravesend, where 72 Sqn was based when Ron arrived in December 1941; note the carefully(!) stowed screwdriver (see Chapters 15, 16 and 22).

Another Gravesend shot of good-humoured B Flight erks (see Chapters 15 and 16).

More B Flight erks happy to demonstrate de rigueur tool stowage at Gravesend (see Chapters 15 and 16).

Two Sgt Robertsons, 30 April 1942. Right, in ATC uniform, is Ron's brother, Alan, who later joined the RAF and was subsequently commissioned (see Chapters 4, 6, 10 and 24).

P/O R.J.H. Robertson RAFVR, summer 1942; the caterpillar tie-pin is a memento of his bale-out a few months earlier (see Chapters 16 and 18).

Connie at home in Woodford wearing her engagement ring, summer 1942, aged 18 (see Chapters 16 and 18).

Connie at home with her parents, Ferdie and Else, in 1942.

Connie and her parents in their Woodford garden, summer 1942.

Sqn Ldr Brian Kingcome introduces Robbie to King George VI at Biggin Hill, April 1942; P/O Owen Hardy is second right (see Chapters 18 and 27).

frustratingly only three of them on 'ops', when he returned early next morning his squadron was due to move from North Weald to Debden. Although 111's new base was only some twenty miles further north, not knowing when or how he'd see Connie again, it felt more like a dislocation than a relocation. In any event, it prompted an immediate resumption in his correspondence.

1 November 1941:

After much rushing about – getting instructions one minute & having them cancelled the next, we eventually started off about 4 pm. We're all pretty fed up with things in general – instead of keeping our sqdn all together we're sharing rooms with other people. The food is OK – the mess is very comfortable (which is just as well if I'm going to spend all my time here) but none of us are frightfully keen on night flying & the chances of getting back to where we were are only 50-50. I wouldn't mind all this if I could only see you now & again. We're not far away as far as mileage goes, but if we get no time off apart from odd hours per day I might as well be in China.

I'll do all I can to wangle a day off later on when we're settled down – the thought of not seeing you for a month when we're really not so far away from each other is pretty awful.

I know I was very spoilt by being able to see you so often but gees! I'm paying for it now alright. I picked up a Daily Express just before writing to you, but even looking at a cross-word puzzle made me feel as miserable as sin. I know this letter is one long moan but once I get it off my chest I'll feel better – I hope we do bags of flying here – if we just sit around all day I'll get pretty fed up . . .

Don't pay too much attention to all this twaddle – things aren't so bad really – it's only the fact that I miss you so much that I look at things in a very bad light.

P.S. I was in such a mess this morning that I rushed off without thanking your mother for all she's done for me in the past four weeks or so – do thank her for me.

A number of comments in this relatively downbeat letter warrant further explanation. First, Ron himself wasn't actually that perturbed with the Debden rooming arrangements; he was sharing with a unique individual. Just 20 at the time, Sergeant Thorsteinn 'Tony' Jonsson was the RAF's only Icelandic pilot, 'an awfully nice bloke, very quiet'. Unable to join the RAF in the land of his birth, he travelled to England on a trawler and took advantage of his English mother to enlist in 1940. Inevitably, he attracted a good deal of publicity. He was regularly asked to pose for pictures: in front of his aircraft, standing on the wing, staring into the distance, taking off and landing – anything, in fact, that would make worthwhile copy. He suffered a good deal of ribbing as a result but accepted the almost invasive press interest with equanimity; his resigned composure rapidly endeared him to his roommate. (Later commissioned, he would end the war flying P-51 Mustangs with eight confirmed 'kills' to his credit.)

Next, the mention of night flying – never popular with fighter pilots – reflects 111 Squadron's autumn assignment to a new role. It explains, too, why their aircraft, much to Ron's surprise, were painted black and fitted with a number of role-related modifications.

But perhaps the most significant aspect of this letter is its tone of barely suppressed frustration. After the privations of more than a year in training, a period during which he falls deeply in love, Ron's introduction to squadron life proves almost too good to be true. When he isn't flying he's able to see Connie almost at will – a situation that creates a false impression of normality. There's a sense here, a foreboding even, of the loss of perspective hinted at earlier on his departure from Hawarden. No matter that it's slight, it's a further sign of what's to come. For now, though, things are about to work out better than he dares hope, thanks in part to over a week when the weather proves too bad for flying.

Turning from the general to the specific, i.e. the difficulties the Debden move posed in terms of seeing Connie, Ron quickly worked out the optimum route: by train from nearby Saffron Walden to London, Liverpool Street, then via Central Line tube to Woodford. Determined to test his latest escape route at the first opportunity, a chance came unexpectedly just a couple of days after his arrival. He left Debden in the early evening of Monday 3 November. However, by the time he reached Connie's home it was after ten and 76 Kings Avenue was in total darkness; there wasn't a light to be seen – hardly a surprise given the blackout.[43] Knowing that Connie slept in a back bedroom, Ron eased his way carefully to the rear of her semi-detached house and began flinging his hat up against what he thought was her window – only

---

43. Blackout regulations, imposed just before the outbreak of war, were designed to prevent the escape of any glimmer of light that might aid the enemy.

to alert her father. However, 'Ferdie' Freeman took Ron's unexpected arrival in good part, invited him in and left the couple to chat together over a cup of tea in the kitchen. All too quickly, though, their assignation was over and Ron set off to catch the last tube back to London. There he whiled away the hours until the first train from Liverpool Street to Saffron Walden, shortly after five in the morning. After hitch-hiking the remaining three miles to Debden, he arrived just in time for a substantial breakfast in the mess. Tired but elated by the success of his proving visit, he felt he'd earned it. His next letter opens with a summary of his nocturnal adventures:

4 November 1941:

I managed to get here quite easily this morning – I went to Bishopsgate cop shop last night but my uncle left at 11 pm & so I just missed him. Anyway – I talked to one of the blokes there till about 1 am – drinking vast cups of tea the while. After that I went to the YMCA & did all the crosswords I could find – Daily Express, Star, Standard – I reached The Times about 4 am but by that time the old brain wasn't functioning so well & so I retired from the unequal contest.

7.45 pm. I was dragged away from my letter this morning to help shoot up some Wellingtons. They arrived here at about 11 am & one Spit was detailed to carry out attacks on the rear gunner. It was quite fun while it lasted and then I formated on the Wimpey to come back. Trying to keep down slow enough to remain with it was a bit of a job though.

This afternoon I hadn't anything to do so I just slept in front of the fire all the time.

Gosh that was a marvellous letter you wrote – I read it through going up to Liverpool St – going to Saffron Walden & again first thing this morning before I started my own letter.

It was worth all the rushing about & travelling last night & this morning just to spend that three-quarters of an hour with you. As soon as I finish this I'm going to have a bath (or shower) & go to bed. I'm due to fly at 5 am tomorrow morning – which means I'll do 1½ hrs night flying – night flying is anything up to 7 am when you still have to use the flare path.

There isn't much more to tell you except that whatever anyone thinks – I'm glad I came down to see you last night . . .

7 November 1941:

I didn't have to do any night flying tonight – only dusk flying, & I finished that half an hour ago, so I can write to you in peace.

Life has taken on a rosy hue nowadays – I've seen you three times in the last week, when I really didn't expect to see you for a month, not only that but as we're going to get our days off as usual I'm almost certain to see you once a week. I say 'almost' because nothing is absolutely certain these days, least of all in this racket . . .

13 November 1941:

The weather's absolutely awful, but so far we haven't been released. As I thought, having Tuesday off, I was unable to get today off as well – still – I managed to see you two evenings this week – so I don't feel too bad. We're all pretty worried at the moment – if we don't get much flying in we may have to stay here a bit longer – which is a cert to send us all crazy.

Yesterday the weather was NBG & so we all went in to Cambridge to see an Observer Corps post. There wasn't much to see & what I did see conveyed little or nothing to me . . .

Unless I'm flying or doing something that takes up all my attention I'm absolutely lost without you. I wouldn't feel so bad if we were doing a good job of work . . . but when we're just stooging – well! . . .

Don't pay too much attention to these moans of mine – after all – I'd be pretty unusual if I didn't miss you wouldn't I?

15 November 1941:

We flew for the first time for about ten days today – it was quite a change to roam around in a Spit. I found your place today – about 12.15 – I couldn't come too low (a) because London is not such an awfully good place to beat-up – & (b) I didn't see anyone in the garden . . .

By the way, my Flight Commander told me he's put my name forward for a commission – it'll probably be about six months before I hear any more about it – after all – I've only been in the squadron about six weeks. I thanked him very much, but I don't care a great deal one way or the other.

30 SEPTEMBER 1941, 111 SQUADRON, RAF NORTH WEALD

Another bright piece of news is that if we don't get sufficient flying in here at night we may have to stay longer – gees – that'd drive me crazy.

21 November 1941:

It's now 5.10 pm or 17.10 hrs so I expect you're well on your way home. I'm perched on my bed listening to operatic records – so far they've been pretty good.

You know, seeing an opera together is about all we haven't done – we must try & remedy that one of these days – if they still run operas . . .

From various things that have been happening during the past few days it appears very unlikely that we'll be coming back – still – wait & see. Maybe this stay up here isn't so bad after all – it's getting me used to the idea of not seeing you so often, so that when we do go far away it won't seem such a great tear . . .

I've looked at it all ways – telling myself there's a war on & we must all sacrifice something if we're to win the damn thing – but nothing at all seems half as important as just seeing you for a few hours . . .

25 November 1941:

I got your letter when I arrived back here this morning . . . Well – now I'll give you all the news of today – at least – of the eleven hours since I last saw you.

I went up & did some dog fighting with that Icelandic chap today – we had quite a bit of fun until the ground station asked if we wouldn't mind giving the ground gunners a bit of practice!

'Wouldn't mind'!! – I ask you! All the A/C (aircraft, to you) in the vicinity fairly rushed back to the aerodrome – after all – it was a glorious opportunity to do an authorised beat-up. We had a heck of a time – kites were coming in from all over the place – it was a wonder some of us weren't smashed up. Anyway – it was damn good fun.

I had a bit of tea & then did a spot of semi-night flying – it was only 'semi' as it was really dusk . . .

It was marvellous seeing you for such a long time yesterday, you seem to get nicer & nicer each time I see you, although I didn't think it was possible . . .

28 November 1941:

I'm so glad you're on the phone – I'd ring you tonight only as your father is fire watching I guess you've both gone to bed fairly early. Anyway – I'll have phoned you before the weekend's over.

There are bags of rumours floating around as to where we're going – but nothing of NW [North Weald]. *Every time I hear one I get an awful sinking feeling – I'm counting so much on going back & being able to see you every night . . .*

Gosh darling – I wish rumours hadn't been invented – I know we're bound to be separated sooner or later for a few months – but just to listen to all the tales floating around & not know whether I'm going to be able to see you soon is awful. At any rate – I should be able to see you on Monday or Tuesday . . .

I'll have to go now as – if the weather's OK – I've got to be up at some fantastic hour in the morning to do some air-firing.

Ron's letters dry up for the next ten days, albeit for good reason. Shortly after his return from seeing Connie fleetingly overnight on the Monday, he found that he'd been given three days' leave later in the week. But on returning to Debden the following Monday, 8 December, he was in for a shock: he was posted from 111 Squadron with immediate effect.

The background to this unexpected move was that Headquarters No. 11 Group had been trawling Spitfire units with a view to boosting pilot numbers on 72 Squadron, a unit that had suffered more than its fair share of recent losses. As a result, and after barely two months on his first front-line squadron, Ron and a colleague found themselves surplus to requirements. He was understandably depressed but, given the circumstances, he knew exactly why he'd been chosen. Any boss required to give up a couple of pilots would normally select the least experienced amongst recent arrivals, so Ron was an obvious choice. He wasn't to know, of course, but it was an approach that would later work to his advantage. For now, what particularly irked him was that it meant sacrificing his Christmas leave. He'd been one of the lucky winners of the 111 Squadron holiday lottery, the fairest way to allocate such a coveted prize. Partial compensation came by way of his log book assessment on posting: 'Above Average' as a fighter pilot – a considerable accolade for one with minimal operational experience.

30 SEPTEMBER 1941, 111 SQUADRON, RAF NORTH WEALD

He was given just a few hours to collect his flying gear, pack up whatever else he needed and deposit everything in a 15-cwt truck that was about to depart for his new location. It was to be Gravesend, one of Biggin Hill's satellite airfields. There was hardly time for any goodbyes before he set off by train for his new home. Never one to miss an opportunity, after an overnight stay with his parents, next morning he travelled with Connie to her office before heading for London Bridge and the train to Kent. No sooner had he arrived at Gravesend than he found himself released once again: surplus to requirements for another four days. *This posting lark is turning out alright!*

Chapter 15

7 February 1943, 94th General Hospital, Algiers

Robbie's mood improved considerably once he began receiving Connie's letters again. As they followed his various moves, they were taking even longer to reach him than before and sometimes arrived out of sequence, but it mattered not. Nor did the fact that everything he received had been written prior to his accident. At least the pair were back in contact.

If it was difficult to keep his spirits up, he consoled himself with the thought that he was in very good hands – those of the Queen Alexandra's Imperial Military Nursing Service.[44] Despite being worked off their feet caring for the injured – wounded whose numbers seemed to swell by the day – with a word here and a quip there these nurses seemed to find time to make each and every patient feel just that little bit better. Their encouragement was a major contributory factor in Robbie's slow recovery. But while his physical condition continued gradually to improve, his mental state remained a concern. He was desperately worried. He simply had to know Connie's reaction to the news of his accident.

Aware that he needed distractions to take his mind off his plight, he made a concerted effort to engage with those others in a broadly similar predicament and indeed to see the funny side of things. Just such a diversion was provided by a bizarre form of ceremonial. Together with most of the British contingent, Robbie was much amused by the sight of an American officer wheeling a small trolley around the wards. It was full of purple hearts – medals rapidly and unceremoniously distributed to wounded members of the US military. He couldn't help but reflect on yet another difference between two ostensibly similar nations fighting side by side. These same Americans were the butt of more leg-pulling from a Royal Navy commander who'd been shot down whilst carrying out an aerodrome patrol. He'd just completed a lap of Algiers harbour in his Swordfish, and was

---

44. As of February 1949, Queen Alexandra's Royal Army Nursing Corps.

about to start another, when American ack-ack (anti-aircraft) guns opened up and consigned him to a parachute descent. As soon as his wounds were healed sufficiently for him to walk unaided around the hospital, he took great delight in recounting his tale of woe to any American who'd listen, providing free aircraft recognition training into the bargain. It was a tale with which Robbie had more than a little sympathy. Less than a week before his own accident, en route to Algiers with a damaged Spitfire, he'd been threatened twice by the same pair of US P-38 Lightnings.

Meanwhile, the date of Robbie's departure for the UK loomed tantalisingly ever closer. *It can't come fast enough!*

7 February 1943:

We've been given half an hour's notice in which to scribble a letter which is to go by air – so excuse the scribble.

I haven't written for about ten days because I thought we'd be home before my letter – anyway – the ship should arrive any day now so it won't be long before I'm home.

I've had two letters from you today – 28th, 23rd Dec – one from Mum – also earlier in the week one from Alan . . .

I had a telegram from Arthur[45] – He says you're OK – I do hope you're keeping your chin up, darl . . .

There's no more news so at last I can tell you I love you again.

I feel perfectly OK now the old eye – or rather where it was – is feeling much better.

I'm dying to see you again, angel – I must rush off now.

13 February 1943:

I've just written to Mum – there's not much news at all, but as I'm not yet at home I thought I'd better start writing again, although as I said in my other letter I'll probably arrive home before this letter – at least I hope so – I do so want to see you again.

I keep on getting out all the photos I have of you (I've got quite a lot, really), & looking at them over & over again.

---

45. Arthur Youd, a cousin.

How are you Tubs? – Now that I'm fit to travel I get fed up as hell just waiting here for transport to England . . .

There's nothing to do here at all except read & go to sleep in the sun – it sounds nice . . . but it gets awfully boring day after day. We've had one or two bright spots this week – I went to church on Sunday & one of the sisters played beautifully on the piano, so afterwards I asked her if she'd play some more, but she was just going on duty. Anyway she invited two of us to the sisters' mess after tea & she played for an hour & a half to us. Not having heard any music for ages we thoroughly enjoyed it. She played everything under the sun from La Bohème to Bing & Chopin.

Later on in the week an American gave an impromptu recital which was even better – then yesterday we cadged a gramophone & some records from one of the doctors & played them all through. You'll never guess which record I found in the album (& played three times in half an hour) – It's Easy to Remember. Needless to say there was one young lady in my thoughts all the time . . .

Well, sweetheart – I must finish now – it's 'Lights out' for us . . .

P.S. The sister who played to us was between 35 & 40!

Given the imminence of his departure for England, Robbie felt it would be pointless to write again; this note of 13 February was his last for a considerable time. Next day he received a welcome fillip. There at his bedside appeared Chas Charnock, accompanied by another squadron pilot, bearing news that he'd been awarded the DFC. Robbie was reluctant, however, to make too much of this, preferring to await any official notification. It came not long afterwards in *The London Gazette* of 23 February 1943, along with the announcement of Charnock's own DFC to sit alongside his DFM. There was similar recognition for two other members of the composite wing at Souk-el-Arba: Squadron Leader George Nelson-Edwards, OC (Officer Commanding) 93 Squadron, and Flight Lieutenant Derek Forde, OC B Flight on 72 Squadron.[46] But Robbie knew nothing of this at the time; he was at sea, on his way home.

Two days later came another event he would never forget: the arrival of six letters, including three from Connie. He was overjoyed to learn that, as far as his fiancée was concerned, absolutely nothing would stand in the way of their future plans; she simply couldn't wait to get married. His diary

---

46. Later in the war, with at least three confirmed enemy aircraft to his credit, Forde was shot down over France. Although injured, with help from the Resistance he managed to escape over the Pyrenees and return to the UK. See also Chapter 30 below.

entry for 16 February said it all: 'My lucky day'. Almost two months after his accident, fed up with the resulting enforced inactivity and anxiously awaiting repatriation, his mood changed instantly. He could hardly credit that none of his misadventures had made the slightest difference to his fiancée's feelings. He was equally buoyed to learn that her parents, who 'thought the world' of their prospective son-in-law, had given their blessing to the couple's early marriage.

Such acceptance represented a *volte face* from Ferdie's previous stance. The single condition he'd imposed when agreeing to the couple's engagement was that their wedding should be delayed, effectively until his prospective son-in-law was employed in a less hazardous profession. This proviso notwithstanding, as time progressed, and as his overseas deployment loomed closer, Robbie became ever more anxious to tie the knot – witness the tenor of his letters and Vickie Malan's revelation about the couple's future plans. Now that events had effectively nullified Ferdie's proviso, he was already making plans for the great day. However, he would keep them to himself until he could discuss things with Connie, if not face to face then at least on the telephone just as soon as he returned.

Chapter 16

9 December 1941, 72 Squadron, RAF Gravesend

O n arriving at his new base Ron was billeted in a large house, 'Polperro', on the main Gravesend to Rochester road. Here he shared a room with two experienced 72 Squadron engineer NCOs, Flight Sergeants Jack Hilton and Jim Norton, both of whom were destined to become close friends. Once settled in he begins writing again, harping on a familiar theme: his efforts to secure time off. Given that he's just arrived on a new squadron, this would seem ill-advised – premature at the very least; however, it may be that in reality Ron's actions speak less loudly than his words.

9 December 1941:

I caught an earlier train than the one I originally intended to & got here about 9.45. They sent some transport to meet me . . .

We're billeted in a private house just outside the aerodrome & have another private house in the 'drome boundary as a mess. The grub is very good & the billets are very comfortable – we have a fire in each room – in fact it's <u>almost</u> like home.

The chaps here appear to be very nice – there are two chaps in my flight whom I knew at Hawarden & there are two Norwegians[47] who are very pally so I'm very much at home.

I'm doing some air firing tomorrow – I should be good at it by this time. I haven't said anything about my leave yet but if the F/Cdr is in a good mood I'll tell him tomorrow . . .

Those days came as a marvellous break for me – it was good being able to see you when I hadn't the faintest idea about it. All I'm looking forward to now is my next day off – by which time I hope to have some definite news about my leave.

---

47. Sergeants G. Fosse and E.L. Westly.

By the way young lady – re our conversation of a night or so ago – do tell me how you <u>really</u> feel when you write. Don't go & say you're having a marvellous time & things are just grand if you're really feeling pretty miserable & things aren't so good. After all – I'm not the one who needs cheering up – I'm doing a job I like & above all I've got you to come home to . . .

In an echo of these final comments, life on 72 Squadron starts well for Ron. He flies two sorties on 11 December, the second a sweep over the Channel, and once again on both of the following days. Then, when the prospect of a day off on 14 December emerges, he grabs the opportunity it presents to see Connie once again; on the evening of the 13th he sets off to test out his latest travel plan.

15 December 1941:

It's now 10.45 and I'm due to go on a convoy patrol in a short while – just in time for me to miss lunch I expect – anyway it's a nice day so a spot of flying will do very nicely.

I nearly 'had it' last night. The 10.19 arrived at Woodford at 10.24 – consequently I didn't get to Liverpool St until 10.55. Luckily I got a taxi straight away & managed to catch the 11.7 [from London Bridge] with about 2 mins to spare. I got a taxi from Gravesend and got to bed at 12.45 am. I was up at 7.30 – just in time to catch the transport to the mess . . .

It made a great break to have spent so much time with you in the last two days . . .

18 December 1941:

It's now 1.30 pm or 13.30 hrs & another chap & myself are the 'readiness'[48] section, which means we're stuck down at dispersal all the afternoon . . . The Duke of Kent has come in to see us. He was introduced to all of us & asked how long we'd been here – what sweeps we'd done etc., you know – all the usual gubbins . . .

We did another sweep this morning – we saw one or two things but nothing of any great interest happened. I like my new kite – it's only three

---

48. Pilots on readiness sat in the dispersal hut in full flying gear close to their aircraft while fitters kept the engines warm. They would normally be airborne within three minutes of the 'Scramble!' order.

weeks old & goes like the devil. I'll give you all the gen when I see you – although, as I explained yesterday the chances of my getting your birthday off are pretty remote. Still – don't give up hope, I may get it yet.

Re my wireless – if you can get me a battery which obviates the need for an accumulator I shall be awfully pleased – they can be obtained but they're pretty scarce. Some very odd remarks are floating around re 'Dook' but I can hardly repeat them here . . .

Well darling – I'm still doing my best to see you on your birthday – I do hope I succeed.

The sweep Ron mentions here is entered in his log book as: 'Top cover – 6 Hurribombers – Dunkirk . . . Still nothing doing'. 'Hurribombers' were Hurricanes used in the ground attack role. In addition to their main armament of four 20 mm cannon they carried 250 or 500 lb bombs on hardpoints under the wings.

The circumspect manner in which he deals with 'odd remarks' about the Duke of Kent is only to be expected, given that the King's brother, a keen aviator serving as a group captain at the time, had long been the subject of gossip. There were salacious rumours of various affairs with, *inter alios*, Jessie Matthews[49] and Noël Coward, as well as stories of drug addiction and illegitimate offspring. But whatever secrets the Duke may have had, they died with him. He was killed the following summer, on 25 August 1942, when the Short Sunderland flying boat in which he was a passenger crashed on Eagle's Rock, Caithness, en route to Iceland; of those on board, only the rear gunner survived.

As for Ron's final comment, he did indeed make it home for Connie's birthday – the day before in fact. According to her diary for 21 December, 'Ron phoned to say he would be home. I picked him up at Windsor Rd & we had a marvellous evening. Went to Monkhams.'[50] The next day, her birthday, 'Ron saw me to the office' before heading back to Gravesend.

23 December 1941:

I spent all day yesterday up here at dispersal doing nothing & I've done the same all today – there's a convoy job at the moment but I'm off as I've

---

49. An actress, singer and dancer who starred in a series of popular stage musicals and films in the mid-1930s; she also developed a following in the USA.
50. The Monkhams Inn was their local Woodford pub, within walking distance of Connie's home.

been on every show so far since I've been here. I'm glad I'm not on it,
otherwise I wouldn't have been able to reply to your letter until tonight . . .

I thought I'd just mention that owing to the fact that I've had fiddle-
all time off to get to the shops I haven't been able to get you a Christmas
present – so I'll organise that as soon as I get 48 hrs – I haven't forgotten
it by a long way . . .

There's a relatively long gap before Ron's next letter. It's written not
from Gravesend but from Manston, near the Kent coast. He flew there on
28 December for a series of convoy patrols which effectively put paid to
the idea of any New Year celebrations. Not that he was in the mood. He'd
had a couple of unfortunate experiences. On Christmas Eve he was tasked
with delivering an aircraft for a minor engineering check but, after landing,
his Spitfire ended up on its nose. His log book entry says it all: 'To Brize
Norton – crashed at South Cerney . . . port leg u/s [unserviceable].' Although
he was convinced that the collapsed undercarriage wasn't his fault, and
miraculously the propeller was undamaged, once he returned later that night
he found it hard to persuade his flight commander that he was blameless.

For his troubles he was despatched on a similar errand next morning,
Christmas Day. His return that same afternoon to Gravesend left him feeling
he was cursed. Once again his log book tells a succinct story: 'From Brize
Norton – crashed at base . . . No brakes – A/C just rolled downhill.' Unable to
stop after landing, he continued across the perimeter track onto rough ground
close to some building works where his aircraft once again ended up on its
nose. It did nothing for his peace of mind that first to arrive at the scene were
members of the squadron he'd joined only two weeks earlier; to make matters
worse, the boss, Squadron Leader Cedric Masterman, was amongst them.

Ron found the next few days deeply dispiriting. Eventually, however,
both incidents were attributed to engineering problems – problems that in the
second instance his own private investigations brought to light. He certainly
wasn't prepared to sit idly by and take the blame for accidents he felt sure
weren't his fault. After three of the most miserable days in his short RAF
life, the reasons for his twin debacles were revealed. Moreover, far from
being one-off incidents, both problems were subsequently found to affect
a number of other squadron aircraft. In the first instance, despite cockpit
indications that the wheels were securely down, a worn nut prevented the
undercarriage leg from locking fully in place. In the second, a wiring error
meant that when the brakes were applied, although things felt normal to the
pilot, nothing happened where it really mattered: at the wheels themselves.

The relief Ron felt at these explanations, his standing amongst his new colleagues hopefully restored, was palpable. Failure to mention any of this in a letter is easily explained. Connie's diary for Christmas Day reads: 'Ron phoned – he had crashed two planes.'

His nomadic existence then continues. On 29 December he deploys to Manston, flies a convoy patrol from there, lands to refuel, then returns to Gravesend. The following day follows a broadly similar pattern: early deployment to Manston and then two more patrols. His log book entry for the second of these reads: 'Scramble – 20,000' over convoy . . . saw nothing. Landed at Manston in thick fog. Visibility 50 yds – up to 1500'. Last to land!!' These lines hardly do justice to an extraordinary performance on the part of the formation leader, Flight Lieutenant Cyril Campbell.

As the squadron returned from covering the convoy, the weather at Manston closed in alarmingly. With thick fog up to a considerable height, the formation 'all got a case of the jitters' and thought they'd have to bale out; they literally 'couldn't see a thing'. Campbell asked Manston to release a series of pyrotechnics to give him some idea where the airfield was, but only a single red flare emerged through the top of the fog bank. However, it seems that he could see better than the rest of his formation so he proceeded to take each individual aircraft, in turn, down on his wing. Once he'd delivered his charge to the end of the runway and seen him land safely, Campbell climbed back up to collect the next formation member. Finally, only Ron was left. But at the *moment critique* he ran out of visibility and was forced to overshoot – much to his leader's evident disgust; however, he somehow managed to circle the field and land safely. Given that his predecessor crash-landed outside the airfield boundary, albeit escaping unhurt, Ron had every right to feel vindicated. More so Campbell himself, who eventually brought his own aircraft down after a supreme feat of airmanship and leadership. His performance that day doubtless contributed to the DFC he was awarded shortly thereafter. It would prove scant recompense, however, for spending the latter part of the war interned in a German prison camp after being shot down over France – an irony that would not have escaped an ex-policeman.

31 December 1941:

The weather's still lousy & we're still stuck here. At the present I'm doing 'readiness' in our dispersal hut – just what for– nobody knows, as I'd hate to try & fly in this stuff – altho' if they let me have a crack at landing at

NW – I'd be off like a shot . . . At the moment I've just got the clothes I fly in, a towel, tooth-brush & soap – the last items were sent down by car from Gravesend . . .

Last night four of us took a bus into Ramsgate & went pub-crawling – there's nothing else to do. We met some naval chaps off one of those motor launches & it turned out that their crew had rescued one of our pilots when he dropped into the Channel recently. One chap came from Walthamstow & another from Aberdeen – where one of our four lives so we had quite a long talk.

Actually – although it passed the time – I got fed up with it. I still don't like beer – although I had one or two during the evening & kept remembering that I should have spent Monday with you instead of wandering around here.

It's nearly driving us all crazy just stuck here doing nothing . . .

I'd give anything just to see you tonight – even for just half an hour – Gee, darling – I do miss you. I've got your photo in my pocket – I always take it out of my wallet before handing the wallet & letters to the orderly before going on a sweep – it means an awful lot just to have it with me . . .

Well, darling – this is a pretty morbid letter but I feel much better now I've written to you – If I can't phone you tonight I'll just put this little bit in here – I hope you have a very, very Happy New Year . . .

Ron and his colleagues finally left Manston for Gravesend on New Year's Day. After a convoy patrol early next morning, he made his way to London to meet Connie. According to her diary, it was a 'Lovely evening – Ron asked me again about getting engaged. We are going to ask Dad.' Given that she turned 18 less than two weeks earlier, it was a sensible precaution. Then, on 5 January, when Ron arrived after securing a forty-eight-hour pass, she wrote, 'Ron asked Dad about our engagement & he agreed – much to our surprise.' Connie would have been less surprised had she been aware of the rider to her father's agreement: a 'delay clause'. In a private conversation Ferdie put it to Ron bluntly that he had no wish to see his only child become a war widow; while he was happy to see her engaged, the wedding itself would have to wait.

9 January 1942:

I had a letter from Dicky this morning – he's messed one of his ears up through high-flying. So far he's been told by the MO it's not a permanent injury & in a week or two it should be OK. It's caused through rapid change of pressure – caused by a dive or something like that.

101

I've been on to the Adj[utant] about Groupie & he told me this morning that Wing Co. Tuck[51] said I could have my leave – I may not even have to see Groupy. So you can <u>almost</u> bank on the fact that I'll be home on Tuesday night sometime . . .

I enjoyed my 48 hrs more than ever I imagined I would. I wish Easter would hurry up & come along – I should be almost due for another leave then – so if I explain things to my F/Cdr then (not now) maybe he can arrange to get my leave to coincide with Easter! . . .

I haven't the faintest idea what to write about – all I can think of is Easter.

When I got to the middle of 'faintest' I was dragged off to do some dogfighting with another chap. I hadn't flown for about a week until today – I thoroughly enjoyed it & did tons of things I never thought I could do with a Spit – some intentional and some definitely not!

When I got back dozens of copies of the Kent Messenger had arrived. I bought one to read all about '72' . . . They say we're a terrifically good squadron – modest & all that – If you read about it you have to take it all with a large portion of salt . . .

I love you so much, dear, that I'm certain I'll come through this job OK – so don't worry too much.

The individual mentioned in the opening line here is Dicky Huband, a close friend from ITW days at Torquay who goes on to figure regularly in this correspondence. A welcome visitor to the couple's homes, he endeared himself to both sets of parents. Like so many, his early ambition was to fly fighters; however, he ended up on Hampdens, medium bombers where the loss rate was relatively high. Almost half of those built, 714, were lost on operations with 1,077 crew killed and 739 reported missing.

This is Ron's last letter for some time. Brief extracts from Connie's diary tell the story of a few days' leave:

13 January 1942: 'Ron home about 7 o'clock. He had tea & then we listened to the wireless & played some records. It was lovely.'

14 January 1942: 'Ron met me for lunch & then we went back to his place for the evening. He wasn't feeling too good but he felt better after we had a little time to ourselves. We are both of us terribly happy.'

---

51. Wing Commander R.R. Stanford Tuck DSO DFC** AFC, a Battle of Britain veteran, was eventually credited with 29 confirmed enemy aircraft destroyed.

15 January 1942: 'Ron met me from the office. We went to see Yank in the RAF – fair. We then went to the Queens & had a really lovely time – eating, drinking & dancing. Lovely evening.'

16 January 1942: 'Ron met me from the office & then we met Mum & went to see Ships with Wings. Home to supper.'

17 January 1942: 'Met Ron & Neil at Tottenham Court Rd – Neil went to England v Scotland. Went to see Two Faced Woman at the Empire & then had tea in Old Vienna. Had a marvellous time at a dance at the Majestic.'

19 January 1942: 'Ron met me for lunch. We met [various of Ron's relations] at Piccadilly Circus. Started at the Lotus, then Captain's Cabin & then finished the evening at the Queens. A really marvellous time. Showed how Ron means just everything to me.'

20 January 1942: 'Ron got up & came to the station with me & met me in the evening . . . went to the station with Ron. I do hope it won't be long before I see him again. I can't bear him to go away.'

No sooner is he back at Gravesend than Ron begins writing once again. Connie will soon receive her first letter for nearly a fortnight.

21 January 1942:

I've never known any of my leaves go so quickly as my last – I had such a wonderful time with you the hours just flashed by – even now I can't believe I've had a week with you . . .

I got my wireless organised & it's going great guns at the moment . . .

Re the night flying. Apparently we're not moving as a whole sqdn – six of us are going to the other 'drome each night to do a spot of flying. This means that we're stopping at G – d for a while at least although the cancellation of days-off seems to remain in force . . .

We've got another chap from 111 here. He was the chap who got a bit smashed up when night flying at Debden. He got a transfer as soon as he learnt that 111 was on that job for good. He used to be a sergeant & is an awfully nice chap – I'm glad he's got here.

By the way – when I got back I found that the taxis had been stopped owing to lack of petrol. Luckily one of my pals was Orderly Sergt & he organised some transport for me.

26 January 1942:

I really missed you tonight as I was told I was night flying at 4 pm – but having rushed over to have tea & come back to dispersal at 4.30 – I was told it had been cancelled. I was very relieved as I've only done about 2 hrs flying in the last two weeks – still – I expect I'll have to do some tomorrow night . . .

I flew this afternoon about 5 pm – took a camera film of another Spit & then came back. There was a terrific wind blowing & it was as cold as blazes.

I managed to see the CO this morning and told him all my plans for a transfer. He didn't seem to mind a great deal – in fact he understood things pretty well. Actually I think there's very little chance of the other business coming off but he's gone up to London today so I may be able to let you have some more news later.

It's a wonderful feeling to know that you're back at home thinking of me & waiting for me to come back. I'm sure I'll come through this job alright whatever happens . . .

This is a telling letter. What lay behind the extraordinary idea that a newly arrived sergeant pilot should make so bold as to tell his squadron commander of *his* plans for a transfer? How could he possibly justify such an approach barely two months into his time on 72 Squadron?

Ron's behaviour was driven by a combination of factors. First and foremost, he was desperate to avoid being separated from Connie. According to her diary, three days before, 'Ron said he would probably be going to the Far East. It makes me thoroughly miserable.' He was obviously feeling the same emotions, concerned about rumours driven by the cumulative effect of recent Allied reversals: the losses of HMS *Repulse* and HMS *Prince of Wales* off Malaya in December 1941, soon followed by the Japanese invasion of Burma and the Dutch East Indies and capture of Manila and Kuala Lumpur.

Although he felt that by now he'd largely established his professional credentials, he still harboured nagging doubts about the implications of his two accidents over Christmas – no matter that he was eventually cleared of any blame. Had they after all left a stain on his professional reputation? He couldn't be one hundred per cent sure. The everyday frustrations – the sheer boredom that becomes more evident in later correspondence – was another factor. Moreover, Ron hadn't yet had an opportunity to test himself against the enemy. There seemed to be something of the phoney war about what he was doing.

During the sixty or so hours' flying he'd managed in nearly four months on the front line, only eleven of sixty-seven sorties (some sixteen hours) were logged as 'ops'. He'd seen neither hide nor hair of the Luftwaffe and only rarely crossed into enemy-held territory. The grey, foggy winter weather had also taken its toll. His obsession with seeing Connie at each and every opportunity didn't help either. Efforts to resolve the conundrum posed by competing demands for his time seem to have prompted his attempt to secure a move, ideally to North Weald, with Woodford just a few miles away. To his mind this would reduce or, ideally, preclude any possibility of a move overseas.

One can only wonder what his squadron commander must have thought of Sergeant Robertson's audacity. That said, a man who 'did his best to keep up morale' and 'always had the interests of the squadron at heart', Cedric Masterman would almost certainly have been aware of what lay behind it. However, what Ron took as benign acceptance on his boss's part may have owed less to sympathy and more to the fact that he was about to move on. In a few days' time, on 9 February, he would be replaced by an individual Ron would come almost to hero-worship, Brian Kingcome. It was a change that would be marked by a welcome increase in operational tempo too.

30 January 1942:

I'm so glad you enjoyed Wednesday night – Derek & Kay are, as you said, two very charming people & make nice company. They (& I) think I'm terribly lucky meeting someone like you – I feel as proud as anything with you . . .

I did a convoy job again today & beat up the same place as we did the other day – the fishermen must be getting quite used to us. That's the sum total of my day's work so there's not much else I can tell you . . .

<u>*31.1.42.*</u>
It's now 6.30 pm or 18.30 hrs & I've got my wireless fitted up to a new accumulator – at the moment it's going very well.

I rather hoped we'd get released today so that I could come up to Covent Garden & meet you. However – the big bugs had other ideas & we've been on duty all day. I flew this morning at about 9 am – the weather was shocking & no one did anymore until tea time when a couple of new blokes were taken up to do some formation stuff.

I'm getting very bored with not doing much apart from the odd convoy job – I wish they'd buck up & get this war either started or finished so that I'd either get some action or else be able to come back to you – personally I've lost all ambition to be a hero – my greatest ambition is to be able to get back to my normal life – which is just you.

By the way – do you remember Derek & I saying we hadn't read of Jack [Ranger] in the casualty list? Well – it's in this week's Aeroplane[52] – Jack's reported 'Killed in action', & his brother is mentioned in a new list of DFCs, then by his name they've put 'since deceased' – what a war! It all seems such a hell of a waste when you think about it – so the best thing to do is <u>not</u> to think about it. I've been getting more & more morbid as this letter's gone on, but I feel so much better after I've told you – it's <u>almost</u> as good as talking to you.

Ron was still managing to get up to London regularly; occasionally he was even able to stay the night at either his or Connie's home. What she described as a 'marvellous evening', the Wednesday (28 January) meeting with Derek and Kay, is a case in point. He returned next morning, but only after accompanying Connie to her office. Afternoon visits to London followed on Monday and Thursday of the following week; in between he squeezed in an overnight stay on the Tuesday, even though it meant setting his alarm for 5.30 next morning.

6 February 1942:

I arrived back here OK last night – luckily the MO was on the same train & had transport waiting for him. He took me right up to 'Polperro' so once more I was saved about 4/- [20p].

Believe it or not I actually flew today! It was such an unusual thing that I got strapped in the plane before I realised I'd forgotten my 'Mae West' – so I had to get out & start all over again. I took two new chaps round the sector – just general stooging.

I had a marvellous time this week – it's almost been like old times seeing you so often. If we don't get released at all next week it's going to seem an awful long time till I see you on my '48' – still – just hope & pray.

---

52. A monthly aviation magazine that began life as a weekly publication in June 1911.

I'm enclosing this letter from Derek – I'm going to drop them a line tonight . . . to thank old Derek for the 10/- [50p] – say we had a good time & tell them it's hardly possible to see them until I get 7 days' leave again – We might manage a couple of days up there [Grantham] if you like . . .

Ron's 6 February sortie was his first for nearly a week. Two more followed a couple of days later. He concluded the second of these, an air test, by disturbing what would otherwise have been a quiet Sunday afternoon at the Freeman family home – enjoying himself thoroughly and delighting Connie in the process. It gave her a feeling of immense pride when 'Ron shot us up about 2.30 pm.'

11 February 1942:

We did another convoy job this morning – it was glorious flying – the sun was as bright as anything – too bright for our liking – we couldn't look up into it to see if we were going to get 'jumped' – needless to say – we weren't.

This afternoon we didn't fly & so I spent some time with my revolver – I actually managed to hit a tin a couple of times – one of our other pilots shot a rook with his sporting gun . . .

With the fine weather coming on I don't expect I'll be able to see you even as long or as often as I do now and sooner or later we're bound to get shifted up north somewhere & I may not be able to see you even if I get a '48' then, so we'll just have to get used to it. I've just looked up the railway map & the place we usually go is about 300 miles from London – which means that I can't see you even if I get a '48'– still – it'll be some time before we go – if we go – so there's no point in crossing our bridges before we get to them. All sorts of things can happen before then . . .

The following day was a frustrating one for the squadron – and a tragic one for the Fleet Air Arm. On Thursday 12 February an entire formation of six Swordfish aircraft (together with thirteen of eighteen aircrew) was lost in a vain attempt to halt progress north through the Dover Straits of a huge German convoy, one that included the battleships *Scharnhorst* and *Gneisenau*.

Ron was frustrated not to be part of the 72 Squadron formation, led by the new boss, ordered to rendezvous over Manston to provide cover for the Swordfish attack. Another four Spitfire squadrons were similarly tasked but in the event only 72 made contact with the 'Stringbags', as 825 Naval Air Squadron's aircraft were affectionately known. Kingcome's formation was an aircraft down too; one pilot failed to take off but there was no replacement scheduled. It wasn't clear why this aircraft returned to dispersal and aborted the mission, although Ron had a somewhat disparaging view of the South African concerned: 'He wasn't exactly a do or die character.'

Following a successful rendezvous near the Kent coast in poor weather, 'beneath a swirling cover of low cloud and rain . . . with visibility fluctuating between zero and a few hundred yards',[53] the combined formation ran into overwhelmingly strong German fighter defences, mainly Fw 190s. It was the squadron's 'first contact with . . . a first-class performer destined to supplant the Me 109 as Göring's most deadly answer to the Spitfire'.[54] In such circumstances protecting the Swordfishes proved impossible. Slow and vulnerable, they fell either to German fighters or to the ships' defensive armament. The pilots of 72 claimed three enemy aircraft destroyed and four damaged against no losses, but with one exception they could do little for those they were sent to protect. A lone Spitfire remained circling a ditched Swordfish crew, covering them as they clambered aboard their dinghy, until it was nearly out of fuel.

Later that day another 72 Squadron formation was sent to hunt for the same German convoy. Once again the South African failed to get airborne. At this Ron took matters into his own hands, leapt into an aircraft and caused considerable consternation by taking off downwind in an effort to catch up with his colleagues. Unable to locate them in the misty conditions that still prevailed, he eventually encountered a couple of Bristol Beaufort torpedo-bombers. These he assumed were also searching for the *Scharnhorst* and *Gneisenau*, so he provided cover for them until his own fuel ran low.

Thus ended another frustrating day. He'd still had no contact with the enemy. He wasn't to know it, but things would change in the next twenty-four hours with his first experience of 'some flak' during a sweep over Gravelines and Dunkirk.

From a British perspective the Kriegsmarine's 'Channel Dash', from Brest to the haven of their home ports, was something of a debacle, prompting Prime Minister Churchill to launch an immediate enquiry. But according to Kingcome:

---

53. Kingcome, op. cit., p.119.
54. Ibid., p.120.

There was a Whitehall cover-up. I attended a couple of inquiries, but nothing came out and the operation, a German naval and propaganda triumph of the highest order was heavily and correctly exploited to the full in Germany. It passed largely unknown and unremarked in Britain, which was scarcely surprising. For three German battleships[55] to have outwitted our intelligence and sailed in broad daylight up the English Channel and through the Straits of Dover before escaping into the wilderness of the North Sea was barely credible. It was certainly an event Whitehall preferred to have swept quietly under the carpet then and thereafter.[56]

Connie's diary entry for 12 February provides a pithy summary of the day's events: 'Ron phoned – there had been "Bags of Flap" in the Channel.'

18 February 1942:

Do you remember that letter you wrote me when I went back to Hawarden? You know – I've always kept it in my wallet. I read it over and over again today – that was the first time you ever said that you cared about me – I just imagined that I was back on Euston station at 4 pm that day – it was easily the nicest send-off I've ever had at any time. I've had a wonderful time with you ever since . . .

My last 48 was marvellous – I enjoyed it no end. I knew you'd be a great success with the odd members of the family you hadn't yet met, but even I was staggered by the exact reception . . .

22 February 1942:

I'd better explain now that (I hope!) I've got from midday Friday to midday Monday – so if all goes well we should have quite a long weekend.

We've done no flying since I last phoned you except for about 20 mins this afternoon – I took a new chap around the sector but the weather was u/s & so we came back.

---

55. The third of Kingcome's 'battleships', *Prinz Eugen*, was in fact a heavy cruiser.
56. Kingcome, op. cit., p.122.

I did dawn readiness this morning, dusk readiness until 7.15 tonight & I'm on dawn again tomorrow – still, as long as I get my weekend I don't care if I do all the dawns & dusks there are. I think I'm going to get my own kite again – I can't have 'R' as we only go from A – K[57] – but the CO is having a new kite – 'K' – he used to have 'C' – so I'm doing my best to get 'C' – for obvious reasons . . .

I can't get over the fact that we're going away next weekend – I do hope nothing comes along & messes it up . . .

Do you think you can wangle Saturday morning off? – There's a train at 5.30 pm on Friday that gets to Grantham at 7.43 – Anyway – I'll ask you on the phone – if the damn thing ever rings!!

25 February 1942:

As things are at present it seems very unlikely that I'll get my weekend . . . I'm pretty fed up about it at the moment as all I've had in five weeks is one 24 & one 48. Not only that – but you'll be kept wondering right up to the last minute as to whether we're going or not & Derek & Kay will be expecting us – in fact things are in a pretty mess all round . . .

I wish I could have been with you when I told you that my leave was a bit shaky – you sounded so miserable . . . still – even now things aren't as hopeless as they might be.

Think of all the times my leave has been just as shaky as this & yet things have always turned out alright. You see – after having spoken to you I'm looking on the bright side already.

P.S. I've got my own kite now – it's got to be repainted – & when that happens I'm having 'Connie' painted on it.

A relatively long gap before Ron's next letter is explained by leave arrangements that were off, then back on again. While this put paid to the idea of a weekend with the Olvers in Grantham, all was not lost. After Derek and Kay's own plans changed, on the Saturday evening the two couples met for dinner in London: another 'marvellous evening' according to Connie's diary.

---

57. The 72 Squadron identifier was RN, followed by an individual suffix; thus Kingcome's aircraft would be RN-K.

4 March 1942:

Did I tell you last night about my beautiful kite. I'll tell you again anyway – it's being re-doped today & I've got the F/Cdr's permission to have 'CONNIE' painted on the side. We've got a signwriter in our flight & he's going to do it. I got ragged like blazes yesterday over it, but I don't give a toot as long as I'm allowed to have it on there . . .

There's really no news – I only left you on Monday – I phoned on Monday night – you phoned me last night & so I can't tell you anything new.

Ron was still taking any and every opportunity to see Connie, as her diary entry for 5 March confirms: 'Ron came home unexpectedly. He met me at the office. It was marvellous seeing him again. I had a letter from him in the morning. He went back early in the morning about 5 o'clock.'

8 March 1942:

I took my beautiful 'H'[58] complete with 'CONNIE' on the side, on two shows today. The first was very quiet but the second was fairly warm – it was also the farthest I've ever been into France – but 'H' did its stuff like an angel & the scarf was a great success – so you see, dear, you bring me luck even when you're not with me. I'm afraid this won't be a very long letter as I've only been away from you for 23 hrs . . .

I'm as tired as blazes at the moment so I think I'll crawl into bed after I've spoken to you . . . with luck I should see you on Wednesday – I stand a fair chance of getting the time off.

There's more to be said about this latest letter. The second 'show' mentioned early on involved accompanying six Bostons (the RAF designation for the American Douglas A-20) to bomb Abbeville. Ron's 'fairly warm' comment relates to the flak he encountered that afternoon. Penetrating some twenty miles into France in a relatively large formation he fully expected to be intercepted by enemy aircraft but it wasn't the case; his log book confirms 'No E/A (enemy aircraft)'.

Next, there was a reason for the 'great success' of the white silk scarf Ron wore for the first time that day. The subject of occasional mockery

---

58. Ron was unable to acquire 'C', so his aircraft registration became RN-H.

from those outside Fighter Command, this item of apparel (or something like it, as with Chas Charnock) was deemed essential by pilots forced to keep swivelling their heads around, searching for enemy aircraft. Rearward vision was difficult enough without the impediment of a uniform collar and tie. Wearing a scarf solved the problem of the sore neck that otherwise resulted; in theory it also offered a way to attract attention in the event of a ditching. This last was an uncomfortable prospect for aircrew, not least because Van Heusen officer pattern shirts were prone to shrinkage in contact with sea water. Wearers of a collar and tie stood a chance of being throttled in the unlikely event that they survived much longer than four hours or so in the Channel during summer. Thus Ron's new silk scarf was much more than mere affectation.

His final admission that he's 'tired as blazes' reflects the fact that he'd flown three times that day – a welcome change after sitting on the ground for the previous four. Given that he flies three times again next day, then contrives to see Connie four out of the next five, cumulative tiredness can't be ruled out either – not that Ron would have been concerned, given the events of a momentous week . . .

13 March 1942:

I got back here at 10.45 am & rang up to see if there was anything doing. Unfortunately, or fortunately, the chaps had just left on a 'do', so I'm afraid I won't be flying today unless they come back early – we've no other kites serviceable.

I got your letter when I came back – it sounds awfully good to hear you speak of us as 'engaged' – I wish my next leave would hurry up & come along, although I've only left you for 5 hrs I'm aching to see you again.

I told you yesterday how much I enjoyed Tuesday – I keep thinking of it now – actually I'm awfully glad we didn't make it our official engagement as we can still look forward to Easter & have the same pleasure all over again. Besides, it's nice to think that people will congratulate us & say all the 'usual' things at Easter, when we two know that we've been engaged for three weeks by then – it's just something we can keep to ourselves . . .

I'm still upside-down over Tuesday – it all seems so marvellous I feel I want to sing & kick up a terrific row just because I feel so good.

The squadron's serviceability problem is reflected in the fifteen-minute air test Ron carries out later that day. But the real news here is the story of the couple's unofficial engagement, fleshed out in Connie's diary entry for 10 March, 'Ron came up to the office unexpectedly & we went to K&D – & got my ring. It's a beautiful one. We went to see Louisiana Purchase at Plaza & then went to Queen's. Just between Ron and I we became engaged. I was ideally happy & always want to stay like it.'

She was much less happy four days later. 'Ron phoned from Shoreham – he had to bale out. Thank you God for keeping him safe. I can't write all that I feel for his safety here.' His log book summarises the story: 'Sweep. Le Havre . . . Took 6 Bostons. Got Glycol leak on way back. Caught fire. Baled out.' The entry concludes with a drawing of a tiny stick man dangling from an equally small parachute. What Ron failed to tell Connie was that on this particular sortie his formation, bombers included, had encountered a fair amount of enemy flak – the root cause of the problems that finally forced him to abandon his aircraft.

Unwilling to trust his fate to the icy Channel, or crash-land on beaches that he thought might possibly be mined, Ron coaxed his stricken Spitfire[59] to the relative safety of dry land before finally parting company with it. His parachute opened at about 1,500 feet, giving him just enough time to take in a panorama of the Sussex coast near Brighton. Dangling below a huge white canopy, he was struck by the unusual serenity of his predicament. His only real concern was his smoking, abandoned aircraft which, for a brief moment, seemed alarmingly adjacent. Minutes later he landed in a copse, where he was dragged backwards through several trees before finally coming to a halt. Releasing his harness, he lowered himself carefully to the ground, confirmed that he was unharmed and headed for the nearest road. After climbing through a hedge he was surprised to be greeted by an offer of a cup of tea from a lady of a certain age. She seemed entirely unperturbed by this unusual turn of events. Ron could only assume that what was a first for him was a relatively common occurrence in this part of the world. Equally sanguine was the second woman he encountered – a doctor who offered him a lift to the nearest military base, a Canadian dental unit. Here he was treated to a meal, a glass of whiskey and a cigar (the pipe that was his constant companion was back at base) before being driven to Shoreham military hospital for a check-up and overnight stay.

---

59. Serial AD183, a Mk Vb, finally impacted near Haywards Heath.

Next morning, no worse for the experience, he was flown back to Gravesend in a Lysander. In fact he 'felt quite the little hero' as he walked across to dispersal, where he was congratulated by the CO on his escape. His chest puffed with pride until Kingcome added, 'There is one point, Robbie, you don't have to tell the whole bloody German Air Force you're going to bale out!' It was then that he recalled the last few minutes of his fateful flight and a lengthy discussion on the pros and cons of baling out over the sea. His number two, convinced it was the right option, had urged him to abandon his doomed aircraft. But seeing below him 'enormous waves which had great white tops on them, [he] didn't fancy finishing up in the drink at all!'

Thanks in part to more bad weather, it would be some time before he climbed into the cockpit of a Spitfire once again.

16 March 1942:

I saw you at 9 am this morning – I'm phoning you on Thursday evening – so what can I say now? . . .

I got your letter this afternoon (very nice) & also one from Dicky. He says he's got 12 days' sick leave & has already written to you so I expect he's shot you a terrific line about being a hero & all that. Anyway – he hasn't had to bale out yet – I'm going to gloat like blazes when I write to him.

I wrote to the Irvin 'Chute Co. today telling that I'd baled out. The CO will have to confirm it for me & then I should get my badge.[60]

Well darling – my new kite's arrived & was tested this morning early. The chap who flew it said it was a real honey – the ground staff say it's about the best kite we've ever had, so I'm pretty pleased all round. 'Connie' is going to be painted on first thing in the morning & then it's all set.

Five days elapse before Ron's next letter confirms the devastating news (in a brief note from Kay) that Derek Olver has been killed in a flying accident. They'd been close since their first meeting at Kidlington and his thoughts went back immediately to all the fun they'd had there. The image clearest in his mind was of Derek, proud owner of a motor-bike and sidecar, transporting five of them to local pubs of an evening. The Trout at Godstow and the Bear at Woodstock were favourite haunts, albeit they were

---

60. A small gold caterpillar pin with amethyst eyes and the individual's name engraved on the back.

occasionally disappointed to be met with a sign outside that read, 'No beer this week'. He could picture the scene now: Kay and 'little Brian Talbot' in the sidecar, Derek on the petrol tank driving, Ron in the saddle and Jack Ranger behind him on the pillion. At other times Derek would ferry them to Parson's Pleasure on the Cherwell at Oxford, where they'd spend lazy afternoons swimming – without Kay though. The location was notorious as one of the few public places in the UK that allowed nude bathing. Even more poignant was the memory of their dinner together in London just a couple of weeks earlier, Connie's 'marvellous evening'.

At the time of the accident, on 15 March, Derek was a flying officer instructor on Oxfords at 12 SFTS, RAF Spitalgate, near Grantham. Shortly after a formation take-off, heading into a low sun, the aircraft he was flying with an American student, Sergeant J.L. Wyatt, collided with one flown by Flight Lieutenant R.J. Jouault DFC and his Dutch student, First Lieutenant W.B. Straver. There were no survivors. It's a measure of the resulting damage – both aircraft were written off – that Kay was never allowed to see her husband's body.

21 March 1942:

I phoned Kay tonight – I scarcely recognised her voice – it seemed utterly lifeless – there was nothing I could say to her that would really mean anything.

I told her that you'd love to have her stay with you for a while, but at the moment she's trying to shut up the Kensington flat & take another near her mother . . .

There isn't much I can tell you now – I'll do my best to see you just as soon as I can & we can both go over & see Kay.

Do try & buck up, dear – I didn't know what to say to you tonight – if I'd been with you it would have been easy to just hold you in my arms & let you have a good cry – it would have been so much better for both of us.

It was as much as I could do to stop my own tears – it seems such a shocking waste for a chap like Derek to be taken. I've never had such a really good friend & I've never met two people, apart from ourselves, who meant so much to each other.

We must, as you said, do all we can to make things a bit easier for Kay . . .

This sad missive was the last Ron sent from Gravesend. In fact, after his bale out he never flew from there again. The very next day 72 Squadron relocated to Biggin Hill.

Chapter 17

18 February 1943, HMHS (His Majesty's Hospital Ship) *Newfoundland*

Built in Barrow-in-Furness, the RMS (Royal Mail Ship) *Newfoundland* began life in 1925 plying the transatlantic routes between Liverpool and Boston via St John's, Newfoundland, and Halifax, Nova Scotia. During the early part of the war she was pressed into service on similar routes, carrying wounded troops from the UK to Canada and bringing rehabilitated troops back home. The transition to hospital ship complete, painted entirely in white except for large red crosses amidships and on the funnel, she then began returning injured Servicemen from North Africa, many of them Eighth Army soldiers. After what seemed an eternity of waiting and any number of false starts, on Thursday 18 February 1943 Robbie at last embarked on what was now HMHS *Newfoundland*.

Before he finally left his ward he made a point of bidding farewell to a lanky American with a huge wound in his thigh. So tall was Captain W.M. Hamblin, aka 'Kentucky', that his foot extended well beyond the end of his bed. It thus proved something of an obstacle for regular passers-by, but he suffered the resulting pain without complaint. His stoicism was one of the qualities that endeared him to Robbie, who was surprised and delighted when Kentucky bequeathed him his Zippo lighter as a parting gift. It came with a note: 'Just to remember me by. Lots of luck whatever you may do.' It was a gesture that touched him more than he cared to admit.

During what proved a slow and sedate voyage he developed a considerable affection for the ageing vessel that was to return him safely to the UK. So it was with a hint of sadness that he learned of her eventual demise, albeit some considerable time after the event itself. The *Newfoundland* was delivering over 100 American nurses to the Salerno beaches in September 1943 when, together with other clearly marked hospital ships in theory protected under the Geneva Convention, she was attacked a number of times by German bombers. Fortunate not to be damaged, together with three other hospital ships, she retired some forty miles offshore for the night. Then, in the early hours of the morning of 13 September, lit up like a Christmas tree to signal her status, she suffered a direct hit in another attack. After fires, explosions, and the loss of all medical officers on board as well as six of fourteen British staff nurses (all the Americans survived), the vessel was scuttled next day.

All this was still to come, of course. Meanwhile, two days after leaving Algiers, late on Saturday night Robbie was surprised to find the *Newfoundland* docking in Oran, some 220 miles south-west of Algiers. Frustrated by this unexpected delay, there was partial compensation in the discovery of a radio which allowed him to indulge his passion for music. The hospital ship eventually left port the following Tuesday morning, 23 February, in beautiful weather. He then settled into his regular routine. After a good night's sleep in a bed that was a vast improvement over some in which he'd found himself of late, traditional English breakfast was followed by lazy mornings ensconced in a deckchair reading and dozing in the sun – that was until the weather turned colder as the vessel made its way north of Spain. Afternoons were spent watching films and playing poker, solo and cravatte, a card game he'd been taught by a Czech airman. He recorded his winnings and occasional losses in his *Collins Handy Diary for 1943* – a traditional birthday present, this one was inscribed with 'Fondest Love & Best Wishes. From Mum, <u>Sept 18 – 1942</u>'. Evenings meant chats with crew members, fellow invalids and the odd nurse, plus the occasional very welcome beer.

One of the compensations of having time on his hands was that Ron was able to pore again over the small stack of correspondence that had accumulated during his time away. It was Connie's, of course, that gave him the greatest thrill, albeit he was frustrated by the absence of several letters from her numbered sequence. (Some wouldn't reach him until much later, after following his trail between various medical facilities.) On 4 January 1943, in 'No. 23 letter', she mentioned that she'd 'finished reading that book *Ten Fighter Boys*. It was "Wizard" – (I think is the correct epithet). I'm now reading *Spitfire*. I have to "keep up" with Fighter Command somehow & as you're not here to enlighten me I've taken to reading about it.' It was the first Ron had heard of a book first mentioned in Connie's previous letter, another of those yet to reach him. There she'd written: 'Our office boy has lent me a very good book called *Ten Fighter Boys* – have you read it? It is the individual stories of ten Spitfire pilots.' Little did she know that one of these 66 Squadron pilots, Jimmy Corbin, was with Ron at Souk-el-Arba. By the time Collins published the book in 1942, five of the original contributors had been killed, as had the two editors, a wing commander and a squadron leader. In 2007 Corbin penned his own aptly titled account, *Last of the*

Ten Fighter Boys, and a year later wrote the foreword to another edition of the original. He eventually passed away in December 2012.

After what seemed a never-ending journey home, but one in which Robbie felt that his eye had improved, his ship finally docked at Bristol on Tuesday 2 March. He wasted no time whatsoever in phoning home and couldn't believe his luck in finding Connie there, visiting his parents. As they chatted animatedly for the first time in more than four months, Connie confirmed what Robbie had first heard from Chas Charnock: he'd been awarded the DFC. Earlier that same day Connie had received a telegram from Vickie Malan. The message was short and simple: 'CONGRATULATIONS ON DECORATION HAPPY REUNION = VICKIE.' Of all the things he and his fiancée discussed that memorable day, including tentative wedding plans, this seemed to Robbie the least important. He was simply ecstatic to be reunited at last with the woman he loved, even if it was just by telephone.

For the nurses who had done so much to make a voyage of nearly three weeks almost bearable, one last responsibility remained. After a final, unexpected night on board they ensured their charges were loaded safely onto yet another hospital train. As in Algiers, these indefatigable ladies had more than proved their worth. It was therefore with some regret, and no little emotion, that Robbie bade them farewell and began the relatively short journey to the 67th General Hospital at Taunton, some forty miles to the south-west. Activated less than six months earlier as an American Army hospital staffed by the US Army Medical Corps, it was scheduled to host the next stage of his recovery. However, just two days after arriving at Taunton he was notified of yet another impending move. He cabled Connie:

5 March 1943:

'DARLING HAVE WRITTEN ONE LETTER BUT AM REWRITING OWING TO NEW GEN HAVE TO GO TO NEW HOSPITAL SOON BEFORE I CAN GET LEAVE I LOVE YOU = RON'

This move would bring him nearer London, to the Mount Vernon Hospital at Northwood. But that could wait. First, he managed a brief spot of leave. The couple's much anticipated reunion came the very next day. The moment he arrived at Liverpool Street Ron called Connie and arranged to meet her at Forest Gate station in an hour. So eager were the pair to embrace when they met that, as Ron wrapped his arms eagerly around his fiancée, he promptly knocked off the smart new hat she wore for the occasion. It hardly mattered. There could have been no happier a pair in the entire country, nay, probably the world.

Chapter 18

22 March 1942, RAF Biggin Hill

As soon as 72 Squadron was established at its new home, Biggin Hill, Ron secured an overnight pass for Sunday 22 March and left immediately for London. There he met Connie and the pair set off to see Kay Olver, who was now living in Osterley with her mother. It was a day of mixed emotions. Their delight in being together was tempered, inevitably, by a natural despondency. For an 18-year-old who'd never before come face to face with such tragedy, it was a particularly difficult visit. Connie's diary entry that day says it all: 'I do feel dreadfully sorry for [Kay] but she is so awfully brave. Ron & I want to do whatever we can for her.'

After an unusually sombre journey back across London, the couple returned relatively early to their respective homes. They were physically and emotionally exhausted. Next morning Ron set off at 6 am in order to arrive in good time for his first flight since baling out nine days earlier. That evening he rang an anxious Connie to let her know he'd returned safely. Given her state of mind – even more worried than usual – he did the same the following day. Neither call did much to reassure her. She was still deeply affected by Derek's untimely death and their visit to Osterley. It didn't help matters when Ron mentioned in passing that seven aircraft had gone missing that day, an unguarded comment that simply exacerbated Connie's unease – witness her diary entry for 26 March: 'Ron phoned me about 8.20. I was so relieved to hear him – I had been so worried all day. There were hundreds of planes about. Mrs Robertson phoned as she was worried about Ron.'

His next letter is unusually reflective. While he was still feeling Derek's loss, his mood also owed something to the nature of his first two sorties back on operations. They exemplified the potential Luftwaffe threat. On the first, a sweep to Dunkirk, St Omer and Neufchâtel-Hardelot, he 'Saw lots of E/A', albeit 'Nothing happened'. During the second, another where he escorted six Bostons to Abbeville, he 'Saw many E/A' but 'None attacked'. The German fighters' apparent reluctance to engage, while in some ways a relief, was also mystifying – a stark contrast with the Fighter Command approach. He would come to understand the enemy's tactics much better as he gained more experience.

25 March 1942:

I haven't done any flying today – just hanging around for the big 'do' – still – it makes a change. I looked up my log book today and altogether I've done 15 sweeps. That includes 9 times when we've actually gone into France to do something & 6 when we've just stooged along their coast. I've also done 12 convoy patrols – so I'm gradually getting a spot of experience at this game – which, perhaps, is just as well.

I'm enclosing a letter – I've had from the Caterpillar Club – I hope the badge comes before Easter.

It <u>was</u> nice on Sunday, wasn't it? – the fact that you were with me made things a lot easier. It's so nice to feel that there's someone always with you, relying on you, and just being there when things are getting you down . . .

It seems funny now – not having Derek to go out with. I just took it for granted that nothing would happen to him & still can't realise that I won't see him again. It used to be such fun going out with Derek & Kay that I hoped we might be able to spend a weekend away with them & then, after the war was over we could go to Oxford & visit some of the places where we'd had so much fun. Still – it just goes to show that you can't bank on anything these days – it seems such a horrible shame & waste in this case though . . .

By the way – we still have to do night flying so if I don't phone you one night when I should have done, don't worry.

29 March 1942:

I felt better after I phoned you yesterday – It seems years since I spent a night out with you – I'm just aching for Easter to come along so that I can get my leave & we can go out together without always thinking of getting up early in the morning to come dashing back here again.

Things have been pretty quiet here so please don't start worrying too much – I know it's pretty bad for you at home when you've only got to sit & listen to the news & wonder what's happening, but all we can do is just hope & pray that things will be alright . . .

I do wish this war would buck up & finish. Just think of all the lovely things we could do.

With Spring coming on & the days getting sunnier we could go for walks in the country or down to Westcliff for a swim – all sorts of things which we took for granted before the war but which seem very marvellous now. As it is – all that Spring means to us is that we'll have to work a bit harder & earn our money now and again.

This was Ron's last letter for nearly two weeks. Released early two days later, he took a train to London and met Connie at her office. After returning home together they spent a convivial Tuesday evening at the Monkhams before Ron set off back to Biggin Hill late that night. His coveted Easter leave was due to begin in another forty-eight hours. Easter Sunday, 5 April, was their special day. Connie's diary records that, 'Mr & Mrs R. & all the family came in the afternoon. It was a really marvellous evening. It was our official engagement & we were both so terribly happy – hope we always stay like it.'

Ron made his way up to town regularly the following week. On the Tuesday, after taking Connie to lunch, he visited his former colleagues at the Ocean. It was more than just a social visit; he wanted to insure Connie's engagement ring – and secure the staff discount to which he was still entitled. The following day the couple arranged to meet Kay in London. It was less than a month since Derek had been killed, during which time she'd hardly set foot outside her mother's home. Connie's diary once again takes up the story.

> Ron came to Stratford with me & then came & met me for lunch. He phoned Kay & then he brought Kay to meet me from the office. We went to see Balls of Fire & then to the Queens. It was a lovely evening – I wish Derek could have been there, but I think Kay enjoyed it. She is wonderful really. She told me she was expecting a baby. I do hope she has one. Ron & I had a lovely evening together – it was his last night & I felt pretty bad about it.

It was a night of mixed emotions. The conviviality of being together again, and the shared joy of Kay's news, couldn't mask the unspoken sadness of Derek's absence. For Ron it was a sadness heightened by the knowledge this would be his last evening with Connie for . . . *who knows?* So before he set off for Biggin Hill next morning, he travelled with Connie to her office. Time together – any time at all – was becoming increasingly precious.

9 April 1942:

I was given bags of news when I came back here but I'm afraid I only half listened to what was being said to me. I kept thinking of Sunday when everyone was 'officially' told of our engagement – how nice you looked, & all sorts of things which happened last week . . .

There have been lots of changes since I left. My pal (?) Bruce has been posted & we're also <u>minus</u> *three chaps. This means, I'm very much afraid, that the likelihood of any days off apart from a release, is rather remote. I can't explain too fully, darling, but you remember the news we heard on the wireless the other day don't you?*

A lot has happened during Ron's time away from the squadron – hence the 'bags of news' opening to this letter and his closing reference to 'lots of changes'. While he touches on the fact that his unit is down on manpower, understandably, he fails to mention the main reason why. In his absence the Biggin Hill Wing had sustained a number of losses. Amongst them was an Australian, Sergeant Al Hake, who'd been with the squadron barely two months – long enough, however, for Ron to form an attachment to a 'monosyllabic character, who used to speak about three times a week'; indeed, he retained an annotated picture of him amongst his memorabilia.

Hake's was one of ten aircraft lost on 4 April[61] when his bomber escort formation encountered a large number of Fw 190s over France. In the resulting mêleé his aircraft was severely damaged and he was forced to bale out. Wounded and burned, he was immediately captured by a German Army unit whose personnel assumed that, as a Spitfire pilot, he was an officer – a pretence he was happy to sustain throughout his subsequent imprisonment in Stalag Luft III. There, after demonstrating his talents as a travel document forger and mass producer of compasses, he took part in the Great Escape – only to be one of the fifty recaptured airmen shot by way of savage retribution. A week after the escape, together with five others he was summarily executed by the Gestapo beside an autobahn near Görlitz.

The news to which Ron refers later in the same paragraph is difficult to pin down. It may possibly have been reports of devastating air attacks on Malta. The almost incessant raids of 7 April 1942, directed mainly at the civilian populace, left Valletta 'a stricken city' and the island's dockyards

---

61. Three of these were from 72 Squadron: Hake, Flight Lieutenant R.R. Gillespie (a Canadian) and Flight Sergeant T. Watson. Gillespie became a prisoner of war while Watson was posted missing, believed killed.

severely damaged. They were the heaviest, most concentrated assaults yet in what was already a long campaign; the island had been under siege since November 1940. With limited defences and Hurricanes increasingly ineffective against the Luftwaffe, reinforcements were desperately needed. The first of these arrived on 7 March 1941: sixteen Spitfires flown in from the carrier HMS *Eagle*. A year later the resulting drain on both aircraft and aircrew was still being felt on the front line. There's evidence for this in Vere Hodgson's 10 April observation that 'We never have enough aircraft'[62] and in Ron's '<u>minus</u> three chaps' comment. It seems likely, therefore, that it's the Malta news to which he alludes.

By way of a footnote to these events, shortly afterwards, on 15 April 1942, 'To honour her brave people', King George VI awarded the George Cross 'to the Island Fortress of Malta to bear witness to a heroism and devotion that will long be famous in history.'

13 April 1942:

I've got enough ink (I hope) to just about address the envelope & no more – so perforce I must continue this epistle in pencil.

I'm glad your people enjoyed 'our' Sunday – I know everyone else did – maybe we can organise some other days like that if I get some more leave.

It'll be rather good when Plaistow starts again – I wonder who'll be there . . . Still, once you get to a Club night it won't take long for the word to get around & the remainder of PUSC [Plaistow United Swimming Club] *will know in a very short time. I don't mean that you'll go around shouting the news to people, but you know how everyone talks to everyone else on a Club night & no doubt after not seeing one another for about two years there's bound to be bags to talk about. I'm as keen as anything to get to one of the old Friday nights – I wonder if the Lunn family will turn up to give us their blessing! . . .*

It's 7.45 now – this time last week we were in the Queens – hope it's not too long before we're there again . . .

My new kite's pretty good – I've got the same crew as I had before – Duncan & George . . . between them they keep it in really tip top condition. I told you I had 'Connie' put on it didn't I?

---

62. Hodgson, op. cit., p.273.

I had my bath last night & crawled into bed about 9.30 & that's all I remember until I was called at 7.30 this morning. I think that's the most flying I've done since I came on 'ops' – about 5 hrs.

My week's leave has done me the world of good – I'm as keen on flying now as blazes – as things are I don't think there's much chance of a day off until a week or ten days – quite a few chaps have put in for 48s for a rest & I've only just come back . . .

I'm proud of the chance to help fight to make the world a better place – after all <u>we're</u> the ones who are going to benefit by it. Think of all the marvellous things we can do after the war – in our own home.

The contrast between this latest note and the despair of barely two months ago is remarkable. Of the reasons for this change, all but one are explicit. Most obviously, Ron's still basking in the excitement of the couple's official engagement. Then there's the sheer enjoyment of regular flying, plus the surge of adrenaline that accompanies operational missions. With batteries recharged and enthusiasm rekindled, he's just flown ten sorties in four days, half of them on operations – sweeps, convoy patrols and a scramble. There's even a sign of his laconic humour. After a 'machine-gun test' on 12 April he writes: 'Aimed at Boulogne. Hope I hit it.' No wonder his mood has lifted.

The missing contribution to this extraordinary turnaround is the influence of an inspirational new squadron commander, a gifted professional and born leader who'd taken over a couple of months earlier. Under Brian Kingcome 72 was a changed squadron. One of the very best of 'The Few', his character was nowhere better summarised than at his funeral in 1994. There, fellow Battle of Britain veteran, Sir Hugh 'Cocky' Dundas, remembered his 'courage, determination, a total lack of pomposity or self-importance and an everlasting lightness of heart and touch'.

Echoing Dundas' reference to the absence of any pretention, Ron would later recall how the new boss introduced himself to his pilots:

> Well, my name is Brian. I don't want any of this 'Sir' business.
> But on the other hand, if I'm talking to the Station Commander,
> I don't want some sergeant pilot walking up and slapping me
> on the back and saying 'Wotcher Brian, how are you?'

If Kingcome was impressive on the ground, in Ron's eyes he achieved almost God-like status in the air. An experience flying as his number two makes the point. Acutely aware of the importance of 'keeping one's voice on the R.T. calm and casual to steady the nerves of the new pilots', Kingcome's response to a call of 'Break right Brian. Break – 109 behind; he's firing at you', became the stuff of legend: 'I know old boy, but just look at his deflection!'[63]

16 April 1942:

I never expected a letter as early as this & so I'm dashing off a reply which will be rather brief I'm afraid . . .

Anyway – I'm at readiness until 9.30 tonight – from 7 pm & it's now 5 pm – so I'll write until 6 pm – go & phone you & Mum & then dash back to readiness . . .

I was DP [duty pilot] *until 8.30 this morning but I was called at 5.15 am to go on a sweep. I'd much rather do a sweep after breakfast – you don't half get hungry before it's all over. We did another one this afternoon & met some 109s but they didn't want to play – so we all came home with our guns unsullied – (I felt such a hero after Tuesday too!) . . .*

I had a letter from Dicky – I haven't answered it because, as you'll read – he's moving . . . as I can't write until he gives me his new address – I'll send you this letter & answer his next one . . .

Ron's 'heroic' Tuesday, just two days earlier, represented a significant milestone: the first time he'd fired his guns in anger. Caught unawares by enemy fighters – another first – his initial experience of air combat proved inconclusive. It's summarised in his log book comments: 'Sweep. Boulogne-Gravelines. Landed Detling . . . Got jumped near [Cap] Gris Nez. Squirted at FW 190 in Channel. My first squirt at a Hun.'

According to Connie's diary he telephoned her twice that day, first 'from dispersal – I was so relieved – though he couldn't tell me much. He phoned again later from the mess. I was so pleased. He has a "probable" Jerry, & is awaiting confirmation.' Not so! Still fired by adrenalin, Ron was exaggerating for effect. He later admitted that excitement got the better of him as he chased the 190: 'I fired like mad at it, but being over-keen, anxious and a rotten shot, I didn't allow enough deflection and all I did was waste a lot of ammunition.'

His unscheduled landing at Detling was due to another 'rookie error'. Focused entirely on the kill-or-be-killed nature of his first engagement – 'it was quite exciting to get chased round and round' – he almost ran out

---

63. Angular deflection is another term for the lead required to hit a turning target: the harder the turn, the greater the deflection required.

of fuel. Once he'd topped up it was a quick fifteen-minute transit back to Biggin Hill, proudly bearing the evidence of his first engagement: the tattered remains of fabric around his gun ports. These dull red canvas patches were a precaution against dirt, dust and, more important, firing mechanisms freezing at altitude; they also provided groundcrew with an early indication of the need for armament replenishment.

The 'letter from Dicky' Huband that Ron forwards to Connie sheds further light on the dangers bomber pilots faced. By this stage of the war Dicky's Hampdens were approaching obsolescence and operating mainly at night. (They were withdrawn from Bomber Command later in the year, although they continued with Coastal Command through most of 1943.) He writes, 'I wish the war were over myself, seems an awful waste of time. We have had another sticky patch – lost more crews. However, that's unavoidable I suppose and we must expect it but it's still a shock.'

20 April 1942:

That was a marvellous letter you sent me – pages & pages of news . . . I can just imagine everyone at club night – I wish I could have been with you . . .

I believe I told you that 'Connie' had been in for inspection – Well – it was repainted today – at least, most of it, the rest will be done tomorrow. You'd have laughed today – we've got some ATC [Air Training Corps] *boys for a week & I got three of them to wash the oil off the underneath of 'Connie' whilst Duncan and George painted the camouflage on & the signwriter put 'Connie' on for the 5th time!*

I've never seen so many people so busy on one plane before!

It's certainly made a difference to the look of the kite – everyone keeps coming up & making rude remarks re the work done on 'Connie' by the battalions of chaps I've scrounged, but it makes no difference to the amount of work put in by the stooges[64] – they're awfully good chaps.

Tubby dear – there's no more news – all I do now is fly – eat – go to bed – write to you & phone you on the odd night. There's no change in my programme ever – the one great exception being when I went out with Jack [Hilton] *& the other F/Sgt* [Jim Norton]. *When the rest of the chaps heard I'd been out they all came into my bedroom & I had to keep on telling them of how Jack got home. They were very amazed that I should leave the confines of the camp – even now I don't know why I did it –*

---

64. The aforementioned Duncan and George, Ron's two erks.

still – it made a change. I'm not likely to give a repeat performance for an awfully long time, though . . .

Things are still very awkward at the moment but I'll do my best to see you just as soon as I possibly can . . .

Ron is less than honest here about the reason for his rare night out. Having learned that he was shortly to be commissioned, his NCO colleagues demanded an immediate celebration and repaired with him to a nearby pub, The Old Jail, behind one of the dispersals. The only way to get there was by bike. After a memorable celebratory session Ron managed the return journey only with difficulty. However, it proved too much for the 'old sweats' with whom he'd shared a room in 'Polperro'. Messrs Hilton and Norton eventually abandoned their cycles in a ditch and walked back. Unable to manage the final leg of the journey to their room, they passed out on the lawn in front of their billet; they were found there next morning, still dead to the world. It was by all accounts 'quite a splendid evening'.

22 April 1942:

There's no news to tell you as I only left you last night so I can just talk to you about nothing in particular.

I'm so terribly sorry about last night, dear – the only thing I can think of is that not seeing you for ages I've got sort of nervy & said things unthinkingly which hurt you. You know I'd never do or say anything willingly to hurt you – I'm so in love with you, dearest – please forget all about it.

I felt much better after I'd phoned you last night – you know it's not at all like us to have such upsets & I'd have given anything for it not to have happened – never mind darling – wait until my next day off and we'll mend everything. 'Mend' isn't the word I want but you know what I mean don't you? . . .

It's impossible to know exactly what caused the upset Ron refers to here. As he suggests, periods of separation may well be taking their toll. Connie's diary entry on 21 April appears to confirm this: 'Ron released & came up to the office about 3. It was so marvellous seeing my darling again. The trouble was we didn't see enough of each other. He left at 9.30 and phoned from Bow Rd [station].' Whatever the cause, such contretemps are a rare occurrence and, in the circumstances, hardly surprising. There's strain on both parties in this romance.

Three days later, on 24 April, Connie's diary entry reveals both good and bad news: 'Ron phoned & said he had shot down a F.W. 190, but the squadron caught a packet.' The story subsequently gets worse, as his amended log book entry for that same day reveals: 'Sweep . . . St. Omer – Dunkirk. Got an F.W. 190', followed by a heavily inked swastika and 'CONFIRMED PROBABLE!!' Some days after Ron's first 'kill' was confirmed by camera-gun film, higher authority determined that because he hadn't seen flames coming out of the aircraft, or seen it crash, it could be counted only as a 'probable'. He was more than a little annoyed at being deprived by officialdom of credit for an enemy aircraft he knew beyond doubt that he'd destroyed. The story of his first airborne success is worth recounting in full.

By this stage of his operational career Ron was well aware of the twin dangers inherent in sweeps over enemy territory: flak and enemy fighters. In some parts of France (Calais, Abbeville and Gravelines in particular) ground fire had become notably more accurate than elsewhere. Enemy fighters were almost equally unpredictable. Sometimes they'd remain at a distance, apparently reluctant to engage; on other occasions they'd arrive in force, as was the case this particular day when the squadron was bounced by more than thirty Fw 190s.

As so often happened in combat, one moment there were aircraft everywhere, the next Ron and his number two found themselves on their own – alone but in company with a pair of Luftwaffe fighters. Faster than the Spitfire and with more firepower than the Me 109, the 190 also seemed to have an almost inexhaustible supply of ammunition. Ron could clearly see flashes from the guns of the lead enemy aircraft as it swept past his number two, an inexperienced American, Pilot Officer R.P. Frahm, who immediately broke formation and set off after his would-be attacker. But it was a trap. The second 190 immediately latched onto the American and quickly closed on him. Alert to the danger, Ron called for him to break off his attack, but to no avail. His increasingly urgent radio transmissions were ignored. All he could do was give chase. It was too late, though. He could only sit and watch as his colleague was shot down.

Fully expecting the second German fighter to follow his leader and head deeper into France, he was surprised to see it turn back. What followed was a lengthy merry-go-round, a turning fight in which the Spitfire's superior rate of turn eventually saw a few of Ron's cannon shells strike home. He'd learned from previous experience and this time allowed plenty of deflection. At this the German decided to call it a day; he broke away and headed for home. Close enough to continue his pursuit, Ron was still firing the occasional burst when smoke suddenly emerged from the Fw 190. It went into a steep, high speed dive, entering cloud at about 2,000 feet. He felt sure the German was doomed. Since there was no future in following him down through the cloud, Ron turned back and headed for Biggin Hill. In the circumstances, the 'probable' with which he was finally credited represented scant reward for his efforts, and no compensation whatsoever for the loss of a colleague – the first and only time he would lose a number two.

By way of a footnote, records indicate that the Luftwaffe claimed ten Spitfires that day. Two of them were 72 Squadron aircraft: those of the American, Frahm, and Sergeant R.P.G. Reilly, a South African. They also show that in the same engagement Fw 190 pilot Leutnant Ortwin Petersen was 'kia' (killed in action), which tends to suggest Ron's original claim was justified. As an aside, in the same engagement a colleague, Pilot Officer de Naeyer, claimed a 'damaged'; it could possibly be the 190 that, according to the same records, eventually carried out a forced landing near Abbeville.

26 April 1942:

It's now 6.10 pm & I think I'm due for a little aviating shortly – I doubt very much whether I'll be able to phone you or Mum tonight but I'll do my best. I'm at readiness now until 9.45 but with luck I'll get some transport to the mess afterwards & phone from there. We flew this morning but it was fairly quiet & all went well. This afternoon I had my preliminary medical for my commission – it won't be long now!

I've just taxied the new 'Connie' up here – it will have to be checked all over and then have 'Connie' painted on it – then be flown & have the guns checked – THEN I can take it on sweeps . . .

Don't think I'm getting used to not seeing you – the only reason I'm not too down in the dumps is that I know I'll see you sooner or later & that makes up for everything . . .

29 April 1942:

Everything's going rather well here at the moment – I think it's because we nearly all have a poop at the Jerries these days & that tends to lift the morale of the pilots & ground crews no end. The only snag is that any prospect of a day off is very remote – I was asked whether I'd like 48 hrs next week but that would mean putting off my leave for at least another three weeks & so I refused it.

I don't know whether I'm glad or not that we're busy – I know you worry when I'm out & yet if my mind weren't occupied with all this I'd just sit around & mope the whole time. As soon as flying's finished for the day I realise how much I miss you – you're so much part of my life now that it doesn't seem logical that I can't see you every minute of the day . . .

The King came to visit us today & we all had to line up in front of our kites whilst he was introduced to us – it was very funny really – there were bags of bigwigs with him – Sholto Douglas[65] etc. etc. & there was also a hell of a wind, consequently the CO would come along – shout in the King's ear 'Sgt . . .' or 'P/O . . .' – the King would holler a question at the pilot (who was wearing his helmet & couldn't hear anyway) & the pilot would yell an answer back & so it went on – the CO was extremely hoarse after it all. I was asked (shouted at) how long I'd been with the sqdn & what I'd got in the way of Jerries – I told him & that was that. By the way – I've got one Jerry confirmed[66] & one damaged to my credit now – Group have just confirmed my claims. The camera film of the cert was awfully good – I know that's a 'line' but it is really.

There's much to add to this, another of Ron's upbeat letters and one that confirms the stimulating effect of operational flying; it's a fillip for the entire squadron. He's clearly relishing the opportunity to close with the enemy – something that brings both risk and reward. First, though, Connie's diary takes up the story of King George VI's visit to Biggin Hill. Her entry for 30 April reads,

> Ron's picture was in The Daily Telegraph shaking hands with the King.[67] I was so thrilled. He phoned me at 3.30 from Bromley and I met him & Geoff @ Victoria @ 5. We went back to 75 [Windsor Road] & then on to the Manor. It was so lovely seeing Ron again & I wasn't expecting it which makes it sweeter still.

---

65. Air Marshal Sir William Sholto Douglas KCB MC DFC, Commander-in-Chief Fighter Command, later Marshal of the Royal Air Force the Lord Douglas of Kirtleside GCB MC DFC.
66. See the notes after Ron's letter of 21 April 1942 above; this is the 'confirmed' later changed to a 'probable'.
67. The same picture appeared in *The Daily Mirror* that day, albeit with a suitably Delphic caption (the immediate identification of individuals was prohibited). It's also included in Brian Kingcome's book, *A Willingness to Die*, pp.126-7, albeit the 72 Squadron individuals concerned are incorrectly identified as '92 Squadron pilots'.

As to the risks Ron faces, nothing illustrates them better than his first sortie a couple of days earlier, on 27 April. His log book hardly does justice to a hair-raising experience: 'Sweep. Landed Detling . . . Escorted 12 Bostons to Lille. Got jumped & chased all the way home.' After flying through flak nearly all the way across France, numerous contrails above the combined formation heralded attacks by wave after wave of Fw 190s. Flying as number two to Jamie Rankin, Biggin Hill's new Wing Leader, as Ron later described it:

> My job was to see that he got home alright. We got jumped as we expected. There was nothing we could do about it and, I must admit, I sweated blood. The 190s would come down in batches of four. Two would make an attack and whilst we were trying to dodge those, the other two would come down whilst the first two climbed up and then came down again. Jamie would wait till the last second before calling out to break.

This nerve-racking routine continued as they were chased all the way from Lille, some sixty miles inland, almost to the English coast. Again he nearly ran out of fuel, hence his second diversion to Detling inside a fortnight. Satisfied in the end that he'd done his job, he was also frustrated; not once did he have an opportunity to fire his own guns.

Turning from risks to rewards, the 'damaged' enemy aircraft to which Ron refers in his letter came the following day. His log book entry for 28 April reads: 'Sweep . . . Gris Nez – Calais. Damaged FW 190', the customary swastika, then 'With "Timber" Woods'. The pair shared credit for damaging the German fighter. Flight Lieutenant E.N. 'Timber' Woods, 'a very experienced chap and a very good flight commander', was a tall, imposing individual who, at the time he was posted missing over Yugoslavia in December 1943, was credited with destroying more than ten enemy aircraft. Underneath his newspaper picture (as a Wing Commander) in Ron's scrapbook there's an enigmatic caption: 'Got DFC in June 42. Later made S/L & sent to Malta. Shot down over Albania. Heard later he was back in England.' Unfortunately, the rumour was unfounded.

This brings to an end the busiest month of Ron's war thus far. Despite an eight-day period at the start of April when he didn't fly at all, he amassed more than thirty-five hours, over thirty of which (twenty-five sorties in all) were on operations. But the increasing pace of events is beginning to take its toll.

Chapter 19

6 April 1943, Mount Vernon Hospital, Northwood

There was no immediate need for letters now that Ron was back on English soil. Communication with Connie was primarily by telephone as he continued what was to prove a lengthy period of recuperation. Much of the discussion was about their forthcoming marriage, arranged for Saturday 5 June 1943. The ceremony would take place at All Saints', Woodford Wells, a church with which Ron was more than familiar. On the edge of the village green, he'd strolled past it many a time on his way from Connie's home up to Woodford High Road as he set off back for North Weald.

The wedding itself, and the reception at nearby Barclay Hall, would be relatively quiet affairs. After all, these were austere times; there was a war on and the number of guests would inevitably be restricted. It would be difficult if not impossible to secure the attendance of those to whom Ron had been closest during his time in the RAF, in particular George Malan. (He wouldn't learn of George's untimely demise until early May.) In any event, 72 Squadron was destined to remain in North Africa for some time before moving on to support the Eighth Army as it campaigned northwards through Italy.

The main reason for those letters that Ron did write once back in England was to confirm contact details, as with this note from London's Mount Vernon Hospital, set up to care for war casualties in 1939:

6 April 1943:

Just a note to let you know I arrived OK – of course I had to do something spectacular getting off the train. I got out & immediately my little case opened & the whole issue fell out on the ground. There I was – probably <u>the</u> smartest Air Force officer grovelling on the ground after handkerchiefs and writing materials – anyway I reached here which is something.

6 APRIL 1943, MOUNT VERNON HOSPITAL, NORTHWOOD

The first impression isn't at all bad – visitors are allowed <u>every</u> afternoon 2-4. There's some talk of a public phone so I'll scout round. That's about all sweet . . .

Take care of yourself and don't worry . . .

During his convalescence Ron renewed a number of old acquaintances, amongst them Squadron Leader Ronald Clifford Brown. Another who earned his spurs during the Battle of Britain, as a flight lieutenant he'd been his first flight commander on 111 Squadron. As the pair reminisced Ron heard a story that was suppressed at the time, for reasons that will become obvious. It concerned a hugely experienced and much admired Czech pilot known as 'Hruby'. Ron could still picture the man who'd taught him to play cravatte: an expansive character, invariably holding a long cigarette holder elegantly in his right hand. He'd been on a rhubarb, a sortie where a pair of aircraft fly across to France at extreme low level in conditions unfit for normal operations, attack any targets that present themselves, then quickly scuttle back from whence they came.

Flying with The Honourable Wentworth Beaumont (later the third Viscount Allendale, known as 'Wenty' or, less respectfully, 'Wendy'), Hruby took off from Debden, flew out low over the sea, then up into cloud before coming down over the sea again. On reaching the coast the pair flew up over some cliffs and almost immediately found a train which they attacked with cannon fire before easing back up into cloud for the return home. On landing they were surprised to be called into the station commander's office. He wanted to know the details of their sortie. What exactly had they done? Nothing out of the ordinary, they explained. All they'd found was a train, which they'd shot up before escaping unscathed. Asked about the outcome, they opined they'd done 'quite a bit' of damage. It then emerged that the train they'd attacked had been just outside Margate!

The upshot of this potential human and PR disaster was that Hruby received an enormous rocket from the station commander – one he pretended to have a great deal of trouble in understanding. Despite the presence of another Czech pilot to translate for him, he appeared blithely indifferent, unmoved by the trouble he was in. As for the future Viscount Allendale, not long afterwards, in May 1942, he was shot down by enemy flak near the Netherlands coast and damaged his leg in the subsequent crash-landing. It proved a blessing in disguise. Captured and imprisoned in Stalag Luft III, he became part of the map-making team for the mass breakout. Along with the forgers of identity papers his team were known as 'Dean & Dawson', after a well-known firm of travel agents. His injury prevented him from taking a more active role in the escape – and almost certainly saved his life.

133

Chapter 20

3 May 1942, RAF Biggin Hill

After a busy end to the previous month, and with tiredness now his constant companion, Ron begins May at an even faster pace: eighteen sorties in ten days, more than half of them in the first five. There's only one day during this period when he doesn't fly, Friday 8 May, but he makes up for it with four sorties the next. It's no surprise, therefore, that his letters become relatively sporadic. He compensates with regular telephone calls to both Connie and his mother, simply to put their minds at rest.

3 May 1942:

It's now 9.30 – I would have started writing before but we've got two Norwegians here & I'm kept busy answering tons of questions about this and that. One chap is very nice but the other isn't so hot. Anyway – why talk about them when I can just keep on writing 'I love you' – it was just marvellous talking to you tonight – I always enjoy talking to you, but I enjoy it much more when I'm finished for the day . . . The N – s are still asking questions!!

I keep thinking of last Thursday[68] – I enjoyed it so much – you make everything so worthwhile – I keep on telling you that – maybe you'll believe it one day.

Tubby sweet – it's nearly impossible to write to you – every minute I have to answer some question that involves going into great detail about sweeps & sqdn formations & try as I may as fast as I answer one question I get another two – still – that's the penalty of being such an experienced type! (dirty great line!)

---

68. See Chapter 18, the notes following Ron's letter of 29 April 1942 and events of the following day when he was released and met Connie at Victoria after his picture appeared in the newspapers.

I'll just drop Dicky a short note to see how & where he is & then I'll crawl off to bed – I've been up since 5 this morning.

Three days later Ron claimed another German scalp but he barely mentions it in his next letter. Connie already knew. Her diary entry for 6 May reads, 'Mrs Robertson phoned. Mum answered. He got another Jerry confirmed. I rang Mrs Robertson later & she told me all she knew.' Ron's log book entry for that day is hardly more expansive: 'Sweep. Landed Tangmere . . . Top cover to Caen – got bounced by 4 190s – got ME 109F [swastika] confirmed.' (Ron has now taken to underlining his confirmed successes in red.) Below this entry are remarks that require further explanation: 'Flying with 'B' Flight – F/Lt [Flight Lieutenant] Hugo Armstrong. "Keep turning, 'B' Flight."'

As a rule Ron flew with A Flight but on the Caen trip he was filling in for a missing B Flight pilot. He enjoyed the relative freedom top cover provided. The alternative, flying close escort uncomfortably close to relatively slow bombers, was much less fun; he always felt more vulnerable. On this occasion the combined formation was nearing Le Havre when four Fw 190s appeared. Ron was more than familiar by now with the Luftwaffe tactics: the first pair would initiate an attack while the second would follow reasonably close on their heels. This is exactly what happened to his two-man section that day. It resulted in the usual turning fight – hence Armstrong's exhortation – which gradually descended to sea level as the Spitfires tried to shake off their pursuers. They were successful in doing so but in the process Ron became separated from his B Flight companion. As for the bombers, they were long gone. Since pursuit would have been futile, he did the sensible thing and headed for home at high speed.

As he weaved from side to side to ensure he wasn't being followed, he suddenly found himself in company with two Me 109s. There was no option but to keep turning at wave-top height in order to survive. Eventually, however, the Spitfire's ability to outturn the 109 led to the pursuers becoming the pursued and Ron worked his way into a firing position. This was too much for one enemy aircraft which broke off and made for the safe haven of France. Left with just a single adversary to deal with, it wasn't long before Ron saw his first rounds strike home, sending the Me 109 crashing into the sea in a mass of seething white foam.

His troubles, however, were by no means over. Once again he was dangerously short of fuel; but he reckoned he could just make Tangmere. As luck would have it, he arrived with the Wing readying for take-off. *That's all I need!* Fortunately, they were held in place while he landed – absolutely drenched in sweat.

There are a couple of sad footnotes to this story. First, a chance encounter while waiting to be refuelled at Tangmere brought Ron news he could do without: further details of the loss, months earlier, of another close Kidlington friend, Beaufighter pilot Jack Ranger.[69] And second, his leader that day, the Australian ace Hugo Throssell Armstrong, was shot down and killed over the Channel only nine months later. Highly respected, particularly as a leader, he was by then a squadron leader with DFC and Bar. Courage, it seems, ran in the family. His uncle, Captain Hugo Throssell, was a Gallipoli VC.

8 May 1942:

There's not much in the way of news – it's the same job every day – sometimes sticky, sometimes not. I could shoot you a 'dirty great line' about my hun[70] but that would take up an awful lot of space & I'd rather tell you when I see you. Actually we (the four who got chased) got complimented by the Wing/Co today – he said it was a good show getting back etc. etc.

You know the Daily Express shot quite a line about our 100th Hun the other day – well – we've had newspaper types here ever since – we also had telegrams from Sir A[rchibald], Sinclair, the Air Minister, & also the AOC our group.[71]

Just look at all this tripe, Tubby – I've written two pages about the sqdn & never mentioned that I love you. I'd swop all the Huns, telegrams from Air Ministers & the rest for one short note from you. There's no comparison.

It's now 2.30 pm – I suppose you're at your desk fiddling with figures whilst I've got to sit here writing letters – wouldn't it be marvellous if we could only chuck our jobs & go for a walk in the country or down to the sea – I get quite morbid thinking about it – never mind, dear – I may get some leave soon & we can do all the things we've been wanting to do for weeks – Do you think we can go down to Westcliff for a day – maybe we can get a swim in the Baths!

The delay before Ron's next letter is easily explained: he was given a week's leave. He'd earned it. Although Connie had to work for much of the time, the couple managed to see a good deal of each other. There were lunches in

---

69. See also Chapter 16 above and Ron's letter of 30 January 1942.
70. The confirmed Me 109 of 6 May.
71. AOC (Air Officer Commanding) No. 11 Group, Air-Vice Marshal T. Leigh-Mallory, later Air Chief Marshal Sir Trafford Leigh-Mallory KCB DSO*.

town, the cinema, a show, and those dinners at the Queen's Brasserie they'd come to enjoy so much. Further variety came on a rare day off for Connie: a meeting in London with Kay Olver, who 'looked very well'. After lunch at the Queen's (where else?), Ron was heartened to see the two girls wander arm in arm along Oxford Street and Piccadilly.

The following evening the couple returned to Plaistow for their first swim together for months, made all the more enjoyable by the chance to see old friends again. On Ron's last full day at home, the Saturday, they finally caught up with Dolly at the Lunns' new home; 'it's a lovely house' wrote Connie. Indeed her diary for the week is full of superlatives describing their various activities: 'marvellous evening', 'marvellous time', 'wonderful time', 'really lovely time', 'very enjoyable' and, finally, a less effusive 'very nice'. There's a touching summary of a week to be remembered in her entry on Sunday 17 May: 'My darling has to go back. I shall feel absolutely lost without him. It's so marvellous just going everywhere & doing very ordinary things – it's so different with him. I went up to Victoria and he caught the 11.18 am. I went back to Woodford. I must just trust that Ron comes back safely again soon.'

17 May 1942:

It's not half as nice writing to you tonight as it was seeing you this time last week . . . Tubby, sweet – you <u>do</u> make me happy you know – I've never been so ideally happy in all my life as I have in these last eight or nine months.

Well dear – to return to the 'line' I'm supposed to give Mrs Sutton[72] – I can't tell her which sqdns I've been with or where I've been stationed but I'll give you some idea of what she ought to be allowed to put in & then if she wants any further details you can let her know. After all – you know just as much as I do of what's been going on these last few months, & it'll also let her & any other club types know that <u>we're</u> more or less <u>one</u> if you can tell her all she wants to know. Anyway – rough precis herewith:

ITW	Aug 40-Feb 41	
EFTS	Feb-May 41	'Moths'
SFTS	May-July	'Oxfords'

---

72. Compiler of the Plaistow United Swimming Club News Sheet and contributor to *The Swimming Times*. The final issue of this print magazine was published in January 2019, ending a 95-year association with the sport.

> *Wings & stripes*   *11.7.41*
> *OTU*   *July-Sept.*   *'Spits'*
> *Started ops*   *1.10.41*
> *Done 45 sweeps to 10.5.42*   *Baled out 14/3/42*
> *Destroyed 2 A/C – Damaged one*

Don't put anything about my commission. By the way, I'm having my second medical on Monday – I'll tell you when I phone you how I got on.

I'm rather at a loss to know exactly what Mrs S. wants – I've given you as much as I can without giving away anything. You know how I shot down the E/A don't you – the first shot down a Spit then turned & I got behind him – the second was when I was jumped by two 109s in the Channel. One finished up in the drink & the other pushed off home.

Actually dear, would you send me the 'line' that's going in the Swimming Times so that I can sort of censor it before it goes to print. If anything happened I'd get in a hell of a row & lose my commission.

Well, darling, – it's 9 pm – I'll go & post this & then crawl off into bed – I'm on at dawn tomorrow – 4.40 am!

20 May 1942:

We had our pals the BBC down this afternoon & one or two of the chaps said an odd word or two for the European Broadcasting Service . . . They asked George Malan to say a few words – he did – but not for broadcasting. I'm afraid George is a dead loss to anyone who wants him to shoot a line – he's an awfully self-effacing type.

Re my commission – it's coming along gradually – the CO wrote a 'line' about me to be put on my personal file & now I'm waiting to see the Groupie.

What Ron fails to mention here is that the radio teams latched onto George Malan as soon as they discovered he was Sailor's brother. Keen to hear anything he was prepared to say, they were destined for disappointment. His reaction was just one of the reasons why Ron thought so much of him. At a time when the odd character developed an outsize ego, George's demeanour provided the perfect antidote: 'he wasn't having any; he just disappeared. He couldn't stand anything like that.'

Neither is there any reference, either here or in his letters, to a concern Ron harboured about his forthcoming commission, unease that finally prompted him to request a quiet word with his CO. It harked back to his premature departure from 111 Squadron in December. All too aware of the way that younger, inexperienced crews were offered up when units had to identify pilots for inter-squadron transfers, he'd heard that newly-commissioned pilot officers were sometimes treated in similar fashion: squadrons wishing to rid themselves of unwanted sergeant pilots occasionally recommended them for commissions. He was much relieved when Brian Kingcome put his mind at rest, adding that he considered Ron 'a valued member of the squadron' – a comment that left him feeling more than a little pleased, given the extraordinarily high regard in which he held his boss.

27 May 1942:

I had a new airscrew (propeller) put on 'H' & went on a sweep this morning. Unfortunately something went astray & oil started coming out all over the place. The snag was that we saw some Huns below but I was unable to go down on them as by this time the whole of my windscreen was covered in oil & I couldn't see a thing. I got back OK but I'm afraid 'Connie' is u/s for a couple of days. You should have seen old Dunc's face when I came back – his beloved aircraft smothered in oil. That's about all the news from here. I'll probably tell you all this on the phone but I feel I must tell you the ghastly news – we've all been given cycles & have to pedal to & fro instead of using the transport. If there's one thing I dislike it's cycling & now I have to cycle everywhere . . . I'm afraid I'm going to suffer no end . . .

Once again Ron tells Connie only part of a story summed up in his log book entry for a sweep to Dieppe and Fécamp: 'Missed beautiful chance to bounce. Windscreen oiled up!! Tommy Wright – my no. 2 – very annoyed – had to escort me home – no chance to play!'

One of two Rhodesians who joined the squadron in February, Ron took to Sergeant Tommy Wright immediately; he was 'a great lad, a very cheerful soul'. But there was nothing cheerful about his reaction when Ron was forced to turn down a golden opportunity to attack a pair of Fw 190s that suddenly appeared some 1,000 feet below them. Given the state of his windscreen he had no option but to set course for home, hoping and praying that his engine would keep going – and that his number two, weaving behind, would protect him from any German attack.

Having reached Biggin Hill safely, landing posed a further problem. Ron had to rely on what little he could see of his companion as he led him in formation to the runway threshold. It wasn't the best landing he'd ever made, but at least he was back safely on the ground; importantly, so too was 'Connie'.

A post-script to this latest letter ties together Tommy Wright and the cycles they'd been issued – because 'the powers that be decided that it was no good pilots living in the lap of luxury'. Ron would later concede that 'one good thing about them was that in the summer we used to take 12-bore single-barrelled shotguns, get on our bikes and ride all round the aerodrome chasing rabbits. George and Tommy Wright were pie-hot with a shotgun, they used to pot things left, right and centre.' Owen Hardy, similarly, was 'an outstanding shot' – unlike Ron, who 'never hit a thing'.

2 June 1942:

As Mum probably told you last night I didn't get home to roost until 8.30 & by the time we got settled it was just about bed time . . .

I'll have bags to tell you when we meet again – it's rather difficult writing but as I told you on the phone we had tons of fun the other night – much better than the Ensa[73] show.

We did bags of flying yesterday – 2 sweeps and a bit of stooging afterwards – there was nothing doing but it was nice flying – it was a glorious day wasn't it? . . .

I got dragged up at 5 am this morning to do a sweep so we look like being fairly busy if the weather's good.

That's about all my news – it seems the more we do the less I get to tell you. It's the same thing over & over again – I'm getting a bit tired actually – I keep thinking of getting back to see you & just doing all sorts of odd things.

I haven't heard any more about my commission, but I do hope it comes in time for that gala – I'm looking forward to going there with you – either to cheer you on or just to sit with you (personally I'm all for just sitting with you – gala or no gala) . . .

Echoing a comment in his letter of 8 March, this is the second time that Ron admits to feeling the effects of all the flying he's doing – and little wonder.

---

73. ENSA, the Entertainments National Service Association, was set up in 1939 to provide entertainment for British armed forces personnel during the Second World War.

Since his previous letter he's flown ten sorties in three days, and three more the day he pens this latest note. But he's clearly enjoying the challenge. This much is evident in his log book entry for May 31, a sweep to Dieppe: 'Bags of fun. [swastika] 1 FW 190 destroyed. 1 FW 190 damaged [swastika]. Lovely dogfight – Sqdn. did very well.' Ron and his colleagues were surprised to find an unusually large number of Luftwaffe fighters patrolling the French coast that day – a response they later attributed to events of the previous night: the RAF's first thousand bomber raid, Operation MILLENNIUM, targeted mainly on Cologne.

There's an interesting medical footnote to Ron's letter. Earlier in the month he'd landed from a sweep 'feeling a bit shaky' – in no shape for the pre-commissioning medical he was promptly despatched to undergo. Hardly in the best of moods either, pedalling across to the nearby hospital the logic of this requirement entirely escaped him. *After all, I've been flying happily and coping as a sergeant pilot. Why should anything change when I'm a pilot officer?* But he was in for a shock when it came to the lungs test. It involved blowing into a tube and holding the resultant pressure, measured on a manometer. Try as he might he simply couldn't manage a task that should have been well within his compass; his every effort ended in abject failure. However, the good Doctor White, 'an awfully nice chap', was unconcerned and proceeded to demonstrate a trick that enabled him to clear what he still saw as an entirely unnecessary hurdle.

The examination itself was a precursor to Ron's commissioning interview with Air Vice-Marshal Trafford Leigh-Mallory at Bentley Priory. On the morning of 21 May, together with other would-be officers, he found himself waiting, slightly nervous, in a small ante-room outside AOC 11 Group's office. When the conversation turned to people and places, as it so often did, he was surprised to learn that the most accomplished pilot on his Hawarden course, Irishman Pat Rusk, serving with 222 (Natal) Squadron at North Weald, had been killed. Apparently the wing came off his Spitfire in a steep dive during an air test and it ploughed straight into the ground, giving him no chance to escape. Sad though he was at this news, after losing two of his closest friends in Derek Olver and Jack Ranger, not to mention members of his own squadron, he was becoming inured to such tragedies. While it was impossible not to ponder his own future lot, Ron repeated to himself a familiar mantra . . . *these sort of accidents happen to other people, not to me.* Little did he realise what fate had in store.

6 June 1942:

It's only two days since I saw you so there's almost no news to tell you.

I thought I'd be able to see you today but instead of getting a release we got sent to look for a bomber crew in the drink. Hugo's flight found them & they were picked up by a launch so our afternoon wasn't wasted.

It was so marvellous being able to see you on Thursday – it made a wonderful break for me & you really were a great hit with all the boys here . . .

I'm writing to you dressed in my pyjamas. In due course I'm going to the local to have a few shandies after I've phoned you – then bed. We're released until 9 am tomorrow morning so I'll be able to lay in bed tomorrow.

There's more to be said about the search for the bomber crew Ron mentions here, a lesser known aspect of operations logged as a 1 hour 40 minute 'air sea rescue' sortie. Once the five crew members were located in a dinghy near Ostend, a section of Spitfires provided overhead cover whilst another protected the rescue launch as it set off from Dover. Ron was impressed. 'It left a wash about half a mile long, it was really moving.' What followed 'was exciting to watch':

> Once it got out to the dinghy, it swung around, hooked up . . . grabbed the chaps aboard, all without stopping and belted for home. Now by this time as we thought we were obviously visible from Ostend we'd be surrounded by 190s and we'd probably have a decent little fight. In actual fact nothing came over to have a bang at us, so we escorted the launch back, landed at Manston, refuelled and went back to Biggin. Sometime later we received a letter from the bomber boys, enclosing £1, and saying please have a drink on us. They were more than pleased at being picked up.

Connie's diary also reveals more about the events of two days earlier, Thursday 4 June, when her introduction to the squadron proved such a success.

> Ron phoned and I went down to Bromley to meet him. Tea at the Gaumont, & then we sat in the park. We went to [the] White Hart and met half of 72 Squadron, George M, Bruce, Tommy etc. It was marvellous & I did have a lovely time.

The White Hart at Brasted, 'as congenial a place as any',[74] which Connie visited for the first time that evening had become a second home to the Biggin Hill squadrons. It was a connection evidenced in a blackboard bearing the signatures of several celebrated Battle of Britain pilots. Originally a blackout precaution, it was later preserved in a glass frame and retired to a museum, to be replaced by a replica that remains there to this day. Amongst the easily recognisable names are those of Neville Duke, J.E. (sic) Johnson, Brian Kingcome, Sailor Malan, Bobbie (sic) Oxspring and Jamie Rankin. For one not given to self-promotion, Kingcome's bold moniker comes as a surprise; it stands out prominently, central amongst so many illustrious paladins.

9 June 1942:

I haven't flown today, but I had a game of cricket with the ground crews. I was never any good . . . it served to pass the time until we went to tea, anyway . . .

By the way dear, we've had orders to delete '72 Sqdn' from the address on our envelopes, so will you try & remember that . . .

Well, darling girl, there's not much else for me to say – I'll try & see you again as soon as I can although as I told you there's not much chance for a week or so – never mind, dear – I love you always – you know that don't you.

Connie's diary now takes up the story. On Wednesday 10 June she arranged to see Kay Olver again. They 'Met at Piccadilly. Went to Plaza [and] to Universal Brasserie afterwards.' More pertinently, the pregnant 'Kay looked very well'. Two days later Connie records that,

> Ron phoned me at the office & he & George met me at Bromley stn in the car. Went to the Gaumont. Drove to Westerham through Biggin Hill . . . Came back to the White Hart. A really lovely evening & we were all so happy.

Such sentiments, evident too in the opening of Ron's next letter, reflect not just the camaraderie of life on a fighter squadron; they also recognise the singular contribution of the White Hart's 'matchless hostess', Kath Preston.

---

74. Kingcome, op. cit., p.183.

13 June 1942:

I had a wonderful time last night, darling – right from 5.15 pm onwards – George thoroughly enjoyed it too. For your information I drove the 'Meteor' from the Sgts' Mess to Madame's – we dropped into the mess to get a bite to eat – George was starving (so was I when I got there) so we ate a few cakes & <u>then</u> I drove. All went well – except that George had to start it three times as I had some small difficulty in getting it into 1st gear – I must practise . . .

Darling girl – you did look beautiful last night – I could hardly keep my eyes off you. As I've told you before, but not in this letter (yet) I'm terribly in love with you, dear. I can't think of anything that could be half as wonderful as being married to you – honestly sweet – that's all I think of these days . . .

The 'Meteor' Ron refers to here, the car mentioned in Connie's diary earlier, is George Malan's tiny two-door Austin 7. His ability to keep it running owed something to his pre-war job with Austin in Birmingham – experience he's soon to draw on in restoring the Freeman family car to roadworthy condition. It's a story for later. Meanwhile, Ron is about to receive some welcome news.

Chapter 21

5 June 1943, Woodford Wells

Once he returns to the UK, notes in Ron's pocket diary become few and far between. There's nothing whatsoever between the entry for 6 March, 'Met young Tubby at Forest Gate Stn.!!!!', and that on Saturday 5 June: 'Married young Tubby at 12.30 pm – Everything went according to plan.' Ron's only concern about the great day was how he would look with only one eye. It was something the medical profession had been working on for months; indeed, they would continue to do so. He needn't have worried. Pictures of the wedding party – both sets of parents plus bridesmaid, Violet Freshwater, and best man, Arthur Youd – show his face wreathed in smiles, damaged eye neatly hidden behind a knitted white eye-patch.

As was the fashion in those days, extensive details of the wedding (dresses, bouquets etc.) and the subsequent reception (location and speeches) were recorded in the local paper. The *Stratford Express* of 11 June reported the events under the heading, 'West Ham DFC Holder Weds.' The couple left afterwards to spend their wedding night at the Strand Palace Hotel in London. Next morning, after paying a bill for the princely sum of 18/3d (91p) they set off for Cornwall on honeymoon. There's a surprising footnote on their hotel bill: 'No tips – visitors are asked not to offer tips to the employees, who are adequately paid by the management.' Yet this was wartime, with rationing in force!

After a few days in Newquay, far enough from the focus of wartime activity for the happy couple to enjoy time on the beach, Ron begins a nomadic existence, shuttling between medical appointments while the RAF decide what to do with him. Connie, meanwhile, remains with her parents in Woodford. His initial two letters to Mrs C.R. Robertson come from the Officers' Mess, RAF Uxbridge. The first of these opens with the pious hope that letter writing will soon become a thing of the past. Far from it; hundreds more were to follow. Like the second, too, it highlights Ron's ambition to sever his links with the RAF just as soon as he can – an important revelation that colours almost everything he does in the next three years or so.

6 July 1943:

Here's my first, and I hope, one of the few letters I shall write to you now we're married. I love writing to you but being married to you I earnestly hope that I shall not long be in such a position that instead of telling you I love you I'm forced to write it. As soon as this war gets straightened out in Europe & I get my discharge I'll be back with you and never go anywhere without you again.

We were talking last night about where everyone's going to live after the war. I enjoyed it an awful lot because I thought how grand it will be when we two can get together and decide where to live – and what to do about the garden – where to put the wireless and all sorts of things. I imagined coming home to you at night and boring you with all the office gen – in fact – having you with me forever. Darling, you're such a lovely wife – I want everyone to meet you – I'm so proud of you.

I'll always love you and I promise I'll do all in my power to make you happy . . .

27 July 1943:

I feel I must write to you – even though there won't be any news. If I'd had a pad I should have written to you last night. I wasn't exactly miserable but very restless – I've been thinking of you more than usual – I wanted to be with you – I feel tired of being in uniform away from you so often. I wanted the war to be over & myself back with you forever. It was such a grand weekend – everything went off well – not even a little squabble over anything. Won't it be grand when we can make plans for a fortnight or a month ahead & know that nothing is likely to come in between and spoil everything? As it is we're not sure from day to day what's going to happen to me and how often I'll be able to see you. Still – it shouldn't be too long before best part of the war is over & maybe I can get out and lead a normal life again . . .

Shortly after this letter the Service finally comes up with a posting for the ex-Spitfire pilot: to the ATC staff in South Wales.

Chapter 22

16 June 1942, RAF Biggin Hill

On 16 June Ron's log book contains a unique entry. Against his second sortie that day, a short return flight from Lympne, he writes, 'Told my commission had come through.' The back of the envelope containing his next letter, number 124 in Connie's sequence, indicates that the sender is 'P/O Robertson'. It's no surprise, therefore, that his elevation to the officer corps is mentioned at the outset. What is a surprise is that it contains nothing about another unusual log book entry, on 19 June. That said, he'd already chatted to Connie on the phone about what she records as his 'poop at a ship'.

That particular day Ron and George Malan comprised the second element of a four-aircraft sweep to Dieppe and Le Tréport, Normandy, led by Timber Woods. It offered little by way of potential targets until they passed a couple of smallish vessels that Ron thought unworthy of their attention. His leader, however, thought differently and ordered an attack. Ron began his strafe run in somewhat half-hearted fashion, followed by the remainder of the formation, who riddled the boats with cannon and machine-gun fire. On landing back at Biggin Hill they were surprised to be met by the Station Commander, Group Captain Barwell, and the Intelligence Officer, Squadron Leader de la Tour, and invited to debrief the sortie.

Apparently their radio transmissions had been heard back at base, leading to concerns that they might have attacked two small French vessels. Ron later recalled that Woods was 'most upset about this and by the time he'd finished explaining to the two senior characters what we'd been doing you would have thought we'd shot up a destroyer. But they seemed fairly happy about it – so long as we hadn't upset the French.' As Barwell and de la Tour left the dispersal, Woods turned to his colleague with a stage whisper: 'Robbie, next time we'll break both their bloody oars!' Nothing more was ever said. The 'Channel recco' sortie entry in Ron's log book reads, 'Damaged two small boats'; it's followed by a couple of tiny yachts in full sail, inked in, as with the swastikas that accompanied each successful enemy engagement. (He added the same symbol after attacks on coasters, for example, but on this occasion the symbol is noticeable only by its absence.) Above this entry is another comment: 'With "Timber" – "break both their oars!"'

No doubt there were wry smiles when his flight commander and boss, Messrs Woods and Kingcome respectively, noted this entry and its accompanying artwork when signing off Ron's log book summary at the end of June. It was his busiest month yet: forty-six sorties and more than forty hours' flying. Add to this his regular fleeting meetings with an increasingly concerned Connie – he'd just warned her that a squadron move was in the offing – and it's no wonder he was becoming exhausted.

There's more to be said about the station commander mentioned here, the 'much revered' Group Captain Philip 'Dickie' Barwell. The previous August his engine had cut out shortly after take-off and he was forced to crash-land his Spitfire in a valley just beyond the runway, severely injuring himself. But 'nothing so trivial as a broken back inhibited his zest for partaking in operations and for several months he flew sorties with his body encased in plaster.'[75] Then, on 1 July 1942, in a 72 Squadron aircraft,[76] he became the victim of a tragic accident. Flying with Squadron Leader Bobby Oxspring, he was misidentified by an inexperienced 129 Squadron Spitfire pilot and shot down. With flames pouring from Barwell's aircraft, Oxspring 'could see him desperately trying to open the canopy to bale out'. But 'with his body still strapped in plaster to protect his cracked vertebrae, Dicky probably found it too severe a handicap either to abandon his aircraft or even to jettison the canopy.'[77] His aircraft crashed into the sea fifteen miles south-west of Beachy Head; his body was later washed up on the French coast and eventually interred in the Calais Canadian War Cemetery. The inscription on his headstone reads, 'An honourable and beloved man who gave his life that others might be free.'

A subsequent inquiry revealed that the two Spitfires responsible for this tragedy 'came from an Allied squadron in the Tangmere sector and that, incredibly, one pilot [the perpetrator] was on his first operational sortie and the leader on his second.'[78] That said, 129 Squadron records absolve the pilots concerned of any blame, rather attributing the dreadful error to confusion between neighbouring sector controllers – shades of the Battle of Barking Creek.

---

75. Oxspring, op. cit., p.97.
76. AB 806.
77. Ibid., pp.107-8.
78. Ibid., p.107.

20 June 1942:

It was lovely getting your last letter – my first as a P/O – from you! . . . I love you darling – so get all those odd little notions out of your head about my getting annoyed when you feel blue – surely we know each other better than that . . .

I'm enjoying it no end as a P/O – I told you that Jamie [Rankin] came up and congratulated me – he seemed to know I was 'Robbie' without any prompting – I felt as pleased as Punch – then Groupie [Barwell] stopped me outside & said he was pleased I'd got it at last . . .

The mess is lovely – the grub is really grand – the billet is also excellent – Timber, Ratten[79] & I have all got separate rooms – the rest are all doubles – the bed's miles better than I've had up to now – in fact – if I was given some money & leave I'd be on top of the world (definitely provided that you were with me).

There was a sgts dance last night & two of us were asked to go so I borrowed Jones' uniform (he's a new P/O) & went with him. Actually I only danced one dance & spent the rest of the time arguing with Jack [Hilton] & co. It was too late to go to the billet so Jones & I went straight up to dispersal & slept in the beds up there. When we arrived Timber & Hugo were already snoring like ten men. Unfortunately we were dragged up at 4.30 to go & fly. We got back at 6.30 & so went straight back to bed & didn't get up until 8.50. It was really lovely flying early – we would have enjoyed it no end but some aggressive types across the other side threw a lot of old iron at us so we left in rather a hurry.

We had some fun this afternoon – I got a 'damaged' – it hasn't been officially credited yet so I may or may not get it . . .

By the way, Jamie has been given a bar to his DSO [Distinguished Service Order] . . .

Ron's log book reveals more about these two sorties. On the first, a sweep to Calais and Ostend, he encountered 'Bags of very accurate flak. 0500 hrs!!' On the second, to Neufchâtel-Hardelot and St Omer, he writes: 'Damaged FW 190 [swastika]'.

In a manoeuvre that mirrored Ron's departure from 111 Squadron, the Pilot Officer N.G. Jones mentioned here was destined to spend only a short time on the squadron. His departure was the direct result of Ron receiving

---

79. A P/O at the time, Wing Commander J.R. Ratten DFC later became the first Australian to command a Spitfire wing.

an unexpected posting to the Spitfire OTU. He 'wasn't at all amused, as [he] was having a great time at Biggin and the whole thing suited [him] down to the ground.' The moment he heard the news he confronted his new boss, Bob Oxspring (Kingcome had just been posted), who was with the Squadron Adjutant, Flying Officer 'Tiny' Le Petit at the time. He needn't have worried. With a wink at the adjutant, Oxspring said, 'Don't worry Robbie, other arrangements have been made.' With that, Jones, who boasted just ten hours' operational flying, was despatched to Hawarden as 'a most experienced chap who would be a great help to the OTU.' The irony here is that had Ron accepted this Hawarden posting, notwithstanding the difficulties it would have entailed in terms of seeing Connie, in all likelihood he would have dodged the overseas deployment he later strove so hard to avoid.

Ron's entries for the next week or so begin with a squadron deployment to Martlesham Heath, near Ipswich, for gunnery practice. Given the amount of live firing he's been doing of late, this hardly seems necessary. However, such exercises served another useful purpose. They removed the pressures of operational flying briefly and allowed crews a few days of relative relaxation – opportunities that Ron was determined to exploit to the full. He aimed to escape to London whenever he could.

His plan was based on securing a slot on the early morning wave. He first managed this on Tuesday 23 June and immediately took off on a second sortie, landing at Biggin Hill. Well-practised in the commute from there, he arrived in London in time for a brief visit to his erstwhile employers at the Ocean before picking up Connie and making for Burberry's, where he had a fitting. Her diary notes that, 'He does look marvellous in his uniform.' Not needed until late the following afternoon, Ron was able to spend the night at home and then travel in to work next morning with Connie. After another couple of hours or so at the Ocean, he rejoined his fiancée for lunch. She 'Had a marvellous time. Ron came back to the office with me & left about 2 o'clock for Bromley.' That evening he flew back to Martlesham and immediately put pen to paper. Unusually, it's his last letter for over a week. For the next few days the pair are barely apart.

24 June 1942:

I got back here at 4.30 – just in time to catch the transport for tea . . .
That was quite a nice finish to our day off wasn't it? I love taking you out, dear – it's only natural, being engaged to you – but I still say I like taking you out – the novelty never wears off . . .

I do hope I get some leave shortly – then we can do all sorts of odd things to cheer each other up – especially if we can get the car going. I'll find out (or try to) just how much petrol I can get for 7 days' leave – the only snag is that the Adj, who does all that sort of thing, is at BH . . .

The car Ron refers to here is Ferdie's, on which he has designs – more of which later. The next day he again flew twice. On the second occasion he landed at North Weald and immediately hotfooted it back to London. 'It was such a lovely surprise' for Connie. The couple travelled home and spent the rest of the evening together. Next morning Ron accompanied her only part-way into London, leaving the tube at Stratford to make his way back to North Weald and thence Martlesham. The following day, Friday 27 June, followed the now familiar two-sortie pattern: the first, air firing, and the second a transit to North Weald – this time in company with George Malan who was spending the weekend at Ron's home.

After lunch at Connie's on the Saturday, the three of them travelled up to Euston to meet George's fiancée, Vickie, who was staying with Connie for the weekend. According to her diary, they took a 'Taxi to Leicester Square & strolled around – Captains Cabin & then the Queens.' It was 'A really marvellous evening & we were all so happy.' Next morning, 'We all got up fairly early & went & had breakfast.' Connie and Vickie then 'went with Ron & George to North Weald. We saw them take up (sic) & fly about – we were both so proud.'

The girls would have been less impressed had they known the full story of what took place that morning. After bidding farewell to their menfolk, they waited at the station to see them take off. Keen to impress, Ron and George proceeded to beat up both the airfield and North Weald station. They were thoroughly enjoying themselves when Ron noticed his starboard outer gun-panel was missing; it should have been locked in place before take-off and must have blown off during their manoeuvring. By rights he should have landed immediately. However, since he'd spent ten minutes or so acting the hooligan, he felt he'd be less than popular back at North Weald; so he and George gently made their way back to Martlesham. It's little surprise that there's no mention of this in his next letter. It's from Lympne, near the Kent coast, where the squadron had deployed on 30 June.

For once he found himself accommodated in relative luxury: in Sir Philip Sassoon's palatial home, complete with swimming pool and extensive gardens. While the aircrew weren't about to complain, the reason behind their relocation remained something of a mystery. Ron would later attribute the move to an abortive attempt to launch Operation JUBILEE, the Dieppe raid.

He based this presumption on the fact that, shortly after arriving, he found his aircraft painted in broad white 'D-Day stripes'. His supposition proved correct. Originally scheduled for 4 July, three days later consistently bad weather caused the raid to be postponed, prompting the squadron's immediate return to base and removal of the aforementioned embellishments.

When the Dieppe raid was eventually launched, on 19 August 1942, only a relatively small contingent from the squadron was involved; it included *inter alios* the boss and Sergeants George Malan and Pete Fowler, an ex-Hurricane pilot who'd joined only recently. They were to supplement 222 Squadron as part of a much larger force tasked with covering an amphibious attack by Allied forces on the German-occupied port. Some 6,000 troops and a regiment of tanks were put ashore in northern France to test the feasibility of a landing and to gather intelligence; secondary aims were to boost morale and demonstrate UK commitment to re-opening the western front. However, after less than six hours, mounting casualties forced a retreat. The eventual loss of more than 3,600 men killed, wounded, or taken prisoner, together with 106 RAF aircraft and thirty-three landing craft, turned Operation JUBILEE into a fiasco. This is all the more reprehensible given that the first rehearsal was a disaster. While higher authorities would maintain that the Dieppe experience proved invaluable in the Normandy landings two years later, it was experience gained at a terrible price.

After this brief but necessary diversion, it's back now to Lympne, where the squadron immediately began flying convoy patrols, and to Ron's correspondence.

2 July 1942:

It <u>was</u> rather a good week wasn't it – I thoroughly enjoyed it. It was nice having a night at the 'Queens' again too – that's something we haven't done for ages.

I've just had a swim & am now in the lounge overlooking the sea thinking how marvellous it would be if only you were here . . .

Timber got his DFC last night (sorry – night before last) – he certainly deserves it – he's an excellent leader & very steady type altogether.

I took a new sgt around the sector this afternoon – it was quite nice flying again but he wasn't over-bright – I'm afraid he won't last awfully long . . .

I do wish they'd get this over with so that I could come back to Biggin & see you again. I do so want a week's leave so that I can just have you all to myself again. I asked the Adj. about that car tax business & he knows damn all about it – still – I'll write to the Ocean & see what they know about it . . .

When Ron telephoned Connie, the day prior to his next letter, it was impossible to hide his mood of disappointment. So much had changed in such a short time. He was frustrated by the mundane nature of what little flying he was doing and, inevitably, by their separation – a stark contrast in both cases with the recent past. He couldn't wait to get back to Biggin Hill. His fiancée records that he was 'rather fed up – I feel so sorry for him. I've a feeling something is going to happen . . . soon. Oh please God keep Ron safe & bring him back to me.' Other than their regular calls, the highlight of Connie's week came on 2 July: 'Got Bonus £13.' Given the parlous state of Ron's finances, revealed below, it was probably just as well.

6 July 1942:

I expect that Mum has told you already but anyway – I've had a letter from the bank telling me I've got £71. By the time I've paid Burberry's & refunded the money paid to me as a sergeant, I won't have much left – & I've got about 3 mess bills to pay & telephone calls. Still – I'll just have to start saving again.

Our Intelligence Officer is acting as Adj. here so I asked him to look into that car tax business for me.

I flew for the first time for ages this morning – I did a convoy at 6.30 am & it was such a lovely morning instead of landing straight away I shot the place up for about 15 minutes.

Unfortunately, the station CO took a very dim view of it, as did the 'brown job' [army officer] i/c gunposts & so I got a lecture when I arrived for breakfast – Still – it was a damn good shoot up – even old Timber thought so.

There was nothing else to do afterwards so I spent the rest of the morning lying in the sun & swimming . . .

I had a letter from Dicky today – his must have crossed mine – anyway – he's a Flight/Sgt now. He didn't have much news apart from the fact that he's nearly finished his ops. time and is about due for OTU . . .

This was the last letter for some time. Connie's diary and Ron's log book continue a story that begins with the news that Ron is about to acquire a car.

Before the war Ferdie ran a 1934 Hillman 10, registration BPB 189, but with the introduction of petrol rationing he was forced to lay it up in his garage. As a pilot on operations, entitled to purchase petrol coupons, Ron argued that potentially the entire Freeman family would benefit were his prospective father-in-law to sign the car over to him. To his delight, Ferdie accepted this argument, acknowledging too the benefits of keeping the car running rather than leaving it on blocks. So the necessary arrangements were made. The next step was to get the car roadworthy again.

On Thursday 9 July, at the start of three days' leave for the pair of them, George took Ron up to London in his Austin. They met Connie at Liverpool Street and drove back together to Woodford with the aim of putting the Hillman back on the road. Thanks to George's expertise, they succeeded in no time. There was more good news to come. Ron would soon learn that his groundcrew were more than happy to service his new acquisition; moreover, petrol would prove less of a problem than he anticipated. In a practice that went back to Sailor Malan's time at Biggin Hill, as OC 74 Squadron and subsequently Wing Commander Flying:

> Operational pilots were allowed to use private cars and were given a meagre petrol allowance which was regularly supplemented with the help of the ground crews. 87 octane (used for station transport as well as private vehicles) was regularly syphoned from the bowser and stored in drums in the outhouses behind the aircrew's billets.[80]

Ron wasted no time in taking advantage of his new toy. Next day he drove to London, picked up Connie from her office in Cannon Street, returned for a session at their swimming club and then took his parents to the Monkhams for the evening. The same hectic pace continued all weekend: meetings with Ron's numerous relations, lunches, the cinema, teas and dinners. Then, on the Monday morning, he drove his fiancée to her office before setting off for Biggin Hill. That same evening he phoned with disturbing news, duly recorded in her diary: '"Connie" has gone for a burton.' A partial but not entirely accurate explanation is contained in his log book entry for 13 July: 'Sweep. Dieppe . . . Chased 190 from 17000' - 5000' – pulled out too quickly. Buckled both wings. A/C U/S. Farnborough types very pleased.'

---

80. Bob Cossey, *Tigers: The Story of No. 74 Squadron RAF* (Arms & Armour Press, London, 1992), p.89.

He wasn't aware of the damage he'd incurred until his crew chief pointed it out. The wing-roots had come away, bolts were showing on the underside and the wings themselves were buckled from the cannon outwards, giving the aircraft a peculiar gull-winged appearance.

The damage occurred when he reacted to what he thought was a bounce. After chasing a Fw 190 downwards at high speed he'd eased out of his dive at 5,000 feet to position himself as it recovered from its own descent. Almost immediately there was a loud noise. Thinking it was cannon fire from behind, he yanked back hard on the controls, applied full right rudder 'and hoped for the best'. He must have blacked out because the next thing he knew he was at 12,000 feet, nothing else in sight, in an aircraft that 'felt a bit strange'. Looking around he saw slight bumps at the centre of both wings near the cannon. He wasn't sure he'd ever noticed them before but thought little more of it. Finding that his aircraft 'was a bit rough to fly [he] imagined that one of the trim-tabs had been torn off the wing or the aileron and that was the reason for it flying a bit left wing low.' It soon transpired that the noise he'd mistaken for hostile fire was in fact the loss of a 'knock-out' cockpit 'clear-vision' panel, held in place by split-pins; it had simply ripped off at high speed.

The boffins' delight is explained by the fact that Farnborough had rarely if ever been able to examine a Spitfire overstressed to such an extent; it had been flown – inadvertently tested – far beyond its design limits. By rights it probably shouldn't have survived the incident. Indeed, the same might be said for the pilot, especially bearing in mind the fate of Ron's Hawarden colleague, Sergeant Pat Rusk. His only injury was a strained back muscle, from which he quickly recovered – which is more than can be said for his aircraft, RN-H (serial BM 313). It remained out of service until January 1944 when it was finally restored to airworthy condition and transferred to the Portuguese Air Force.

It's evident from the opening paragraphs of Ron's next letter that he's been badly affected by the loss of his beloved 'Connie'. It wasn't the only thing on his mind either. Two days later his fiancée notes in her diary, 'My darling probably has to go north. He was very fed up about it, also about pranging "Connie".'

The circumstances of another narrow escape prompt a reflection on the way aircrew lived their lives in wartime – on the physical and emotional demands on them too. On the Monday morning in question, Ron rose early, drove from Forest Gate to Woodford to pick up Connie, took her into London and then returned to Biggin Hill. Shortly after parking the Hillman he climbed into his Spitfire to fly an operational sortie, a sweep to Dieppe. A contemporary RAF board of inquiry, let alone a behavioural psychologist, would have a field day examining the circumstances surrounding this potential fatality. The key question would be: where, in the chain of events leading up to the incident, could the sequence have been altered in a way that might have avoided the eventual outcome?

An incident that occurred that same evening involving Pete Fowler's wife, although outside the scope of any hypothetical inquiry, is a clear indicator of stress. Described in Ron's next letter, it suggests that an additional contributory factor would have to be taken into account in considering the aforementioned chain of events: the effect of cumulative tiredness. He's been serving on a front-line squadron for nine unbroken months; moreover, he's just turned down the rest that an OTU posting would effectively have provided.

14 July 1942:

I told you most of the news last night so there's not much new stuff. After we'd finished phoning I went back to the bar and had an odd beer or two but I don't think Pete's wife was very struck by me. She's quite pretty but we didn't get on at all well together. I wasn't in the least comfortable all night & was glad when we came back.

Actually I felt a bit browned off last night – what with just having left you after a wonderful weekend – then smashing up 'Connie' – maybe if we meet again (Sheila) I'll be in a better mood. Apparently I was quite rude to her.

Do you remember Pete Durnford at N. Weald? His squadron [124] came over to see a film with us this morning so we had quite a talk. He's just been given the DFM for shooting down 3 huns. He's got 1 prob. & 2 damaged. From what I hear of it our old squadron went to pieces – I'm just as glad I got out now . . .

By the way – we're supposed to be doing aerodrome defence on Thursday evening & as I've only just been on leave I expect I'll have to be one of those staying – so don't be surprised if I'm not able to see you on Thursday afternoon.

Darling – it was marvellous seeing you over the weekend – I'm never so happy as when I'm with you . . .

Ron trained with Pete Durnford at Hawarden and they'd flown together briefly on 111 Squadron as sergeant pilots. Commissioned in September 1942, two months later he was shot down by enemy flak and ditched off the Dutch coast near Flushing. After spending twelve hours in his dinghy he was eventually captured and imprisoned in Stalag Luft III, from where he was liberated by the Russians in May 1945.

In a letter of 24 November 1942 Connie wrote that she'd heard from a WAAF (Women's Auxiliary Air Force) friend 'that Pete Durnford was missing – ten days after his investiture'. Then, on 19 December, she forwarded a newspaper cutting headed 'In enemy hands'; among the list of six 'airmen prisoners according to German sources' was 'Pilot-Officer Peter Edward George Durnford, 128994, Adrian-avenue, Southall'. He was finally credited with five confirmed and one damaged enemy aircraft.

20 July 1942:

I felt so much better after I'd phoned you this morning – you see, last night I was almost surrounded by batmen & so forth and couldn't say half the things I wanted to – & then I had to shout like blazes to get you to hear anything at all – consequently it wasn't any too good.

Anyway – that's all over now – I'm just waiting for Wednesday so that we can be together again. I do hope it'll be alright – I've never been to one before but I expect there'll be the usual gang of drinking types. Anyway – we can dance & be together & I can show you round the Mess – at least it will make a change for you. I'm not sure what time I'll be able to get off, but I think the best plan would be for you to go to the hotel and wait for me there. It's the Royal Bell Hotel and it's just on the right of the market square as you come from Bromley North. I hope to be able to give you more definite news when I phone on Tuesday . . .

P.S. In case I forget – the room is booked in <u>my</u> name.

There's no mention here of the sortie Ron flew the day he wrote this latest letter, a rhubarb to the area around Le Tréport and Dieppe. It was notable for the amount of flak he saw, eliciting this log book comment: 'No fun! Every little thing had a bang at us.' In any event, he's hardly likely to mention this in a letter that concentrates on a much anticipated social occasion.

In the early evening of Wednesday 22 July Ron drove into Bromley to pick Connie up for their first major squadron event together. The 'do' in the Officers' Mess left an indelible impression on her, as did those individuals who beforehand were no more than just names, amongst them Brian

Kingcome, Hugo Armstrong and Jamie Rankin. Connie's diary entry says it all: 'They are such a marvellous crowd. It is an evening I'll never forget. I'm so proud of my darling, & he makes me so happy.'

What Connie understandably failed to mention was her first encounter with Timber Woods. Keen for her to meet his colleagues, Ron proudly introduced her, first, to his flight commander, 'who by this time was three parts under'. Looking down from his substantial height, he said, 'So it's your bloody name we've got on half the bloody aircraft in the squadron!' While Woods's jocular remark caused the young Connie a mild degree of embarrassment, he had a point. At the time there were two aircraft on the squadron bearing her name, both designated RN-H: Ron's overstressed near write-off together with its replacement.

Next day she commuted from Bromley to her office and returned again that same evening. Ron met her at the station and, after a drive around the local area, they went to an 'erks[81] do' at the Teapot in Biggin Hill village – the venue for many such parties. Although it was mainly for other ranks, a number of those Connie met for the first time the previous evening were there again. She had a 'really lovely' time at a dance that was notable for seventy-two gallons of free beer. Some party!

What state Ron and the erks were in next morning isn't revealed but there's a clue in his log book entry that day, 24 July. It's one of the few occasions he logs the scramble time: 0700. He and Pilot Officer Johnny Lowe 'Met 2 FW 190s. They wouldn't fight – we couldn't catch them.' Maybe it was just as well.

27 July 1942:

It seems ages since I last wrote to you – I only wish it were possible to carry on as we've been doing this last week or so & see you two or three times a week.

I'm so glad you were able to come on Wednesday – I've always wanted the crowd to meet you – I'm terribly proud of you, darling.

I don't think there will be a party here for our "900th"– as we had a sort of a 'do' last night. There was free beer – Brian & some other types came over from his station & we had quite a time. The sergeants were all invited but Tommy, Mac and Al were all in bed early, George was away – & so only

---

81. Airmen groundcrew below the rank of corporal were affectionately known as erks.

*Pete & one or two others were able to get to it. Actually we didn't drink a
great deal but sang many low songs – I'll tell you in greater detail when
I see you.*

George & Pete go to see the AOC tomorrow – I hope they get on OK [in
their commissioning interviews].

*There's an Ensa concert on tonight – so I think I'll phone Mum early &
then go to it. Sweetheart – there's not much else I can tell you, as I saw you
on Saturday – much to my delight . . .*

Despite the milestone of Biggin Hill's 900th confirmed aerial victory – an
Fw 190 despatched by Hugo Armstrong – in flying terms the end of the
month was something of an anti-climax. During a sweep to St Omer on
26 July Ron 'Squirted at Fw 190 – no result'; on the same sortie they 'Lost
S/Ldr Tidd (supernumerary)'. After returning to base to refuel he launched
again on an unavailing Channel search for this unfortunate individual, shot
down by Fw 190s near Calais. (It's a sad fact that only one in five aircrew
who baled out or ditched in the North Sea or English Channel lived to fight
another day – another possible reason for Ron's own reluctance to ditch
four months earlier?) On 28 July he flew his last two sorties for more than
a fortnight: a sweep that involved 'No fun & games' and a scramble via
Canterbury to mid-Channel, when again there was 'Nothing doing'. It was
time for some leave now, before the squadron's scheduled move north.
Fighter Command's practice was to take squadrons out of the front line for
a rest after a continuous period of operations, and 72 Squadron had been in
the thick of things for a year or so. Much the same applied during the Battle
of Britain, although squadrons then were often replaced after much shorter
periods, such was the strain on individuals flying anything up to five sorties
a day.

With the prospect not just of imminent relocation within the UK, but
also a subsequent overseas deployment, Ron devoted most of his leave to
seeing his fiancée. On Saturday 1 August, the day before the squadron was
due to begin its move from Biggin Hill, he rang to check when he was next
required for duty, only to be told there was no need for him to return for
another week. Hardly able to believe his luck, he was determined to make
the best of this heaven-sent opportunity. In addition to their usual jaunts to
the cinema, the Monkhams and the Queen's (including one where Connie
noted wistfully, 'could not get our usual seat'), Ron organised a couple
of day trips to the coast in the Hillman. On the second of these, Tuesday
4 August, he drove Connie and her parents to Southend, where they 'had

a really lovely time'. Having taken no cognisance of the requirement for anyone living or working near the coast to carry a special pass, as luck would have it he was apprehended approaching Southend's famous pier. A policeman strolled out into the middle of the road and signalled for the car to stop. Ron wound down the window. 'You have got a pass, Sir, haven't you?' said the officer with a knowing smile. Patting the empty breast pocket of his uniform, Ron assured him that he had. It was enough. 'Right ho, Sir, carry on.' And with that Ron simply drove away, albeit with a rather worried Ferdie beside him. As an example of the relatively relaxed approach taken by the police when dealing with men in uniform, it mirrored George Malan's experience a few weeks earlier.

With no tax or insurance for his tiny car, and hence no coupons, George relied almost entirely on the Biggin Hill syphoned petrol scheme. He was similarly cavalier about parking. On a visit to London, he and Ron had completed the business at hand and were returning to where they'd left the Austin, in Piccadilly, when they saw a policeman inspecting it closely. Asked about the absence of any tax, George said, 'Oh, I haven't got it. But I've applied for it.' A query about his insurance drew the same unabashed response: 'I haven't got it with me.' And with that the pair squeezed back into the Meteor, George started it up (no mean feat in itself), and left the policeman standing by the roadside. Whether he was satisfied or, more likely, turned a blind eye was of no consequence. The pair's RAF uniforms carried the day.

Towards the end of Ron's leave Connie accompanied him to Fairlop airfield for a lecture to an ATC unit. The evening provided an insight into her fiancé's public persona as it were – she was inordinately proud of him – but was marred by what in the years ahead was to prove an all too familiar hazard: a puncture. The Hillman was mercifully free of such problems a couple of days later when they drove to Biggin Hill. On the morning of Saturday 8 August they said their goodbyes at Bromley station before going their separate ways: Connie home by train and Ron to the mess to begin preparations for the journey north. He was not a happy man.

Chapter 23

24 August 1943, Newport, Monmouthshire

T he first entry in Ron's diary after his wedding appears on 24 August 1943: 'Posted to ATC HQ Wales. To be an inspector of ATC units. Sounds very nice.' Little did he realise then that he would gradually come to loathe South Wales. First and foremost, it meant lengthy separations from his new wife, a problem compounded by having to live in 'digs' and also by geography. Commuting to and from London was nowhere near as easy as travelling between Connie's home and many of the airfields from which he'd flown. And he no longer had Ferdie's car, of course. Then there was the weather. All too often it was dank and grey with rain an almost constant companion, especially in the winter months.

After the camaraderie of a squadron and the excitement of operations, there was little job satisfaction in his new role either. Hardly taxing, it involved dealing mainly with cadets, part-timers and a few older officers effectively put out to grass. If there was little to do at work, there was even less to occupy his leisure time. He was particularly irked by the way South Wales effectively died on Sundays; Newport, like all its neighbours, became a ghost town with nothing open and little if anything to do that day. Having said all this, the letter Ron sends on arriving shows no signs of the frustrations to come. It's the first of many. He writes almost every day, twice sometimes. In the interests of brevity, some correspondence has been omitted. It begins with a few scene-setting letters.

24 August 1943:

Here's just a short note to give you the latest gen. I arrived at 3 pm – the ATC place is only about 100 yds away from the station so that was OK. This is going to be fairly cushy, I imagine. To begin with – I found no reservation of 'digs' for me & so I'm at the Kings Head Hotel for the time being.

Apparently the set-up is this – I'm supposed to be a sort of inspector & tour Wales in a car (another Hillman for me!) seeing that all the ATC places are being run properly. So far as I can see it's money for jam . . .

As regards weekends – we knock off at 1 pm on Saturday till Monday – but I may have to work on occasional weekends. I've not asked about your [rail] warrant yet – I'll get to that tomorrow . . .

Don't worry about me, darl, I'll work like a good boy here & see if I can get back to London soon . . .

I think you may as well address your letters to ATC HQ's Cambrian Buildings, Cambrian Rd. Newport. Because if I start changing my digs I don't want your letters following me all over the place.

25 August 1943:

Little by little I'm getting the gen on this job – which seems rather a nice way of spending the war. It's more or less what I've already explained in my previous letter. There are loads of ATC places scattered all over the area & my job is to go round by car & report on each one. I can suit myself which one I see first but the F/Lt here suggests that whilst the weather's nice I might as well do the sea-side places first. I expect I shall start locally though & get the hang of it. I've got some very nice 'digs' – it's where my predecessor lived & apparently he did very well here so I may do the same. It'll cost me 30/- [£1.50] per wk for bed, breakfast & a spot of grub at night – I'm away all day so I get my meals out. I've joined an Officers Club – I think it used to be a Conservative Club before – however – I can get a very good meal for 2/- [10p] . . . So far as expenses go I think I'll be able to manage although it may be a trifle hard the first month. I'm going to my new digs tomorrow night & I'll give you the new address then. I can't remember it off hand. I asked about you & the old dear said it would be OK for a weekend. There's only one snag as far as I can see that is that the old dear talks like the clappers.

Well sweet – that's all the news for now – now – how about you? Isn't it funny sleeping on your own? – I'm not at all keen on it – still – with a bit of luck you may be down here soon. There's not a great deal to do – still – I may have some more gen by then . . .

Another thing about this job is that as the ATC classes are held at night I do my driving during the day – get to the place – laze about & then spend the evening with the ATC.

Actually I think this will suit me down to the ground because being on my own in a strange place is rather brassing & it will give me something to pass the evenings away . . .

Do let me have a wedding photo & one of those we had taken at Betty's as soon as you can – I want to have one on my desk, as well as one to carry around.

I've just managed to get hold of the railway vouchers for you but they'll have to be stamped, so I'll send you one each time you need one.

Well, darl – I'm going on an unofficial visit to a local ATC place tonight just to get the gen – I must do as much as I can with the ATC at nights here – then I won't have so much time left for feeling sorry for myself at having to leave you. I miss you an awful lot, Tubs – especially when I'm sitting here going through files. I read about a page & then my mind wanders back to you again. Still – roll on that weekend when I can see you.

The Betty mentioned here is Dicky Huband's girlfriend. The relationship between the two couples only really began to flourish once Connie got to know Betty better after Ron's return from North Africa. There's a picture of the four of them together in his photo album, almost certainly the one referred to here. Two happier looking couples would be hard to find. Sadly, it wasn't to last. Dicky had barely a year left to live.

27 August 1943:

I've just sent your book off with a note inside . . .

I've moved into my digs and find them very comfortable. The grub is excellent & there's lots of it . . . It's only about 5 mins walk to HQ – I'm pretty lucky to get anything at all round here as digs are at a premium. I've been told that it's very difficult to get a seat on any train going back to London. The form is apparently to go back to Cardiff (12 miles) and pick up the train there.

Weekend leave seems to be pretty easy here so I'll put in for Sept 18th later on, I think. I'll let you know how I get on as soon as I can . . .

The brief note mentioned in Ron's opening sentence above concludes with an important comment about his return to driving; it's copied below. Losing an eye not only restricts his field of vision, it also affects his depth perception. The resultant disability – one for which he'll eventually receive a compensatory pension – dictates a relatively circumspect approach. However, it's another month or so before he even hints at this.

I went down to St Athan yesterday and had a very nice time – I also started to drive the car last evening – I can still cope OK – which pleases me no end.

29 August 1943:

I'm wondering what on earth you're going to do when you come down here – there's absolutely nothing to do on Sunday & about the same on Saturday. I thought of looking at some place half way between London & here & then meeting you – we might be able to spend a nice weekend somewhere. Do you think we both might meet at Vickie's one week end?

By the time I've been around a bit I may have found somewhere to go but I'll be able to tell you more when I see you. I've got 18th Sept weekend OK, I think . . .

The old landlady here is just about driving me crackers with her talk – I'll give you a couple of examples – & this isn't a 'line' at all. She asked me where I was in hospital – when I said Algiers she said 'where's that, Canada?'!!! When I said Tunisia – she goes even farther and says – 'Now is that Germany or Italy?' – What can you do with her. Actually she's very good to me apart from talking – I keep getting dug into a book but she keeps on thinking up new ones. I almost forgot – at lunch today she asked me why I had 'that little piece of ribbon' on my jacket – she actually thought I'd stuck it on to brighten up my uniform!

While Ron pokes gentle fun at his landlady here, the laugh in one sense is on him: Algiers is the capital of Algeria! The 'little piece of ribbon' that she mentions is, of course, the diagonally-striped, violet and white insignia of the DFC.

30 August 1943:

It's just 2.30 & I've had lunch – this morning I wrote to Jack H, Jim & Chas – read the paper, did the DE [Daily Express] crossword – had morning tea with the G/C [Group Captain], and now I'm trying to finish this & post

*it before 3.30. There you have my doings in a nutshell. Tonight I'm going to
see some ATC unit & give a pep talk.*

*I've got that article you sent pinned up on my notice board & I've marked
up the piece about Sailor, Jamie & Lacey.*

The 'Lacey' mentioned here is J.H. 'Ginger' Lacey, one of the RAF's top
scoring fighter pilots. Credited finally with twenty-eight enemy aircraft
destroyed, five of them in France as a sergeant prior to the Battle of Britain,
he retired as a squadron leader with the DFM and Bar. As a flight lieutenant,
his flight commander at Hawarden, Ron had good reason to be grateful to
him – largely because of the almost cavalier indifference with which he
treated a potentially fatal incident.

During one of his final sorties as a quasi-instructor, Ron was flying with
an Australian who 'wasn't awfully good'. In fact his close formation verged
on the dangerous – so much so that during one turn, to avoid a collision
Ron pulled up and away, and promptly lost his companion as he entered
cloud. With the pair now separated he began a gentle descent through
what proved to be a dense layer. Flying now on instruments, he must have
become disorientated because he broke cloud pointing almost vertically
down, uncomfortably close to the ground. Convinced he was about to crash,
he 'gave the stick a hell of a yank and there was a crunch'. Without realising
it, he'd clipped the top of a hill, flattening the radiator under the starboard
wing. He was extraordinarily fortunate that no other damage was done –
other than to his ego. The same Lady Luck who'd indulged him in the air
was now about to dispense similar favours on the ground. Not only was he
lucky to be alive, he was also fortunate that his flight commander 'thought
it was quite a joke'. Lacey's sense of perspective is only to be admired. His
attitude was a reflection, perhaps, on all he'd already been through: nine
times he was either shot down or crash-landed – once in a French swamp
where he nearly drowned – and twice he had to bale out.

By way of a footnote to this incident, there's no mention of it in Ron's
correspondence at the time – it was September 1941 – or indeed his log
book. Neither omission comes as much of a surprise, though.

1 September 1943:

*As regards the weekend I don't think you'd better come down – I shall be
at this 'do' all Saturday & if the weather's like it is today it would hardly be
worth it anyway – it's been pouring ever since I got up . . .*

I'm getting into the run of things here & it seems quite good. They're trying to find out whether I'm just attached here for a while or whether I'm actually on the strength. If I'm only attached I can't get promoted. Still – if that's the case I'll see if the G/C can get me put on the strength . . .

Hello old plum, only another 17 days & I'll be with you . . .

2 September 1943:

I'm getting quite a 'Staff Officer' here – I write letters & try & look as though I understand everything – I gave a pep talk yesterday – I expect I've got to do another tonight – I'm not sure.

Yesterday I went out in our Vauxhall 16 to help test the speedometer on the Hillman. It was grand driving a big car – I'd like a big one after the war.

I'm trying to arrange to go to Colwyn Bay & Rhyl about the 13th, 14th Sept . . . I've written to the sqdns today but I'm not sure whether they'll be working or still on holidays.

I'm looking forward to seeing you again & having a nice early night – are you getting the morning of 18th off? There's one point though – I must catch the early train on Monday – that's at 9.15 – so I shall have to be up with the lark!

5 September 1943:

I had the best time I've had since I arrived here, yesterday. If only you'd been with me it would have been marvellous. As it was I enjoyed it, but missed you an awful lot – especially when we were being introduced to everyone – it would have been so much nicer if I'd been able to introduce you as – 'My wife'.

Anyhow – to continue. It was . . . a sports do in Cardiff for the ATC. Luckily the weather made a mistake and was quite fine all day. The Group Captain said he'd take me to lunch with him . . . we were supposed to meet Sir Reginald Clarry – MP for Newport but he didn't get there until 1.30 – however – so we started lunch without him & he was full of apologies . . . He'd come from London & the train was late. He's a charming bloke . . .

After lunch we drove down to the sports ground & met the rest of our "staff" – F/Lt Kibbler & his secretary-cum-girlfriend. The sports do was quite a success and Sir R.C. presented the prizes. After this the G/C took Sir R.C. to dinner & left Kib & I & his girl to do as we liked. We'd had an invitation to attend an Ensa concert at the local balloon centre, & so we got along there about 7.45 & were treated to beers. Everyone seemed very nice to us – then we saw the show. It was supposed to have been a variety show but they'd changed it at the last minute & we had a ballet instead. It was a really excellent turn and everyone thoroughly enjoyed it. The whole audience cheered like mad at the end of each piece & I think the artistes were agreeably surprised with their reception, because you get all sorts in the audience, & ballet doesn't appeal to everybody.

It was over at 9.30 & so we all repaired to the mess for sandwiches and drinks. Quite a large crowd of guests were there, wives of officers, army types, ATS,[82] WAAFs, civvies – & us. The ballet troupe came in about 10 pm and stayed until about 10.30 . . . I got talking to three army types who'd been round London in 1940 on AA.[83] One had only one eye – so we had quite a heart to heart talk as you can imagine . . .

7 September 1943:

It's only another 10 days before I come home to see my small plump plum – I'm rather looking forward to having a week end with you – especially as it's my birthday . . .

If only there was something to do on a Sunday it would be grand for you down here. However, I've complained so much about Sundays in Newport that I've been invited to various golf clubs & private houses – just to prove that there is something if you know where.

I may be going up to N. Wales next week – I've had a reply from Colwyn Bay today but I'm waiting to hear what Llandudno & Rhyl have to say before I do anything.

8 September 1943:

Another nine days and I'll be with you – you've no idea how I'm looking forward to it . . .

Well, sweetheart, I had a very nice drive last night – some of the prettiest country I've seen round here. The only snag was it rained like the clappers as I was coming out – still – it had stopped by the time I reached home.

---

82. The ATS (Auxiliary Territorial Service) was the women's branch of the British Army during the Second World War.
83. Ack-ack, or anti-aircraft, guns.

By the way, I wrote to the Wings Club in Grosvenor Place for details of fees etc. & I've had a letter saying all I have to do is apply personally & I get a membership card free. It sounds a very nice place. They have supper dances from 8-11 pm on Wed. & Sat. so maybe we could go there for a change. I'll have to see what it's like when I'm up for any length of time.

9 September 1943:

Your letters are getting brighter & brighter – from the sound of things you're quite enjoying my absence! I don't <u>really</u> mean that – but I'm pleased to have some cheerful letters from you . . .

I didn't tell you where I was going the other night because half the places aren't on the map – they're tucked away in the mountains somewhere. I can't pronounce the words so I normally carry a notebook with the names of the places written in & then show it to some local lad.

A catastrophe happened to me today – my landlady is taking a job so I've got to find new digs. She doesn't go for a fortnight so I've got a chance of looking round. At least it's stopped me going to N Wales – I'll have to stay down here & look for digs next week . . .

12 September 1943:

Once again a weekend comes to a close & I can phone you & then just wait for the week to go until I'm able to see you.

Darl, I do miss you so much – I'm absolutely at my wits end to know what to do with myself. I'm not keen on going out far & I've read all my books – so there you are – still – it's not so bad really. I've got my itinerary planned for tonight – it's just 6 pm now – I'm going to finish this letter, clean my shoes & buttons, post said letter, carry on to the Officers Club – wait until about 8 pm – & then phone you.

Only another four & a half days & I can be with you – Do you think we can spend Friday night at the flat – then we can go to Woodford for Sat & Sunday if you like. Only I do so want to see just <u>you</u> on my first night home – & your bed does squeak doesn't it, darl? Anyway, I'll see what you say tonight . . .

The G/C took me down to his dry docks on Saturday morning. He asked if I wanted to drive – naturally I said 'yes' because he was going in the Vauxhall. Anyway, he showed me all around & then we had a coffee & I drove back . . .

It seems such a pity that I'm able to get a cushy job like this with every weekend off & then not be able to see you. I'll bet that if I got transferred to a nearer place I wouldn't get any weekend at all.

14 September 1943:

I went to see one of the <u>answerers</u> to my advert. (Answerers isn't a very good word is it?) – Anyway, I picked the one in the nicest district & I think I've touched lucky again. The husband is a baker & works from 4 am - 3 pm & has only just married. Now the labour exchange have told his wife she's either got to go into a factory or take a war worker. It's a very nice house – they don't seem to be hard up by any manner of means – in fact entirely the opposite. I'm going to pay 30/- [£1.50] the same as before but the atmosphere is much better. It's hard to say yet really how everything's going to work out but I think it will be OK. I asked about you & they said it was OK any time. I've got a very nice bedroom with a double bed – so I hope everything's going to turn out OK . . .

I had a letter from Chas today – he's got his commission and gave me lots of gen. I'll let you read the letter when I come home.

15 September 1943:

The time's gradually getting nearer & nearer – anyone would think I'd been away for years by the way I'm looking forward to seeing you – but the fact is I'm so used to having you with me that I'm all over the place when we're apart.

I'm gradually getting busier but I like the job and the people are very nice . . .

I had a shocking drive in the rain yesterday – it was absolutely pouring down – still I managed to get home in the light.

Well sweetheart – believe it or not I've got a fair lot to do this morning & I'm going out all the afternoon – so I must leave this now.

17 September 1943:

Good morning, darling, Glad I'm home?

Chapter 24

2 August 1942, RAF Morpeth

No. 72 Squadron's move to Scotland was a somewhat haphazard affair and took place in stages. It began with a deployment to Morpeth on 2 August while Ron was still on leave. Having elected to take Ferdie's car, he was simply required to reach Morpeth before the next stage of the move, a week or so later. But first he had to pick up some 'official' luggage left behind at Biggin Hill, notably that of the squadron commander.

Things never felt quite the same under Bob (Ron could never bring himself to say 'Bobby') Oxspring, although he was 'a nice enough chap'. He had an impressive record too. A Battle of Britain veteran with nine confirmed 'kills' before he took command, and another since, the son of Major Robert Oxspring MC*, a First World War flying ace, had a pedigree to match. But for all his success he 'wasn't really in the same class' as his inspirational predecessor – something Oxspring effectively acknowledged in his autobiography, *Spitfire Command*:

> Brian Kingcome was promoted to take over the Kenley wing. I was lucky enough to be plucked from Hawkinge to take his place as CO of 72 Squadron. As a measure of his status as a leader, he handed over to me what surely ranked as the best drilled, most experienced and aggressive fighter squadron in the RAF . . . [a] cosmopolitan bunch of tough operators . . . about half were British together with two Australians, a Canadian, a New Zealander, a South African, two Americans and two Norwegians.[84]

Using the Hillman as a pseudo removal van turned out to be a boon rather than an imposition because it meant Ron could claim petrol coupons for the journey from Biggin Hill. That said, it took some persuading before he eventually relieved a disgruntled station adjutant of almost his entire supply of these prized possessions. By the time he reached Morpeth the squadron was

---

84. Oxspring, op. cit., p.111.

already preparing for the next stage of its relocation. So, after a brief stay and equipped with another supply of coupons, he set off once again, this time for Ayr. Shortly after he arrived he began his first letter for more than a fortnight.

12 August 1942:

Once again our only (or nearly only) method of communication is by letter. Honestly, dear, I do miss you – I seem to be cut off from everyone & everything here. It's a shocking deadbeat place. Luckily there was an Ensa concert last night which served to take our minds off the place for a while.

The car went splendidly all the way from Morpeth – I didn't have any trouble at all. I had the puncture mended at Cranwell and everything is fine now. The others haven't got here yet – the weather's holding them up so far – but when they do I'll get Jack's chaps to completely overhaul the car – I won't be using it for a while yet . . .

The phone here is right in the anteroom – and the line's awful – I had to phone the CO at Newcastle yesterday and despite the fact that we were both shouting our heads off I could scarcely make out a word . . .

Tubby, sweet, that was a wonderful leave, wasn't it? – just imagine spending the rest of our lives like that – it seems far too good to be true – although if I can wangle it I'll come home just as soon as possible . . .

You remember I said I thought the CO was peeved with me for staying away – well – he was in the mess just as I got back from phoning you – all he said was: – 'Hello Robbie – have a good leave?' – so there you are.

It's time to put Ron's apparent obsession with securing time off into context. Since he joined 111 Squadron at the beginning of October 1941, notwithstanding the odd relatively short period of leave, he's been on operations constantly for over ten months. Whether he realises it or not, this is taking its toll both physically and mentally. The irony of moving to a base where there's little chance of any action is that the attendant relaxation brings acute boredom; each new day contributes to a never-ending routine, a cycle of frustration. As if this isn't enough, the likelihood of a move overseas now hangs over everyone's head like the sword of Damocles.

15 August 1942:

The remainder of the chaps are here now & we're all brassed off to blazes – we're doing more readiness here than we ever did at Biggin & so

171

far as we can gather nothing's come within range to get shot at since war was declared!

Anyway – we play cards, darts – go to the flicks & bind amongst ourselves – it all helps to pass the time.

I took my 'Connie' up the other day – it's not bad – not as good as my last one, but one of the best in the sqdn. The chap who did all the painting has been posted – so I put 'Connie' on. Actually I'm quite pleased with the result. I couldn't do it in copperplate & so I drew it in block capitals in pencil first & then painted it in white. The final result is <u>something</u> like this: – 'CONNIE' – so there you are – at least I feel much better with it on.

I'm at readiness until 8 pm. One flight does it one day & the other the next. We have a pretty easy time really but we'd rather be down south.

Did I tell you there's a chap here very keen on water polo – he's the station MO. There's a rather nice pool at Prestwick on the beach. The only snag is that it's open air. If the weather gets better I hope there's a chance of a game . . .

I'll try & phone tonight if I can – the phone's a shocker still, though . . .

Well – sweetheart – once more I come to the end of another letter. Postings are coming thick & fast. You'd scarcely recognise 72 at the moment – nothing's come up for me yet, though – at least – nothing to get me down south. I do hope I'm able to get down to you soon . . .

The sortie Ron mentions here, on 14 August in his latest 'Connie', is his first for over a fortnight. He and a new arrival, Pilot Officer Jerrold Le Cheminant, were scrambled in search of a 'Ju 88 reported off N. Ireland. Shot down later by N. Ireland boys', according to his log book. After climbing to 15,000 feet they were immediately recalled, their fifteen-minute sorties the squadron's first operational missions since 1 August. To add to Ron's personal vexation, telephone communication with Connie continues to prove difficult.

19 August 1942:

It's now 8.45 pm – I've booked a call to you but there's an hour's delay – I hope it comes before that though.

I'm on readiness until 9.15 pm so I can just sit here & write to you until the call comes through . . .

Fancy our Dorothy[85] being at Morpeth! – I wonder what she'd have said if she'd seen me as a P/O – not that I care, but I think it would have given

---

85. Dorothy (Dolly) Lunn, a WAAF corporal now, was serving at RAF Morpeth.

the Lunn family something to talk about if they haven't talked enough about our engagement . . .

I didn't say much about George before because he isn't here. He's been attached to another sqdn. (+ 5 other sgts) for a while – I'll tell you more later on.

Now – to answer the rest of your questions – the mess here isn't bad – the food is <u>very</u> good – even better than B.H. We all eat like hogs – the quarters aren't at all bad – not <u>quite</u> as good as before, but tons better than Morpeth . . .

. . . I get just over £22 per month – less tax (about £3.10.0 [£3.50]) – less £4 to Mum – so the net result is about £14. With luck I should be able to save about £9 of that, so we should have quite a bit by <u>Christmas</u>!

It was awfully funny tonight . . . Chemi & I (Chemi – is a new chap, Le Cheminant) went to the local pub for one or two beers – some of the locals asked us to play darts and so we agreed. The locals were awfully good – but Chemi & I seemed to be unable to do anything wrong. We both got fantastic scores & completely wiped the board with the three teams we played. Actually I hadn't played darts for years & never was very good, but these locals thought we were terrific. We played for pints but won so much we couldn't drink it & so we had to start giving our 'rivals' some beer. Old Chemi and I have been laughing about it ever since. The whole point is that if we play them again we probably won't win a game – still – it gave us some fun to pass the time . . .

I've just finished phoning you & feel miles better – I'll pedal home to sleep now – so goodnight darling . . .

24 August 1942:

It's funny that you should send me that Stratford Express cutting, as only today I received a letter from Bill Edwards, which had been forwarded to me from home, saying that Dorothy[86] had written to him telling him that she'd married Ron[87] on the 12th. It is rather staggering news isn't it . . .

The rest of the sgts – George, Pete etc. and the CO arrived yesterday – they went down south for that show [the Dieppe raid]. *None of them fired*

86. See letters of February 1940 (Chapter 4) and May, June, July 1941 (Chapter 10) plus WAAF Corporal Dorothy Lunn's mention in the letter of 19 August 1942 above.
87. Sub-Lt Ron Hawkey RNVR.

even one burst – old George is binding like blazes over chances missed. Tommy Wright has his commission now & looks quite a pretty little boy as a P/O . . .

The weather's lousy again this afternoon so we're going to have tea & go and see My Favourite Blonde – Tommy & Chemi are dressing up preparatory to having a beer or two in town but George & I are coming back to letter-write. It's 2.50 pm young Tubs – do you realise it's fifteen days since I last saw you! . . .

Well dear, I'm afraid the news question is getting worse & worse – this is such a dead hole & our activities are so limited that there's nothing worth writing about – except that I must keep on telling you that you're in my thoughts always and I miss you terribly . . .

Ron wasn't sorry to have missed the Dieppe debacle. For the squadron's part, restricting patrols to relatively low altitude (4,000-8,000 feet for the first sortie and pegged at 6,000 feet for the next three) had proved a 'tactical handicap'. This was particularly unfortunate because the boss had wanted to use the opportunity to blood some of the newer crews. Turnover had been considerable during the squadron's latter days at Biggin Hill. As Ron later recalled:

> We lost several very nice chaps and good pilots. In fact some were lost before I even met them. I went on leave for a week once and when I came back two chaps had been posted to us; one had been shot down and one had crashed on coming back and he hadn't even unpacked his gear.

Bob Oxspring's return to Ayr was greeted with a degree of relief. In his absence, Squadron Leader Archie Winskill had taken temporary command. One or two minor incidents, taxiing accidents and the like, reinforced his reputation as 'a bit of a miserable character'. But after threatening 'the direst of penalties for the next person who did something really bad', Ron was delighted 'that the next person who had a taxiing accident was Sqn Ldr Winskill!' He hit a small roller near the edge of the perimeter track, damaging both aircraft and propeller. Thereafter, little more was heard from a man who, it must be said, deserves a more positive appraisal than the foregoing might suggest.

As OC 222 Squadron, shot down over France in August 1941, Winskill escaped capture to become the first man to return home via Spain and Gibraltar – an experience that precluded him from flying over France for the remainder of the war (an embargo imposed by the Air Ministry because of his contacts with the Resistance). In January 1943 he was shot down again, this time off the Tunisian coast. After baling out for a second time, he returned to his squadron through German lines, becoming one the few individuals to escape capture twice. A distinguished career came to an end when Air Commodore Sir Archibald Winskill KCVO CBE DFC* AE retired in 1982 after fourteen years as Captain of The Queen's Flight.

Back at Ayr, on 27 August there was a break from routine in more ways than one when Ron flew to Northern Ireland on convoy duty. At Eglinton it was his turn for a taxiing accident, recorded in his log book thus: 'Hit lorry – by perimeter track – <u>absolved</u> of all blame.' The only damage to RN-H (serial BM 413, transferred from 611 Squadron some three weeks earlier and the latest to carry Connie's name) was to a wingtip navigation light – and to his pride, of course. He and three colleagues, Flight Sergeant Patterson and Sergeants Fosse and Menzies, remained on the ground, deeply frustrated, for three days. Their putative task was to provide top cover for the *Queen Mary*.[88] He'd seen the ship just a fortnight before, a magnificent sight steaming up the Clyde towards Glasgow, leaving behind both a beautiful wake and, it seemed, a number of her escorts. Bad weather in the end precluded activity that would have made a welcome change. It's no surprise that the letter Ron writes immediately on his return to Ayr is notably gloomy.

30 August 1942:

As you can see – we eventually got permission to return & eventually arrived here at 11 am this morning. Never in all my life have I been to such a deadly hole. I thought Ayr was bad but it's like Biggin compared with Ireland. There's nothing to do at all there & the only papers you get are the Northern Whig & such like – English papers arrive at night on the next day. I got there on Thursday night just in time for Wednesday's papers. We did absolutely nothing & apart from hitting a lorry whilst I was taxying I didn't exactly cover myself in glory. It wasn't my fault and the aerodrome control officers who saw the accident put in a report for me. It's not very serious & I'm not unduly worried about it – so don't <u>you</u> go & worry, young lady.

George & I are trying to get to Sailor's school of air firing – for various reasons. George flew over there the other day but Sailor was away so he had to leave a note. I hope something comes of it, but I'll keep you posted with all the gen anyway. It's three weeks since I've seen you, dear – it seems ages & ages ...

---

88. They were misinformed. The *Queen Mary* sailed for New York on 11 August and didn't return for a month.

What little flying there was in August came mainly by way of short training flights; Ron flew only twelve hours in sixteen sorties during the month. Inevitably, in circumstances where time passed so slowly, the overseas deployment rumours rapidly gathered pace. If the prospects of a move concerned the entire unit, they seemed to hit Ron and George hardest of all. Neither individual relished the prospect of separation from his fiancée. Their efforts to avoid the anticipated move culminated in the discreet but vain appeal for help from George's illustrious brother Ron mentions here. Little did the two friends know that their future was effectively pre-ordained.

As Bob Oxspring later recalled, he would soon have much to do 'as the unit expanded to become self-sufficient in transport, tentage, field kitchens, medical facilities and airfield defence'. But his most immediate need was to 'replace recently posted officers' to serve alongside experienced individuals like Ron and George, whom he was keen to retain. He'd already 'submitted a list of names to a sympathetic AOC 13 Group, AVM Jock Andrews,[89] who somehow overcame obstacles' and prised 'half a dozen old sweats' from various locations, mainly OTUs, 'for their second tour of operations'.[90] Notable amongst these names were Chas Charnock, Pete Fowler, Jimmy Corbin and the aforementioned 'Chemi' Le Cheminant.

The last named pair had spent time together at Biggin Hill in 1940-41, serving on 66 and 92 Squadrons respectively; but it was subsequently, as instructors at 53 OTU at Llandow in South Wales, that their lifelong friendship began. They both knew Oxspring of old and Le Cheminant may well have been instrumental in securing Corbin's posting to join him on 72 Squadron. Like his 'best pal', the latter had had more than enough of instructing. Notwithstanding its inherent dangers (witness Derek Olver's sad demise), the 'job of teaching others to fly had become increasingly tedious and dull'; he needed some excitement. In fact, he was 'ready to rejoin the war'.[91]

3 September 1942:

Wish I had some news to tell you dear – I'm sure you must be tired of reading 'there's no more news' but actually life is pretty deadly up here & there's nothing really that would interest us.

---

89. Air Vice-Marshal J.O. Andrews CB DSO MC*.
90. Oxspring, op. cit., p.114.
91. Corbin, op. cit., pp.151 and 152.

We don't even fly much these days – as a rule George, Jack Hilton, Johnnie & I play poker down at dispersal, go to see a flick or have a beer at night & then go to bed.

We miss Tommie rather, although we never had much to do with him apart from seeing him all day – I mean George & I very rarely went out at night with him – he was always looking for a 'Popsy' but he was an awfully nice kid & had some really good points.

He was sorry to leave, but as he said, the sqdn isn't what it used to be & sooner or later we'll all go somewhere or other, so there it is.

By the way – if you see that First of the Few before I come home look out for Brian Kingcome – he took part in it & I understand he's in one or two scenes – if I know anything of Brian he probably commanded the screen for quite a while.

Kay makes me laugh with her infant – anyone would think she was going on a picnic – I do hope everything's OK for her[92] . . .

I just can't get used to the idea of being so far away from you – it seems all wrong that I'm not able to dash up & see you when I'm released now . . .

9 September 1942:

There's only one thing to write about & that, I'm very much afraid, is now a certainty. My one real hope is that Sailor can do something, but there's no point in my trying to buoy your spirits up with any false hope – so I must tell you that I don't think anything can be done. I asked the CO today if I could have a posting somewhere on to anything at all, but his hands are tied & he just couldn't do a thing.

It seems as though the whole bottom has suddenly dropped out of my world. I can't even think past you & now this has happened I feel completely lost. I can't realise even now that we've got to separate – you're my whole life and if I can't have you I don't care what happens. This past year has seemed so very wonderful it just doesn't seem right that we should be made to feel so sad . . .

We've got to do a certain amount of flying before we can go on leave but it shouldn't be more than a week before I see you – that is if the weather keeps fine.

---

92. Six months pregnant at the time, on 4 December 1942 Kay Olver would give birth to a son, Derek John, named after her late husband.

Darling – there's not much more I can say is there? -- Don't give up hope completely, dear, – after all – we've been pretty lucky so far and maybe something will turn up . . .

Ron had warned Connie about his impending move before this last letter – by telephone on 7 September. Her diary entry for that day reads, 'My darling rang to say he was going abroad. Oh please God grant that he will not have to go. I just can't go on – without seeing him until the end of the war. <u>Please</u> don't let him go.' Her mood in the days that followed wasn't helped by the fact that such an important letter was delayed in the post.

11 September 1942:

I've just received your letter & am trying to catch the afternoon post – if I do you may get this on Saturday evening.

I can't understand why you haven't had my last letter – it should have reached you on Thursday at the latest . . .

I'm trying to get through the flying we have to do as soon as I can & then get back to see you just as quickly as I can.

The flying to which Ron refers brought to an end a quiet, truncated month in which he flew less than eleven hours. Amongst a dozen or so short training exercises, two lengthy cross-country flights stand out as unusual. The second of these, his final sortie before a period of leave, was a portent of things to come. However, it would be more than two months before he understood the significance of the two-hour, 400-mile navigation exercise he flew on 13 September: 'Shaky do – bags of mist'. In retrospect he added a post script: 'With F/Lt Le Cheminant DFC'.

In due course the squadron would return south to Ouston; meanwhile, he's about to head the same way in the Hillman.

14 September 1942:

I'm starting this letter in dispersal & hope to finish it in the Mess at lunchtime, by which time your letter should have arrived.

I've been looking up your 'AA' book – it's only about 160 miles to Doncaster – and as I shall start at dawn I should get there, or rather to Scotch Corner, by about 10 am – I hardly think it's worth your while to come all the way up there if I can be rushing nearer home at the same time.

Don't think I'm trying to put you off, dear, but my idea is to get to you just as soon as I can and I think it would be better if I just came straight home. I wish you could be with me – it was very sweet & thoughtful of you to suggest meeting me, darling.

I've just heard that this is all the leave we're likely to get <u>before</u> – I think they're counting it as embarkation leave – I'm terribly sorry to have to tell you this, my dear, but it's so much better if you've got some idea of what's happening before I see you.

God knows how long I'll be away but all I care for is that you'll be waiting for me when I come back.

There's not much more I can put on paper – but we'll have so much to talk of when I come back – I just can't get used to the idea that I'll have to leave you – I can't even think of it because it just doesn't seem possible.

Ever since I've known you I've loved you and now when everything seemed to be going fine I'm taken from you – it seems as though nothing matters now at all.

I'll leave this now until I read your letter.

<u>It</u> was there when I came up to lunch, and, darling, it really was a wizard letter – I love you more & more. I didn't realise you meant spend a night in Doncaster – I thought you meant to come straight home. Anyway dearest – I think the best thing to do is to wait until I phone you tonight – we can talk so much better then . . .

When Ron spoke to Connie that night it was the first time for a couple of calls that she managed not to cry. She sensed that Ron was a little happier, although by no means reconciled to the enforced separation that was to come. He left the car at Doncaster and caught a train to London on the morning of 16 September. His plan was simply to spend as much time as he could with Connie and his immediate family before embarking for . . . well, he still had absolutely no idea.

The couple spent their time visiting both sets of parents and catching up with friends and members of Ron's large, extended family. In the evenings they gravitated regularly to the Monkhams, where Ron was occasionally persuaded to lose to Ferdie at snooker. There were regular trips to favourite London haunts too, including lunch with a heavily pregnant Kay Olver who, Connie noted, 'looked awfully well'. They even squeezed in a quick trip to their swimming club. When Connie saw Ron off at Euston on 25 September his ten days' leave had gone so quickly it felt like an extended weekend. If this wasn't exactly their final goodbye, it was by no means clear when they'd see each other again.

Once he's picked up the Hillman, driven to Ayr and returned almost immediately to Durham, laden once again with others' kit, it's from the mess at Ouston that Ron writes next.

27 September 1942:

The chaps were still at Ayr when I came back but were due to go on Saturday – so I drove over here as I expected.

I had to have <u>one</u> piece of bad luck before I got here – I had a puncture about 20 miles from Ayr & had to sit in the middle of the road & change a tyre. I didn't mind that so much as the time it wasted, because I had to drive to the nearest garage & get the bad tyre fixed. Anyway, I finally got here with about 2 ozs of petrol to spare – they don't give you very much on a duty run. Apart from that the car went like a little dingbat – By the way, when I paid my mess bill at Ayr I had over £2 to pay on the telephone accounts – I'll have to be a bit more careful in the future.

I think I'm getting leave in a day or so – so don't reply to this letter until I phone you . . .

I do hope you're able to come up here and drive down with me – although your office may take a pretty dim view of all the holidays you've taken.

I gave George the tobacco & he was very pleased with it – he sends his thanks & best wishes to you. He'd bought me some tobacco for my birthday – so it was a good thing you thought of getting him some.

Sweetheart – there's not much more I can tell you – didn't my leave go quickly though – I expect it's because I love you so much I don't notice what we do or how long it takes – the time just seems to fly. If our married life goes as quickly we'll be grandparents before we realise we've had our honeymoon. Tubby, darling – I do love being with you – I begrudge every minute I'm away from you.

Just try & make the best of things until I'm home for good & then we can go our own way – just keep smiling darling – it won't be long now.

Ron's peripatetic existence continues. His next letter is again on Officers' Mess headed paper – this time from Ayr, the station he's just left.

P/O Jerrold Le Cheminant, wife
Eileen and best man Jimmy
Corbin (left), 28 February 1941.
Both 72 Sqn pilots survived the
war unscathed (see Chapter 24).
(David Le Cheminant archive)

72 Sqn pilots at dispersal, Biggin Hill, April 1942. Australian Flt Lt Hugo
Armstrong is seated on the china mascot with Robbie (plus pipe), chatting to P/O
R.C. (Rene) Kitchen. Another who survived the war, Kitchen left 72 to join 65 Sqn
in August 1942.

Except where noted, all pictures are from the author's private collection.

The first in a series of informal pictures Robbie took of his colleagues is another Australian, Sgt Al Hake. Shot down on 4 April 1942, he was executed by the Gestapo on 31 March 1944 after escaping from Stalag Luft III (see Chapter 18).

A relaxed Hugo Armstrong. Kia 5 February 1943 when OC 611 Sqn, his name is commemorated on the Runnymede Air Forces Memorial (see Chapters 18, 20 and 22).

Above left: Yet another Australian, P/O J.R. (John) Ratten. He survived the Luftwaffe only to fall victim to meningitis on 27 February 1945; he was a Wg Cdr at the time (see Chapter 22).

Above right: Flt Lt Franz Ferdinand Colloredo-Mansfeld, who took over from 'Timber' Woods as OC A Flight. Son of Austrian nobility, he was kia on 14 January 1944 when CO of 132 Sqn; his grave is in Boulogne Eastern Cemetery (see Chapter 27).

Rhodesian Sgt R.A. 'Tommy' Wright. As a P/O he left 72 Sqn for 1435 Sqn in Malta and was killed when his Spitfire crashed at Luqa on 1 November 1942 (see Chapters 20, 24 and 28).

New Zealander Flt Sgt J.G. McCutchan who, according to 72 Sqn records, on 25 April 1942 'failed to return – he was seen to go down in a controlled dive.' It was his second sortie of the day and the Sqn's third fatality in forty-eight hours. He's buried in Etaples Military Cemetery near Le Touquet, not far from where he crashed, at Enocq (see Chapter 18).

New Zealanders P/Os Owen Hardy (left) and David Waters. Waters was killed returning from a sweep on 9 May 1942 when he 'was seen . . . to go into the sea'. He's another commemorated on the Runnymede Memorial (see Chapters 7, 20, 26, 27, 28 and 30).

A picture that exemplifies the close squadron relationships: Sgt F.M. (Francis) Browne with B Flight groundcrew. Kia on 5 December 1942, he's buried in Beja War Cemetery. Sgt Alan Mottram, killed the same day, is buried 30 miles away in Medjez-al-Bab War Cemetery (see Chapter 28).

P/O Francis de Naeyer left 72 for
602 Sqn and was kia on 25 May
1943. A Flt Lt at the time, he's
buried in Abbeville Cemetery
(see Chapter 18).

Sqn Ldr Cedric Masterman (left), Robbie's first 72 Sqn CO, at Gravesend, 9 November
1941. Behind him is the original Spitfire named Connie, RN-H (AD183), destroyed
when Robbie baled out. (Cedric Masterman Memorial Collection).

'Mac' Macdonald and 'George' Malan as Sgts, summer 1942 . . .

. . . and later as officers: left to right, P/Os J.W. Macdonald, J. Le Cheminant and F. Malan at Ayr, September 1942. Macdonald was kia on 5 December 1942 (one of three 72 Sqn pilots lost that day) and Malan on 26 April 1943 (see Chapters 13 and 27).

HMT *Staffordshire*, which took half of 72 Sqn's pilots, plus their crated aircraft, to Gibraltar in November 1942, albeit in no great comfort (see Chapter 26).

Above: Two Polyphotos Connie sent to Ron. On the back she wrote, *'All my dearest love - Connie. Dec. 1942.'*

Left: Robbie carried this photo with him as part of his escape gear, for use with a forged passport.

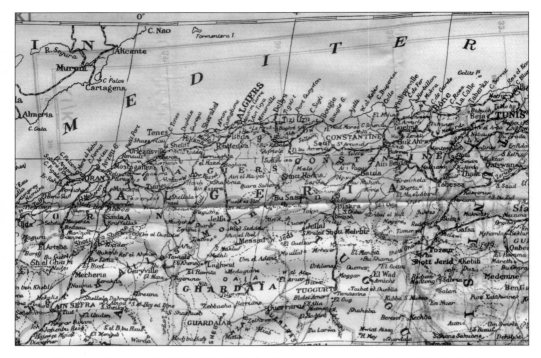

This small scale (1:6,000,000) folded silk map was part of every North Africa pilot's escape package. The reverse provided larger scale (1:1,657,000) coverage of Cyrenaica, the eastern coastal region of Libya.

Hauptmann Erich Rudorffer in 1944, aged 27. Two days before Robbie became his forty-seventh victim, on 18 December 1942 Harry Charnock, the grand old man of 72 Sqn, was Rudorffer's forty-sixth (see Chapter 30). (German Federal Archive Image)

Above left: Connie with bridesmaid
Violet Freshwater in her Woodford
garden (see Chapter 21).

Above right: Mother and daughter
at All Saints', Woodford Wells (see
Chapter 21).

The happy couple, 5 June 1943
(see Chapter 21).

The beach babe! A Cornwall honeymoon picture (see Chapter 21).

F/O & Mrs Robertson with Dickie Huband and Betty, at Betty's home, summer 1943 (See Chapter 23).

The last, poignant scrapbook picture of Ron's long-standing friend Dicky Huband (see Chapters 16, 18, 23 and 27).

Taken in June 1943 in her parents' garden, on the back of this photo Connie wrote: *'We three!'*

One of his proudest possessions, this 72 Sqn shield was effectively gifted to Ron during his time as an ATC Inspector. The Welshman who carved it would accept only the cost of the wood.

Ron's brother, P/O Alan Robertson, in a picture sent from Italy, May 1945 (see Chapters 4, 6, 10 and 24).

Flt Lt & Mrs Robertson during a 1945 visit to Ron's parents' home in Broadstairs (see Chapter 29).

This Leonard Bridgman drawing of 'Supermarine Spitfire VBs, No. 72 (Basutoland) Squadron 1942', torn from a magazine dated 13 June 1958 (possibly *The Aeroplane*), was pasted inside the rear cover of Ron's scrapbook.

Ron & Con Robertson arriving for a Battle of Britain hangar service, RAF Wattisham, September 1986.

Ron & Con Robertson in the mid-80s – Con wearing her RAF wings and Ron his coveted caterpillar tie-pin (see Chapters 16 and 18).

Hunter pilot Chris Golds' painting of Robbie's Spitfire – a present from the author.

The bench above Ron and Con's beach hut at Frinton-on-Sea (see Epilogue).

The dedication fixed to the Frinton bench (see Epilogue).

2 October 1942:

As you can see I've started travelling again. I got your letter just as we started off back here – everything seems to be upside down at the moment. Six of us have come over here to relieve another sqdn – only when we arrived the other sqdn had pushed off – so six of us are doing readiness the whole day – at least it passes the time but we don't seem to be getting nearer any leave. The continual changing of plans & general messing about is getting on everyone's nerves – especially when I think of the car sitting at Ouston – the Adj. says we're all bound to get leave but I'll believe it when I see you . . .

Ron would have been feeling a lot less sorry for himself had he been aware of the news Connie learned from Kay Olver the day before he wrote this latest letter. In fact it wasn't until the following day, 3 October, when he telephoned her that he heard of yet another fatality: Derek's cousin had been killed. There was simply no escaping the impact of the war on those around him, those closest to him.

6 October 1942:

I'm sorry to hear about Derek's cousin – that family seem to have had more than their share of worry & trouble this war . . .

All I do these days is read & go to the flicks – we work the readiness so that we each get the maximum of time off each day, which helps us do something apart from just sit in dispersal all day. Even this isn't bad really – the six of us often get together down here & play cards – I lost about 3/- [15p] at poker the other day, but later on I taught them how to play cravatte & so far I've won about 10/6 [52.5p] – so I can't grumble. Every time I play cravatte I think of North Weald & how I used to rush off each night to see you.

Tubby sweet – we've really had a good run for our money haven't we? We don't know what's in store for us in the future but I know that wherever I go & whatever I have to put up with, the memories of the past year will help to make things a whole lot better . . .

This was the first of Ron's letters to be censored. The envelope bore a message posted across the left edge where it had been slit open. On the back in thick capitals 1 cm high it read: 'OPENED BY'; then, folded onto the front was 'EXAMINER 835'. However, it was the exception rather than the rule; only a couple of the next half-dozen he wrote suffered a similar fate.

To say Ron was frustrated and bored back at Ayr once again would be a considerable understatement. Marriage is constantly on his mind and he's coping less and less well with separation from Connie, a situation exacerbated by strictly limited flying opportunities. In the first ten days of October he manages just four sorties – three hours in total – only one of which could remotely be classed as operational: a convoy escort mission. Then, without warning, on 11 October the detachment is recalled to Ouston. It would be his last sortie for over five weeks. Typically, he pens a brief note as soon as he arrives back.

11 October 1942:

As you can see we've been rushed back here. We were told at 1 o'clock to be ready to come back at 2. Actually we didn't get here till about 4.30. No-one knows anything at all – although there are rumours of bags of p.t. & exercises etc. The thought of it fairly chills me but I suppose it'll do me good. As soon as I can gather what the form is I'll bid for some leave – everyone's got the same idea so I expect we'll get to know what's happening shortly.

There's transport coming to take us to the local pub in a minute. We're all going to get together & down the odd pint or so. I'm going because I haven't seen George or anyone for ages & there's almost bound to be some gen floating around.

As soon as I get anything definite I'll give you a ring. Excuse the rush darl, but I'm trying to tell you everything I can before the bus comes . . .

I never thought there'd be anything as important in the world happen to me as to get married to someone like you. I'm terribly lucky having you, sweet – I pray every night for a speedy end to the war so that we can carry on our lives in our own way – not caring whether I might have to leave you & go far away . . .

Two days later, on Tuesday 13 October, Ron sped home in the trusty Hillman, destined soon to be laid up again in Ferdie's garage. Together with the rest of the squadron he'd been sent on embarkation leave, with firm instructions to remain contactable by telephone at all times – a stricture that in no way inhibited his activities. He spent every second he could with

Connie. Even though she was at work that week, he travelled up to London on a couple of occasions so that they could enjoy lunch together. Evenings were usually spent at the Monkhams. An exception was his second night back, which found Connie at Ron's home sewing wings, buttons and other accoutrements onto his battledress. Given the special circumstances, she took the Friday off so that the couple could spend more time in each other's company. Next day she joined a large party of Ron's immediate family for lunch and it was only with difficulty that they eventually managed to extricate themselves. They wanted to be on their own; besides which, they had a dinner reservation at the Queen's Brasserie.

The couple travelled up to London later the same afternoon. But no sooner were they seated at their favourite table than the moment arrived they'd been dreading. The bandleader called an unscheduled halt mid-melody and announced a telephone call for Pilot Officer Robertson. It was from Ron's brother, Alan, who read out the contents of the recall telegram: 'IMPERATIVE YOU REPORT UNIT IMMEDIATELY REPEAT IMMEDIATELY = 72 SQUADRON'. Dinner was abandoned as the couple returned at once to their respective homes. It was hardly the romantic last evening they might have wished for; however, they arranged to meet next morning and travel to London together.

Connie was touched that her father wanted to accompany her as far as the rendezvous at Forest Gate. Ron was both surprised and delighted by this – even more so by the outcome of a brief, emotionally charged conversation with Ferdie. Standing distanced from his daughter, he not only wished Ron good luck, on the assumption that the couple would be apart for at least two years, he agreed that they could marry as soon as Ron returned. With that he turned, waved a final farewell and headed back for Woodford.

As she sat on the tube next to her fiancé Connie tried desperately to avoid any sign of her growing anxiety, but it was impossible. It wasn't long before she and Ron found themselves on the platform at Kings Cross – standing together like so many couples before them in similar circumstances, couples whose lives the war had interrupted, couples whose futures were clouded with uncertainty. For people who normally chatted so animatedly together, they were strangely uncommunicative. Both found it difficult to find the right words. Finally, after hugging each other for what seemed an eternity, they reluctantly kissed goodbye; Connie then turned away, hiding her tears, and Ron boarded his train. As it pulled out, Connie stopped, turned back and watched transfixed until it disappeared. Rooted to the spot, her mind raced as she rehearsed her perennial concerns about the dangers Ron would inevitably face. She had her own uncertainties too. Where and when would she see her fiancé again? In a way, though, such questions were immaterial. All that really mattered was that he should return home safely. Before she could tear herself away from the platform she offered a silent prayer to this effect – one echoed in her diary for that day, Sunday 18 October: 'When I'll see my darling again I don't know but please God keep him safe wherever he goes and bring him back safely soon for good.'

Once he lost sight of the distant speck that was the woman he loved, Ron's mind went back to the previous evening at home. It hadn't exactly been the prelude to departure that he'd imagined; he knew why though – at least in part. For the first time he'd told his mother that he intended to marry Connie the moment he returned on leave. She seemed less than delighted, taken aback in fact – so much so that it rather soured their farewell. There was much more to be said, he sensed, but there simply wasn't the time. In any event, his mother seemed disinclined to pursue the matter. Given her normally forthright manner, this was a surprise. But with other things on his mind, he thought little more of their brief discussion. That was until he read his mother's letter of 21 October. It was one of the first he received in North Africa and explained a good deal.

She'd written, 'When you said "You don't appear to approve of my marriage Mum" – I wanted to say such a lot – but was too choked.' Having striven hard all her life, 'sacrificed myself . . . working every hour God sends . . . for the love of my boys', Ron's mother was concerned that 'when young folks are in love – as you and Connie are, they are so apt to view life through rose-coloured spectacles & overlook the ordinary side of life.' What followed, from a woman who readily admitted to being 'strictly business-like' about such issues, was effectively a polemic – a discourse on a husband's financial responsibilities. 'I have <u>had</u> to get like this to over-rule our disasters . . .'. The declared aim of what his mother openly acknowledged was a sermon about marriage, was to ensure Ron had his 'eyes opened – & [was] not going blindfold into it'. But having cleared her mind of any potential misgivings as it were, Ron's mother made it clear that, ultimately, she and her husband would support whatever decision he made.

Little did she know it was a decision already made much easier by Ferdie when he wished Ron bon voyage that morning at Forest Gate.

Chapter 25

21 September 1943,
Newport, Monmouthshire

L ife as an ATC official may lack the excitement of Ron's previous life, but travel the length and breadth of Wales is beginning to relieve at least some of the tedium of his new existence.

21 September 1943:

It was a marvellous weekend wasn't it! I felt absolutely marvellous when I was with you . . .

The train was about half an hour late so I couldn't write to you in time yesterday – by the way – I saw Jessie Matthews at Paddington. She was standing in front of me wearing yards of silver foxes – but her face & voice!! – Either would have stopped a clock . . .

I'm returning your book & gloves, one of us must have a very bad memory. I also forgot my hair tonic and 'me eye' – so could you try & remember them when you come down? I'm going to swap 'digs' this morning – actually I'm very busy for some reason – I wrote various letters before I went away & all the replies seem to have come in today.

22 September 1943:

My new billet seems very good – I've again asked about the weekend & they again said – OK – so there you are. I'll let you have a voucher in this letter.

I asked about the food question & they said it would be OK but I'll leave that to you . . .

I'm going up north tomorrow, but what time we'll be back on Sunday is up to the G/C. I hope it's pretty early. I've arranged to go to Swansea district next week but I'll be back on Friday morning – so I'll be in time to meet you . . .

How are you, sweet? That weekend has put me in a good mood for quite a while – a bit disappointed with everything in Newport though!

23 September 1943:

I'm just waiting for the car to come & pick me up & then we're off to N. Wales . . .

I've looked up a train for Friday week & it appears there's one about 5.50 which gets in about 9.1 – I can't find anything which gets in at 7 pm or thereabouts – still – I'll have another look. I won't be able to let you have as much chocolate when you come down next – I won't be able to get to the officers' club to get it . . . I'll do my best to get some when I'm back on Sunday or Friday next.

24 September 1943 (a postcard from Betws-y-Coed):

Being kept very busy – driving all day & seeing ATC at night. Very nice, though – the scenery's very lovely – I'll <u>try</u> & write a letter if I get the chance – I'm a sort of ADC & have to keep the CO up to all his engagements.

27 September 1943 (first of two letters):

This is in a great hurry as you can imagine. I've got 3 days' reports to get in – & prepare to rush off to Swansea – also see the CO when he comes in. I'll try to write tonight & give you all the gen . . .

You'll get this on Tuesday – then it will be only three days before I see you – marvellous!!

27 September 1943 (second letter):

I'm sorry my previous letter this morning was so rushed but I had a lot to do in a short time. As it is it's just 1.30 – I've had lunch but the car won't be ready for a while – something's up with the starter – so I can start a letter to you.

I had a marvellous time with the G/C in N. Wales but I missed my daily letter. Still – I had three when I came back, so that's OK.

Well, darl – I'm off any minute (I hope) so I'll continue later on.
<u>5 pm.</u>

I've reached Swansea OK – although the car isn't going at all well – it scarcely seems to have any 'go' at all. However, as long as it gets me back to Newport I don't mind.

We visited one of the CO's houses (he's got 2) on the way up – you'd love it. There's lots to tell you about our little tour – I'll wait until I see you on Friday before I can give you all the details. By the way, it's very chilly down here so bring your woollies.

The G/C did say that if you wanted to go with me on a tour it would be OK – but since then I've tried to get the gen & and it seems you're not allowed in an RAF car – still – I'll see what the G/C can wangle. By the way, sweet, will you bring down my book of insurance rates – it's in the hall stand at 76 – I may be able to get a life policy for one of the chaps down here . . .

The last sentence in this latest letter is revealing. Ron has maintained contact with his previous employers since leaving the Ocean three years before – and not just because there's the prospect of a return once the war is over. He's always been happy to use his experience and contacts in the insurance business for the benefit of friends and acquaintances, a benefit that manifests itself as a small discount.

28 September 1943:

I'm on my travels [at Llanelli] *still as you can see. I thought I'd be able to save tons of money with the £1 per day I get on my travels but it takes nearly all that to get digs and food where I go. I think that all the hotels are descended from a long line of pirates – still – I'm not losing money, yet.*

I forgot to tell you that when we went on our tour with the G/C we had lunch with the Lord Lieut. of Flintshire – he's an old chap by the name of Admiral Rowley-Conwy[93] – he's a typical old sea dog & made us very welcome – he nearly got us to stay the whole evening but we had to get away.

You'll have to tell me all about this pub my folks are thinking of taking – it sounds pretty unlikely to me – still we've done some pretty peculiar things all told . . .

4 October 1943:

I had a marvellous time over the weekend – it was wonderful having you with me again – now all I've got to look forward to is the weekend after next . . .

---

93. Rear Admiral Rafe Rowley-Conwy CMG, who'd just turned 78.

I asked Mrs Taylor about paying & she said she wouldn't take anything as you brought your own rations & were <u>very</u> welcome at any time!! – so there!

Apparently you were quite a success at my digs – what a wizard wife I've got! . . . I've been quite busy this morning seeing about that insurance policy. I had a long chat with the manager of the local Ocean branch & he's invited me down to his place one night. He seems quite a nice chap . . .

5 October 1943:

I'm so glad you managed to get home in good time – it's such a bad finish to a holiday if you're a long time travelling.

Well, sweet – it seems ages since I saw you last – I'm counting the days again for our next reunion. Only 10 more!

I think I'm working tonight – the G/C's gone to London & said I could have the Vauxhall . . .

By the way, sweet – I've got £8/8/- [£8.40] due to me for expenses for Sept so I think I'll put it towards a new uniform – I do really need one – it's very awkward only having one & I'll never get another if I don't buttonhole this 8/8/-. What do you think of the idea? I thought I'd go up to Austin Reeds when I'm up next & then we can go straight to the Wings Club – how about that?

I'm almost earning my money now – I've got a fair bit of paperwork to do . . .

6 October 1943:

I visited another unit last night – but I'm glad the driver came with me. I enjoyed driving there but coming back in the blackout wasn't very nice – so as he knew the road I let him drive.

These remarks confirm the intimation just a few weeks earlier that Ron is very aware of the challenge driving now represents. Although he's gradually learning to adapt to his visual limitations, caution remains the watchword. Given the regularity with which he goes on to mention his motoring experiences, it's a challenge that's always at the back of his mind.

7 October 1943:

I had no visit to do last night so I went to see Mr Hodges – the chap we were supposed to see on Sunday. He was feeling much better – although on Sunday his eyes were so swollen he was quite blind so it's just as well we didn't go.

J.H. Thomas was visiting Mr Hodges when I arrived. He's the chap who left the government some years ago over some Budget business. I always thought he was a terribly common chap but he certainly has a personality & his stories of the House of Commons & Law Courts kept us absolutely thrilled for an hour. He left after tea so we sat in front of the fire & talked shop. Mr Hodges is going up to London Friday week & I think he's staying at the Park Lane Hotel – however – they don't have music there & he thought you'd prefer music with your meals – <u>so</u> if he stays over Saturday night and Mrs Hodges goes with him he asked me if we'd like to have a bit of dinner & dance at the Piccadilly Grill – he'll let me know later if he's stopping up there. I thought we could have tea at the Wings Club & then carry on. What do you think of the idea, old plum? . . .

The erstwhile Labour politician who, much to his surprise, so impresses Ron was a colourful individual. Newport-born J.H. 'Jimmy' Thomas was brought up by his grandmother and began life as a railway worker at the age of 12. He went on to become General Secretary of the National Union of Railwaymen, a position he retained whilst MP for Derby. Known for his sartorial elegance and ability to mix across all levels of society, he was forced to resign as Secretary of State for the Colonies in 1936 following a scandal involving budget leaks. Undeterred, he marked his departure from office with characteristic style and humour. Churchill is said to have been brought to tears by his resignation speech in the Commons. Just turned 69 when Ron met him, Thomas had clearly lost none of his oft-remarked zest for life.

10 October 1943:

Since we'd heard of the London raids I'd been thinking 'Ah, young Tubby will give me all the gen in her next letter' – lo and behold, when the letter arrives – no gen on bombings!

I hope that's because you weren't bothered by them – only I read of a Goodmayes chap getting killed & thought it would be near you – still – I'd rather hear 'nice' bits from you rather than bombs . . .

I had a very nice letter from Jack <u>Hilton</u> yesterday – he's looking forward to a letter from you – he's a grand chap – I hope we can go up and spend a couple of days with him later on.

The raids to which Ron refers, on the night of 7/8 October when thirty-five were killed, came a little too close for comfort. Vere Hodgson described the experience thus:

> Jolly old Wailer set up on Thursday night. This time it was the goods. Gunfire loud and frequent. Searchlights filled the sky and planes caught in them. Lots of people watching. Ladbroke Square gun cracking out. Donned my tin hat – courage returned and I joined the sightseers. All London was doing the same. Shells bursting and amazing fireworks filled the air above us. Went in for the News – then came another wave of bombers. Our bombers were on the way out as the Germans came in – sometimes the searchlights caught one of ours, and sometimes the enemy.
>
> Heard next morning that 30 tons of bombs had dropped. Woodford, Ilford, Grays, Battersea, Hampstead . . . some say Red Lion Square and Vauxhall Bridge. Windows of Woolworths in Kensington High St blown out by one of our shells . . . [94]

11 October 1943:

I received your letter this morning & it certainly sounds as though things are getting a bit more noisy in London. As long as you're OK that's all I worry about . . .

I'm off to lunch now dear – & then I'm away on my travels again. I'm due home every night so my time will be taken up pretty well in driving to & fro . . .

Cheerio – till Friday . . .

---

94. Hodgson, op. cit., p.421.

12 October 1943:

I've been very busy this morning – It's 12.15 & I've only just started this letter to you. It's awfully good being able to see each other every fortnight, as you said. I doubt if I'd be able to have so much time with you even if I got nearer . . .

Darl – will you remind me to bring back here:-

(A) *Flying boots*

(B) *Photo of sqdn*

If I've got to visit gliding sites amid lots of wet grass – then my boots will be a great help. I may be seeing Chas next weekend – I've got to go to his aerodrome for a question on gliding – so with luck I'll be able to have an odd noggin with him.

How's the blitz these days – is our little flat OK? . . .

It's not long to Christmas now – is it, old Tub – just imagine – a whole week . . .

13 October 1943:

Before I go any farther please note that I <u>wasn't</u> peeved over you not telling me of the blitz – I just thought that it would be a spot of news for you to put in – especially as it was so near home . . .

I've got an early job to do today – visit a school unit – so I should have the evening to myself . . .

It's been very nice driving these last few nights – there's been a full moon out & it's been almost like driving in the daytime . . .

I'll be awfully glad to see you sweet – I get rather 'down' about the end of a fortnight. I don't know how I managed to go a whole month at first without seeing you . . .

14 October 1943:

Believe it or not, darl, but I've been kept quite busy these last two or three mornings & I haven't been able to start your letter until about 11.30-12 each day. However – it passes the time & makes Friday seem to come all the quicker – so I can't grumble . . .

Mr Hodges is not staying in London this weekend – he's going to Leicester – so our night at the Piccadilly Grill is off – still – we'll find something to do I've no doubt . . .

I'm trying to catch the 10.38 tomorrow . . .

18 October 1943:

I have to be at Llandrindod early tomorrow afternoon – so I shall have to pop off fairly early tomorrow morning – hence the fact I'm writing to you now in case I don't get time tomorrow.

I'll write tomorrow evening but in the meantime thank you once again for a very happy weekend. I had a wonderful time with you dear – and I'm getting to love you more & more.

19 October 1943:

I'm in the 'interior' as you put it, with a vengeance – the actual place is Llandrindod, as I believe I told you. In peacetime it was undoubtedly a very nice Spa with loads of hotels – but now what aren't taken over for various purposes are full of <u>old</u> fogies & <u>very</u> old fogies & army instructors . . .

I had quite a nice drive here except for one point where I was told to go one way & avoid something or other but I ended up by reaching the top of a mountain & then having to come all the way down again through a very narrow winding road with a damn great drop on one side. However, I got here OK and after inspecting the unit I was invited to the CO's house for tea. He'd invited the other two officers as well. His wife had the tea all laid & left us to it, so we had a very nice bachelor tea & talk & then I came on here . . .

Darl – you should really see the old dodderers here. Some are playing cards, the rest are discussing ailments. It's just started to pour with rain & everyone is discussing it with great vim & vigour. (It's certainly raining very hard, at that!) . . .

20 October 1943:

I arrived here this morning after a very pleasant drive across country & was lucky enough to get a room for tonight.

This really is a very one-eyed dump – the cinema apparently opens only Mon. Tues. Fri & Sat evenings – the local library only once a fortnight & that's about the sum total of life in Presteigne. Actually the hotel itself [the Radnorshire Arms] is excellent. The rooms are large with modern basins etc. & the food is very good indeed.

The beer isn't at all bad. I had a pint with my lunch and feel quite pleased with life . . .

I've been here since about 11 am – I'm due out at 7 pm to see the local unit & after that I'll probably crawl into a chair and read. There are quite a few old people here who were at Bournemouth and suchlike places – found themselves too near the war & so decided to live here for the duration.

It's a marvellous place for rest but I think I'd go crackers if I had to stay here very long. I'm off on my travels again tomorrow . . .

21 October 1943:

It poured with rain nearly all the time I was driving up here, but, nevertheless, it was quite a pretty run & I arrived just in time for lunch. I'm at Llanidloes today, staying at the 'Unicorn' – by the way, most of these places are in the AA book if you want any more gen on them. I wrote two reports out this afternoon & then settled in by the fire to do the 'DE' crossword but needless to say I was asleep in ten minutes & slept solidly until tea time, when I got dirty looks from the three other people here for nearly letting the fire go out . . .

A year ago tonight at roughly the same time & certainly the same weather (raining like Hell) I climbed on board the ship which took us all to Gibraltar. Funny how time flies & what can happen in a short while isn't it?

I felt as miserable as sin & was sure I wouldn't see you for at least 18 months, & tonight, although I'm away from you I'm happy in the knowledge that I'm married to you & can be with you in a few hours if need be – it makes a world of difference, you know.

Every now & again I stop writing and think of one or two things which happened whilst I was abroad – I shall always remember some things.

Do you remember how pleased I was when I had that cable from you & how I wrote and said I'd read it a dozen times, both to myself & other people.

Well, sweet, there's not much actual news – I'm not due at the ATC unit for another two hours so I'll pop out & post this. I'm told there's a post at 6.30 . . .

There are a couple of anomalies here. First, although Ron's letter suggests that he 'climbed on board' his ship on 21 October 1942, both his diary and his log book indicate that he left Liverpool the previous day. Given that he eventually docked on 6 November, and the voyage took 'seventeen anxious days',[95] it's clear that he actually boarded on the evening of 20 October and set sail next morning. Jimmy Corbin's diary confirms as much.

The second incongruity is that while he may possibly have broadcast the contents of Connie's telegram, there's no indication of this in any of his letters. Moreover, it would seem out of character for one who rails against others 'talking about their wives & girlfriends' and prefers to keep personal feelings 'locked away'. Be that as it may, as Ron evokes memories of his embarkation for North Africa, we can turn back the clock a year, almost to the day . . .

---

95. Oxspring, op. cit., p.119.

Chapter 26

19 October 1942, APO
(Army Post Office) 4330

O n Monday 19 October, the day after Ron bade Connie a sad farewell at Kings Cross, he became a combatant in transit. Obliged now to use a surrogate address, the letter he wrote that day amidst last-minute preparations for the squadron's departure was sent from APO 4330 (postmarked Manchester). It would be the last he'd mail to Connie before setting sail. The aforesaid preparations included survival lectures and inoculations, prompting thoughts the squadron might be bound for the Far East. But it was not to be.

When his ship, the HMT[96] *Staffordshire*, sailed from Liverpool's Ellesmere Port, sadly in one sense but happily in another, amongst Ron's colleagues there was no George Malan. He was on honeymoon and it would be more than a month before he finally caught up with the rest of the squadron. Also left behind was the bulk of everyone's kit. All that crews were allowed to take with them was what could be stowed safely in a Spitfire: toiletries, a change of clothes and any other essentials. In Ron's case these included writing materials, inevitably, and one or two pictures. There wasn't even space for his pocket diary; that would arrive later, together with all the other personal effects he had to leave behind.

19 October 1942:

Excuse the pencil & scrawl but I've no ink for my pen & my arm's full of injections.

I arrived back on Sunday night OK & rushed around getting a parachute bag for my parachute – a pair of boots & one injection. We came over to this place this morning – or rather tonight – were booked in & told to prepare

---

96. The *Staffordshire* was designated as Hired Military Transport (HMT), i.e. a troopship.

for another injection. My left arm was so sore from yesterday that I had it in my right – it hurt at first but appears to be dying off now.

I got your telegram today – thanks so much darling – it was so lovely of you . . . Well, sweetheart it's come at last so all we can do is just hope for the best & pray it won't be long before I see you again. You were awfully good at the train dear – I was so proud of you but when you went I almost broke down – Tubby darl – I do love you . . .

The censorship first introduced in early October now comes into its own; 'this place' referred to above was Wilmslow. Ron was part of a small group sent there for further inoculations; it included the CO, Jimmy Corbin, Owen Hardy and Johnny Lowe, and resulted from splitting the squadron into two batches – an unpopular move immediately prior to their deployment and one that prompted the obvious question: why? 'Lowe looked a little shocked' when Corbin explained: 'If we get torpedoed on the way, the whole squadron gets wiped out. By splitting up, at least one half has a chance of getting through and carrying on with the fight.'[97]

In his next letter, the first Ron writes once embarked, the date has been neatly excised by 'Examiner 1,795'; there's no date/location stamp on the envelope either. It might possibly have been written on 20 October, the evening before he sailed. In any event, it would be over a month before it eventually reached Connie, on 28 November.

20 (?) October 1942:

I can't tell you any news because everything I could tell you of the past two or three days would be censored – so you'll just have to wait until I arrive wherever we're going and then maybe I'll be allowed to tell you some of the past . . .

We've got quite a good selection of books and we all spend a good part of the time reading and smoking.

I managed to get hold of quite a few tins of 'Capstan' [tobacco] & stand a fair chance of getting some 'plug' as well – I'll buy as much as I can afford then I'll be able to exist until we get things organised wherever we end up.

I managed to scribble a short note to Dicky before I left just giving him my address. I told him to keep writing to you to get all the latest gen. What do you think of his ideas about getting, or rather not getting engaged? Actually, it does need a bit of thinking about if he hasn't got a job to do when the war's over.

---

97. Corbin, op. cit., p.154.

It's all been very interesting so far & from what we can gather I don't think we're likely to have time hanging heavily on our hands – at least that'll make it go quicker whilst I'm waiting to see you again.

Built in 1929 by Fairfield Shipbuilding & Engineering at Govan, Ron's temporary home, the *Staffordshire,* looked and felt even older. This was in part due to the way the vessel had been adapted to wartime needs. He and his colleagues were housed in one of the holds, deep in the bowels of the ship, where they slept in makeshift wooden bunks. Not only was it uncomfortable, it was also incredibly noisy; they were next to what they assumed must have been a couple of coal bunkers. Almost the final straw was the ship's regular pitching and tossing, which simply added to their discomfort.

Above them on deck were numerous boxed aircraft, each individual crate marked in foot-high letters with the word 'Gibraltar' – the last place cynics thought would be their destination. As they sailed north to the Clyde and joined a large convoy, there seemed to be ships and aircraft everywhere. Small landing craft zipping to and fro and a number of aircraft, mainly Dakotas, overhead made for an impressive sight. Soon, though, they were heading for the Atlantic, still with no idea of how long their confinement would be, or indeed where they were bound.

In an effort to solve this latter mystery, Ron and a colleague managed to gain access to the chart-room, but to little avail. From what they could see, after heading initially towards the Azores, the convoy almost reached New York before turning east again; then, after a couple of pirouettes, it set course for . . . they were still none the wiser. All they knew was that they were part of a mixed convoy of merchantmen with a defensive screen comprising a number of corvettes and an aircraft carrier. In all there were some fifty vessels, many of them laden with aviation fuel and ammunition as well as the crated aircraft lashed on deck. The convoy would make a juicy target for German U-boat packs, which explains its circuitous routing – a necessary precaution given that most vessels were ill-equipped to defend themselves. The *Staffordshire* itself was fitted with only limited armament: Oerlikon 20 mm cannon operated by merchant seamen gunners. Pairs of aircrew spent many an hour in these gun emplacements, scouring the sea for any sign of enemy submarines. If nothing else, it helped pass the time and provided a welcome change from their accommodation in a 'windowless drifting dungeon'.[98] Ron's letters continue the story.

---

98. Oxspring, op. cit., p.119.

26 October 1942:

I don't know whether my other letters have reached you – the first should have done since it was posted before I sailed but I'm not sure of the second. I think they hold back some letters for a time until we're safely away but I'm not too sure.

You'll have to excuse the writing as the ship is rolling like Hell & we have an awful job to eat let alone write.

When we first came on board the Wing/Co decided we should have a sweep on who was sick first – it was rather funny really – the chap who drew the w/co didn't think he had much of a chance but after we'd been floating around in the ocean for some time sure enough the w/co made a leap for the stairs & it was all up.

So far we've been fairly lucky as although the seas have been pretty bad & the ship has been tossing about like a dingbat the w/co is the only one who's been sick.

We read, smoke & play cards nearly all day as there's very little else to do – it's been damn cold & blowy so far but seems to be a bit warmer today.

Actually I'm thoroughly brassed off with ships & I know that once I get home I'm going to sit by the fire and not budge – (until I go to bed!).

The other night I was on deck & the sea was quite calm – I couldn't help thinking about the Embankment & us. The rail is just about the same height as the wall of the Embankment – how I wished I were back there with you.

I'm glad in a way that we came away as soon as I left you – I should have hated to have had to stay in England & not been able to see you again. A quick breakaway seems to get over things much better.

Well, sweetheart, how are things with you? Tubby, dear, I do miss you such a lot – I miss you even more when everyone starts talking about their wives & girlfriends. From the way they talk I don't see why half of them got married – they can't possibly love them wholeheartedly or they'd never mention half the things they do – still, that's their business but I'm hanged if I'd ever bring you into the conversation. What I think of you & just how much you mean to me is something I keep locked away – that only concerns you & me.

There's not much else to tell you at the moment, darling, so I'll pack up for a day or so and continue when I've got a bit more news for you. I don't know when you'll get this but I hope it's soon – I'll post it as soon as we reach a port.

29 (?) October 1942

Good morning darling – I've just had breakfast, had a wash & shave, & can now settle down to a spot more letter writing. I did 'dawn readiness' this morning – we all take turns at going on the bridge & keeping a look-out for subs, enemy A/C, etc. – it was very cold, windy & rough this morning but at least that gives you an appetite for breakfast.

We had quite a good day yesterday – it actually started (the 'good' part) in the afternoon. I was lying on my bunk reading when the W/Co came in & asked me to make up a four at pontoon. I wasn't very keen but I went. Anyway – we played for half an hour & I managed to win 10/- [50p] – then we packed up & later on four of us were playing poker & the W/Co, keen on revenge, asked to come in – he did – & we took another 13/- [65p] from him – bags of fun. Still – he almost had his own back at night by taking 14/- [70p] off me – even so I'm still doing well so can't grumble.

That's about all that's happened to us since I last wrote – we tried to get some gen on where we're going but were unsuccessful. At any rate, we should know something pretty soon.

I won't write to Kay, dear, although if I've bags of time I may drop her one letter – so will __you__ give her my regards & any gen I give you.

Having been on this ship over a week I can understand why Joe [Dobbs – a swimming friend] *got a shore job – I've never had such a brassing time – every day we look out there's just sea all around us going up and down. Why these old salts speak of 'the call of the sea' I can't imagine.*

By the way – there's no doubt that all our letters will be censored so we'd better get one thing settled to begin with. When you write will you tell me how my letters are censored? – Some people just black-out the parts which shouldn't be in & others cut the piece out. If mine are cut I'll only write on one side . . .

There's the end of another chapter – I'll continue in due course.

I think it's the 30th Oct today but I'm not sure. No one seems to care a great deal . . .

We don't have any newspapers or radio – consequently we have only a vague idea of what's been happening whilst we've been ploughing the seas. Not that it matters a great deal to us but I'd love to have a Daily Express crossword to do. I've read at least eight books and even poker is beginning to pall.

Whilst I'm writing two chaps are playing 'Battleships' – so you can see how bored we are.

It's been quite warm today & I was almost tempted by the Wing/Co to hang over the side and get pulled along by a rope, but I had visions of being drawn up the side in a swimming costume & getting all the skin taken off me so I politely declined . . .

It was damn funny the other night – there was a terrific bang and everyone thought at least we'd been torpedoed – one chap was dressed & out the door before I was even awake – another one dressed & shot out but just as he did, the ship gave a lurch and he came hurtling back almost before he'd left. In any case, all that had happened was that an iron gadget had come loose & dropped on the deck making quite a din. All these little things help to amuse us & pass the time but I can still do without being torpedoed – especially tonight – I've just had a bath (more later).

<u>3rd or 4th</u> [November]

Good morning, sweet. We're still travelling – altho' we should arrive at our destination in a day or so & then I can get this posted.

As I've told Mum, – the place is like a laundry – everyone, bar me, has been doing his smalls & all you can see now is a row of shirts, towels, socks and hankies on the line.

We heard that Canterbury had a daylight raid the other day – I wish they'd started something like that when I was down there.

Cravatte seems quite popular these days – especially because it takes such a long time to play out. Old Hruby would make his fortune here – I'm not doing so badly & I'm not very good at it . . .

This morning we saw land in the distance. It shouldn't be long before we get ashore now.

Dearest, I can't tell you how much I've missed you & how I long for this job to be over – whenever I'm away from you everything seems so futile – as though I'm doing something to put in the time until I see you again. The next period in our lives is going to be very trying for both of us but if we can get over it OK, then when we're married everything is going to be just marvellous.

I'll close the letter now, dear, as I think we're docking today & I want to post this as soon as I can . . .

Once their ship docked – at Gibraltar, despite everyone's scepticism – on 6 November, Ron and his colleagues were billeted ashore in Nissen huts. Lacking any information on the next stage of their deployment, sightseeing became the order of the day. A number managed the occasional excursion

200

into Gibraltar town, but it failed to impress. The main street appeared to consist of a number of bars, most of them up on the first floor, where climbing the stairs was fraught with danger. Local bartenders had a unique way of disposing of those who over-imbibed: they simply threw them down the stairs. Ron once found his progress along the street halted by just such an unfortunate, collapsed at the roadside after emerging through a doorway like a champagne cork.

On another occasion, after changing what little money he had into French francs, Ron enjoyed a 'very, very tasty' meal with David Cox. (What was advertised as steak they later learned was actually horsemeat.) A Battle of Britain veteran Ron both liked and respected, D.G.S.R. Cox had joined the squadron in May; in a few short weeks, and in unusual circumstances, he was destined to take over as OC A Flight.

On 12 November Ron sent Connie a Post Office telegram: 'DARLING LANDED AT LAST ALMOST FIRST PERSON I MET WAS BOB MITCHELL AM GOING OUT WITH HIM TONIGHT THINGS AREN'T SO BAD WITH ME HAVE WRITTEN THREE LETTERS THE LAST ONE MAY TAKE SOME TIME REACHING YOU WILL CABLE AGAIN IF POSSIBLE ALL MY LOVE.' Truth be told, he'd seen neither hide nor hair of the individual mentioned here. However, he knew that Connie would be aware that Bob Mitchell served as a flight lieutenant on the meteorological flight at Gibraltar; it was mentioned in one of their regular swimming club news sheets.[99] It was simply his way of letting her know where he was.

He needn't have bothered with this subterfuge. Connie had a Cable & Wireless contact who was soon able to confirm the telegram's origin. Then, two days later, a second telegram arrived, this time via Cable & Wireless, clearly stamped 'Gibraltar': 'MY OWN DARLING I SENT TWO MORE LETTERS YESTERDAY STILL OK NO MORE NEWS I LOVE YOU HOPE EVERYTHING WELL WITH ALL AT HOME I LOVE YOU AGAIN.'

Delighted to be in contact at last, Connie was prompted to try cabling Ron in Gibraltar. On 16 November she sent a brief message: 'DARLING HAVE RECEIVED TWO CABLES WRITING REGULARLY ALWAYS THINKING OF YOU.' But she was too late. By the time it arrived the squadron was already en route to their new location. Ron managed one last letter before they left for Algiers.

---

99. This same information subsequently appeared in *The Swimming Times* of November 1942.

12 November 1942:

This won't be a very long letter so if it arrives before the one with all the news in it don't think I'm dodging my letter writing – you should get quite a stack of correspondence in the near future. I wrote 14 pages to you on the boat but the letter didn't go Air Mail so I'm not at all sure when you'll get it.

The photos I've got are the ones we took in our garden when I was a sergeant. You do look sweet darling – I spend all day thinking how grand it's going to be when I get home to you again. This life just wouldn't be worth living if I didn't have you to think about. The war doesn't seem to be going too badly at the moment – although it can't go too quickly for me. The sooner I'm back with you the happier I'm going to be . . .

Keep smiling, darl – we're in this lark & have just got to take things as they come, but everything's going to come out right for us in the end . . .

Four days after this final despatch from civilisation, Ron picked up his flying kit and reported to the airstrip along with the other 72 Squadron pilots. Here they were confronted by a strange sight: Spitfire Vbs devoid of registration numbers or identification lettering and modified for tropical operations. The give-away in this latter respect was the large Vokes air filter under the nose, just behind the propeller boss. Another unfamiliar appendage was the 90-gallon long-range fuel tank fitted beneath each fuselage. Full of fuel it weighed some 750 lbs and posed a dilemma for pilots who'd never flown with one before – which was everyone. *How would the aircraft handle? How does the tank actually work? Should we start with it selected, or with the main tank and then transfer to the auxiliary?* There was no time to address such questions; the imperative was to get moving.

Ron quickly removed the armour-plating behind his seat, stuffed the parachute bag containing his few possessions behind him, replaced the panel and followed Bob Oxspring as he took off. Little did he know, but his squadron was now part of the Allied invasion of North Africa. Operation TORCH, commanded by US General (later President) Dwight Eisenhower, had begun just a few days earlier, on 8 November.

Gibraltar may have been a hive of Spitfire activity when the squadron left, but when Ron arrived after a flight of nearly three hours, Algiers was something else altogether. The port itself had been a primary TORCH objective. Its huge airfield, Maison Blanche, captured only days before, was already packed to the gunnels with different types, from huge American

B-17 Flying Fortresses to tiny French Tiger Moth lookalikes.[100] Confronted with something that resembled an ants' nest, and with no idea where to park their own aircraft, the squadron simply taxied to a relatively quiet area near the runway, shut down and awaited developments. They came by way of an individual who noted everyone's details and, somewhat unhelpfully, told them to find somewhere to eat and sleep. The first problem was solved courtesy of a café near the airfield boundary, which provided a distinctly unappetising greasy meal but at least it was food. Beds were more of a problem. Everyone ended up sleeping on a hangar floor, wrapped in what little clothing they had with them. Aware that the airfield was now an important enemy target, it proved a worrying and less than comfortable night for all concerned; mercifully, though, it was free from interruption.

Next morning, Tuesday 17 November, the squadron was tasked with mounting patrols over the airfield and nearby docks, activity designed to discourage Luftwaffe attacks, typically by Ju 88 bombers or Me 109 fighters; occasionally, though, it was both. This commitment lasted just twenty-four hours. Next day the entire squadron was sent to Bône, another airfield/port complex nearly 300 miles further to the east, close to the Tunisian border. The contrast with Maison Blanche could not have been more marked. Bône's runway bore a striking resemblance to a single track road hacked out of rough terrain; everywhere else was simply a mass of stones, holes and dust.

Ron was amongst the first to arrive and taxi to a rudimentary dispersal, no more than a concrete block house. It was a rude awakening in more ways than one. A pair of Me 109s suddenly appeared and began strafing the airfield. Ron's first instinct was self-preservation but, other than the single concrete building, there was nowhere to hide. He felt incredibly exposed. *How did this happen? Where's the top cover?* A pair of 72 Squadron Spitfires was supposed to be providing airfield protection, insurance against just such an attack, but the aircraft were nowhere to be seen. While the squadron survived this assault relatively unscathed, the unexpected intrusion brought an uncomfortable reminder of just how vulnerable both aircraft and personnel were on the ground. It was a danger the squadron was to become acutely, and indeed tragically, aware of in the weeks to come.

Not long after six in the evening, darkness arrived. In the absence of any administrative support, together with his colleagues Ron made his way into the nearby town in search of somewhere to sleep. His luck was in – in

---

100. The Belgian Stampe-Vertongen SV4, built under licence in France.

more ways than one. Not only did he find a hotel, he ran into an instructor he'd known at Hawarden, 'Jimmy' Baraldi,[101] who'd arrived just a few days earlier. A flight commander on 111 Squadron, he spoke French well enough to arrange a number of rooms. That said, the absence of any lights, or even candles, meant that it was a case of every man for himself. After blundering around for some time searching for somewhere to lay his head, in the end Ron found himself sharing a double bed with Johnny Lowe. Sadly, his overnight companion would be killed only ten days later.

Back at the airfield next morning, together with Owen Hardy, Ron was scheduled for the first patrol of the day: protecting the aerodrome and harbour. But there was a problem. Like all the squadron's aircraft, their Spitfires were still fitted with long-range tanks. Just as they had no idea how the tanks operated, they were equally clueless about how to remove them. After exhausting every possibility inside the cockpit they decided the only solution was a two-man enterprise: one to operate the appropriate cockpit lever, the other to deliver a mighty kick in order to free the tank from its 'moorings'. Having found a workable solution, lest others should find themselves similarly hamstrung, the pair proceeded to exploit their new-found technical expertise and similarly disencumber all the remaining aircraft. This done, and feeling mildly pleased with themselves, they finally set off on patrol.

Relatively early in their sortie, while operating close to the airfield, an Me 109 suddenly appeared at extremely low level. It carried out a single strafing run then turned east for the safety of German-held territory. With Hardy in the lead both Spitfires immediately gave chase, but the Messerschmitt was proving difficult to catch. Not only had they little height advantage to aid their acceleration, unbeknown to them the Spitfire's tropical modifications, especially the new air filter, brought performance limitations, reducing both top speed and rate of climb.[102] Eventually, however, Hardy manoeuvred close enough to fire a couple of bursts from directly astern, the second of which saw the German fighter engulfed in flames before it crashed to the ground. It was the first confirmed 'kill' of 72 Squadron's North Africa campaign. The excitement whetted Ron's appetite for action. Tasked with a sweep later that same day over enemy-held Beja, some eighty miles to the east, his log

---

101. Ferdinand Henry Raphael 'Jimmy' Baraldi left 111 Squadron soon afterwards, in January 1943, suffering from vision problems.
102. To overcome the reductions in top speed (by some eight knots) and rate of climb (by 600 ft/min) the outboard cannons were quickly removed, reducing weight and producing a small increase in speed.

book entry reflects frustration at the lack of enemy targets: 'Nothing repeat nothing seen.'

The next day he seemed to have been in bed for scarcely more than five minutes when the call came for everyone to get up and get packed. A task that would normally have taken a matter of minutes took considerably longer in the pitch dark of an unfamiliar hotel bedroom. Eventually, weary crews emerged into a surprisingly cool morning – it seemed much colder than the 50°F (10°C) indicated – heaved their parachute bags into a number of trucks and motored back to Bône. Tasked once again with sweeps over Beja, the continuing dearth of targets proved frustrating for a squadron primed now for action. Returning crews were further piqued by airborne instructions to land at a different base, Souk-el-Arba. Less than halfway back to Bône, apparently it would be easy to recognise: there was a crashed aircraft, a French Potez, in the centre of the airfield. And so there was. But it was like no airfield anyone had ever seen before. Reflecting on his arrival there, Ron likened it to 'landing on the moon. It was rough, hard mud with the usual dust and potholes and we wondered how long our tyres would last.'

Souk-el-Arba itself, no more than a large village, sat at one end of the runway, joined to the airfield by a road with ditches either side that ran straight through the middle of the field. It therefore seemed sensible to park all the squadron's aircraft on one side of the airfield, away from the nearest ditch. Conscious of the inviting target a dozen or so Spitfires represented, pilots congregated on the other side of the ditches and once again awaited developments. Eventually troops arrived, together with supplies of petrol and ammunition. This came both as a relief and a surprise. They had no idea that another unit, No. 111 Squadron, was already in residence. With nothing else to do, the aircrew set about helping to pile four-gallon petrol cans into the ditches, partially hidden under trees; there were no other storage options. It was an inauspicious welcome to their new home.

Chapter 27

22 October 1943, Welshpool

Despite numerous travel opportunities that break the monotony, with little to do in his Newport office Ron finds plenty of time for contemplation – soul-searching that's about to produce a change of heart that might, on the face of it, appear surprising. However, reading between the lines there have been signs of dissatisfaction, of disillusion even, in his correspondence for some time. But there's none of this in his next few letters. They're unusually upbeat. For the first time in a year or so he's hoping to meet members of his old squadron.

22 October 1943:

My programme today was almost identical with that of yesterday. I had an excellent breakfast . . . then I just ambled slowly up here to Welshpool . . .

I rang Chas just before lunch & said I'd be up to see him but he's going up to AM [Air Ministry] *on Saturday to see about a posting – he's very keen to see some action again – after all – he's been at an OTU for nearly six months.*

Anyway – Owen Hardy is up at this place so I'll go & see him on Sat. & then go to the satellite & see Chas on Sunday – he's back at midnight on Sat.

If I can I'll take Owen with me – he can always sleep at Chas's place & fly back the next day . . .

It was very nice where I was yesterday at Llanidloes – although if you haven't a car it would be a bit awkward. It's a very ancient town with a sort of market building on stilts in the middle of the square. The building is high enough to walk under and has about 8 brick supports – it's all beams & leaded-paned windows. Quite a few of the houses have beams – very old like! The country starts almost at the end of the main street – you don't get gradually into it – it's awfully pretty . . .

23 October 1943:

I've had a very good day so far – I arrived at this aerodrome & rang Owen Hardy the New Zealand chap who used to be with us in N. Africa. I believe I've already told you he used to share a tent with George & Lew [P/O H.S. Lewis, an American] *& I – anyway, he was very surprised to see me & we spent much of the lunch hour talking over the old days. After lunch he had to give a lecture & then he took me over to his dispersal & gave me a flip for 40 minutes in a Master.*

I was as pleased as blazes – I took over as soon as we were airborne & had the time of my life. It wasn't strange to me at all – everything seemed to come back naturally – I did one or two rolls and chased other aircraft – it was a lovely afternoon. I'm very glad I can still fly after not touching it for a year.

There's an Ensa concert tonight so we'll go to that & then to bed. Tomorrow I'm off to see Chas but I don't know whether Owen can come yet or not.

You'll be pleased to hear that my old longing to get back on flying is gradually going. I enjoyed my flip this afternoon no end, but I'm getting so used to the life I've been leading lately that I'm quite happy to leave flying alone – although I'm pleased to know that I can still fly . . .

Tubs – I do miss you – you'll probably not think so after what I've said about flying today – but for some reason or other it made me miss you even more than usual . . .

It's now 11 pm & I'm in my room for the night. It's certainly not like Biggin but it's not bad. I realise now what a cushy job I've got & how good it is to live out. The show was very good indeed – the comedian harped mostly on RAF life but it fairly made us roar – I wish you could have seen it.

Ron's sortie with Owen Hardy in the Master is the final entry in his log book: 'First trip since I was shot down. Marvellous!!' Despite thoroughly enjoying the experience, it represents the crossing of a personal Rubicon. He's resigned himself to the end of his flying career and increasingly looks forward to leaving the RAF. If nothing else, bowing to the inevitable will assuage his wife's barely hidden concerns, as he's about to acknowledge.

25 October 1943:

You didn't sound very happy when I told you I flew on Saturday. At least, you sounded quite pleased but I don't think you were – anyway – before you get this you should have a letter from Oswestry explaining just how I feel about it – so I hope that will make you feel better. Anyway – I'll tell you again – I'm quite happy as things are – and my longing for flying definitely takes a back seat when I think of how you'd worry, and then I might not be able to see you so often . . .

Anyway, sweetheart, believe it or not – I do respect your wishes & know you'd worry like blazes if I did much flying – so there you are.

1 November 1943:

Tubs – that was a marvellous week end – I had a grand time!

I shook everyone this morning – I was the first one here – the cleaners had a large fire in my room so I sat in the armchair reading the paper.

The CO came in at 9.30 – the earliest he's been in for years – it's a good job I was a busy little bee or I might have had a raspberry. However – all was well – he asked me what we did and whether you had a nice time.

4 November 1943:

The CO is going up to London for the weekend & said I could go with him if I like. Of course – 'I liked' – so we're coming up on Friday morning & going back on Monday afternoon. I'll try & phone you this evening & explain a bit better – but I'm so excited I scarcely know what I'm writing. Fancy seeing you two weeks running!!

I still think I can get the following week too!

9 November 1943:

Well, sweet, – I arrived at the Mayfair OK & had lunch with the CO, Mrs B.[103] & Taffy Jones. Taffy was a famous last war pilot – he stutters like mad & knows all the chaps in 72. I believe I told you of him before. He's a hell of a good egg. Anyway – apart from a slight mishap on the way back everything was fine. We just scraped another car but damage was nil on both sides so that's OK.

P.S. We met S/Ldr Learoyd V.C. at the Mayfair as well.

---

103. Mrs B's husband, the CO, is referred to elsewhere as GB or the G/C; however, he's never identified.

Ron has just spent time in company with two men whose place in RAF history is assured. They deserve more than a simple name check.

Group Captain Ira 'Taffy' Jones DSO MC DFC* MM served, and indeed flew, in both world wars. An ace in the first, with more than twenty-eight confirmed 'kills', he provided a link with one of Ron's early heroes: Edward 'Mick' Mannock.[104] Firm friends when they flew together on 74 Squadron in France, Jones remained close to Mannock after the latter took command of 85 Squadron. In fact, less than twenty-four hours before Mannock was killed, Jones drove over to his base for one of the regular chats they'd promised themselves now that they were on separate units; little did they know that it would be their last meal together.

Jones rejoined as soon as war broke out once again. At the time of his most celebrated feat he was commanding No. 7 Bombing and Gunnery School, RAF Porthcawl. Flying an unarmed Hawker Henley (a two-seat Hurricane derivative used for target towing), he attacked a Ju 88 with the Very pistol normally used for firing flares and drove it off. Later in 1940, as commander of No. 57 OTU at Hawarden, he came to know many of Ron's Spitfire colleagues. He particularly admired Brian Kingcome, which gave the pair plenty to talk about over lunch.

Acting Flight Lieutenant Roderick 'Babe' Learoyd earned his VC in August 1940 during a night low-level Hampden attack on an aqueduct on the Dortmund-Ems canal, a strategically important target. In the face of intense fire that destroyed two aircraft and damaged a number of others, his own was hit several times and badly damaged. He nevertheless pressed home his attack at 150 feet before nursing his crippled aircraft back to Scampton. With damaged undercarriage and flaps, he circled until first light to reduce the chances of injury to his three crew members during the eventual landing. The citation for his award noted inter alia that Learoyd had 'repeatedly shown . . . complete indifference to personal danger'.

10 November 1043:

Well, sweet, I wasn't sure whether I could get up to London until I saw the G/C this morning. He's not going up on Friday but he said I'm to take the car up & get the glider & come back on Monday – so that's worked out fine. I expect to be up at Woodford about 3.30 on Friday . . .

---

104. Major E.C. Mannock VC DSO** MC* was credited with 61 aerial victories; he died in July 1916, the victim of ground fire. Jones later published a biography of his greatly admired friend, *King of Air Fighters*.

11 November 1943:

I think it's a much better idea if we stay home on Saturday – I don't suppose Vickie would care to go up to town after having travelled from B'ham the same afternoon. We can show her some of our Bing.

Well, old darling – I must put on a show of work, so I'll bid you a fond farewell.

16 November 1943:

I'm so glad you enjoyed the weekend darl, I'm sure Vickie did & I certainly did. I'm going to drop a note to Vickie sometime today – & also one to Owen about George's decoration.

The issue of 'George's decoration' was one that weighed heavily on Ron's mind. While there's no record of any gallantry medal for him, it's entirely possible that he'd been recommended for a DFC but was killed before it could be gazetted. Such awards weren't granted posthumously until 1979.[105] In any event, Ron was determined to pursue the matter further.

There's a strange codicil to this story. At the start of Ron's diary, under the heading '72 Squadron North Africa', is a list of individuals in rank order, starting with the boss and two flight commanders. Each name is in effect a signature, to which Ron has later added any decorations. Malan's name is one of those followed by 'DFC'. Beneath this same list, at the bottom of the page, is a summary: 'Decorations awarded for N. Africa, 10 DFCs (2 Bars to DFC), 1 DFM'. Originally Ron wrote '9 DFCs' but later upped the total to ten. While it's tempting to suggest that this reflects support for George's putative DFC, it may also be that, in the absence of his own name, initially Ron forgot to include his own award. Sadly, we'll never know.

17 November 1943:

I've just started this letter to you & it's nearly 12 o'clock. I wrote to Vickie yesterday saying that I was very glad she was able to come down &

---

105. See also below Ron's letters of 14 and 15 December 1943 and the explanatory notes to that of 18 March 1944.

hoped it wouldn't be long before we all met again. Then I wrote an airgraph to Lew – I'll write to Owen tomorrow – I haven't time today.

I've just looked in my log book – this time last year we'd been in Algiers one day & I'd done a patrol over the harbour with Johnny Lowe.

The sortie Ron mentions here was his first in North Africa. He'd arrived from Gibraltar the previous day after his longest ever Spitfire flight: 2 hours and 50 minutes. Now he knew why he and Chemi had been tasked to fly that long navigation exercise at the end of their time at Ayr!

21 November 1943:

I've just come back from phoning you & I feel much happier. Now I'll give you all the gen on the weekend.

There was a big do at Port Talbot – Sir R. Brooke-Popham[106] came down to inspect the ATC there. An invitation came for the G/C & Staff Officers but Kibbler wrote back and accepted for only 1 officer, but didn't tell me anything about it . . . anyway – Mr Hodges came in on Saturday & read the invitation then played hell with Kibbler in front of GB[107] for acting as he did. So GB asked Hodge to take me down in his car – so at a quarter of an hour's notice I had to go off to Port Talbot. GB introduced me to Sir R. B-P. and he talked to me for quite a while about N. Africa – how we got out there, extra petrol tanks, ground crews – etc. he was quite interested in all our doings.

However – Hodge drove me back & we had a few beers with Kibbler who was trying his best to be nice to me . . .

23 November 1943:

I've not written to Owen yet – I must try & do that soon – maybe I'll do it while I'm waiting for you on Friday. I'm giving a big lecture on how I won the war on Wed . . .

I'm going in to work (?) on Saturday morning – from about 10 until about 11.30-12 – then they can't grumble at me – F/Lt K. would very much like to haul me over the coals in a nice quiet way if he could . . .

---

106. After retiring from the RAF for the second time in May 1942, Air Chief Marshal Sir Robert Brooke-Popham was appointed Inspector-General of the ATC.
107. Hitherto identified as the G/C or CO.

24 November 1943:

Before I forget – I'll do my best re the chocolate but there's not a great deal down there lately – so far I've only got two bars of Mars . . .

There's not a great deal of news from this part of the world, although I had a nasty trip last night. I had to go 30 miles up the valley & it was simply pouring down, & as black as the pit. However, I got home about 10.15 so it wasn't too bad . . .

Did I tell you I had a letter from Vickie – I won't answer it – I only mentioned before that I was glad she came down – I don't want to start a great correspondence with her – so could you just mention that I have received her letter – I'll leave you to write to her regularly . . .

25 November 1943:

I've just had three letters back from N. Africa. One of Alan's, one of Dicky's & one from the bank.

It's funny to read them now when they're nearly a year old. However – better here than there! . . .

29 November 1943:

I arrived here [the Castle Hotel, Haverfordwest] *at 1.30 this afternoon & after seeing the bank manager at Lloyds – who is one of the District Inspecting Officers . . . I intended reading and doing a spot of writing but I went off to sleep . . .*

I'm due out at 6.45 & it's just 6 now so I'll do a bit of this letter & then carry on with it when I come back.

Well, darling – I do hope you had a good trip back – I'm glad you managed to get a seat anyway. I felt terribly lonely when I was driving up here – that little business we had made me realise just how much I love you – perhaps it was a good thing . . .

Do try & come down again if you can, sweet, – I do so want to see you before Christmas & I don't want to come up to London for fear of messing up my Christmas leave.

Tuesday morning.

I met the DIO [District Inspecting Officer] *& went to see the unit last night – then came back to his place & just talked shop . . . I may be staying here* *until Friday morning but I'm not sure yet – It's a very dead hole – I'll be glad to get back to gay (?) Newport.*

30 November 1943:

I was supposed to be at Fishguard tonight but I got a telegram saying there was no parade so I'm stuck here for today . . .

There's absolutely nothing to do here. The hotel is full of old dears with some disease or other – flu is very prevalent & there's a general discussion on illnesses all day. I always seem to find places like this – at least most of them are English (Very English too!) & so my ears aren't assailed by the Welsh language. I think most of them came to escape the bombing in '40 & just forgot to go back, & hibernated here . . .

I'll try & phone you tonight sweet – although I quite expect in a primitive spot like this I'll have a hell of a job getting through.

I had two surprises yesterday – I was saluted by two Americans – that's the first time I've ever had that happen to me – I was absolutely staggered.

1 December 1943:

I'm still at this 'home for the ailing' – I expect I shall be here until Friday morning – I'm going to Pembroke tonight but I've got to get near here on Thursday so I might just as well use this as a kind of base for operations. I tried to phone you last night between 6.30 – 7.10 but although I heard the ringing tone nobody answered . . . Anyway, I toddled off to the flicks after that and saw To the shores of Tripoli – in colour – it wasn't bad – it helped to pass the time at least. I came back about 10 & watched the two old dears play bridge with another two old dears they'd asked in. I felt quite sorry for them – it must be pretty awful to get as old as that & only have this sort of life to look forward to. I should hate to finish up, old & solitary in an hotel . . .

2 December 1943:

This is my last day here – I'm off to Tenby tomorrow – & then home to Newport on Saturday. I'm jolly glad I decided not to stay at Pembroke Dock last night – it's a dreadful hole . . .

It's been quite a rest cure for me this week – all I've done all day is sit in front of the fire & read & write. I thought I'd be much busier than I am – not having to go to Fishguard made a difference. I was let off two days driving for that. I'm off at 5.30 tonight to visit a unit near here with S/Ldr Edwards the DIO – I wish I were on my way to Newport though . . .

3 December 1943:

Yesterday evening an RAF P/O came in to the hotel at Haverfordwest with his wife – I thought I recognised him & it turned out that he went to the Sec & was two forms below me. He'd crashed in a Beaufort in May 41 & was now on flying control . . .

The only place I could get at Tenby was the Royal Gate House – it's smack on the front & a most palatial place so I suppose they'll sting me a hell of a lot . . .

It's a bit late now so I'll continue this tomorrow . . .

Sunday afternoon –

It's just as well I decided to come back on Saturday – the car was shocking – the farther I went the worse it got – from Cardiff to Newport I did 25 mph! – still I got back by 3.30 Sat. afternoon . . .

7 December 1943:

I had a very pleasant surprise this morning – apart from your letter. I heard that Dicky had got his commission at last – I'm very pleased about it because he certainly deserves it after all that he's done . . .

You remember I was supposed to be put up for F/Lt last week – well – the letter only went yesterday – Kibbler told GB that he'd been waiting for me to come back to give him my personal number – apart from the fact that all the details he required are on a card at HQ! – All he's trying to do is delay it coming through! Anyway – now it's gone it may quite likely be turned down – so I'm not banking too much on it . . .

Won't it be grand to be together for Christmas – my first at home since I joined up & also our first in married life – here's hoping we never miss one together again.

This is the last time Ron mentions Dicky Huband, with whom he, and indeed Connie, stayed in regular touch throughout their different wartime experiences. The erstwhile colleagues thought a lot of each other, witness

Connie's letter of 14 November 1942: '[Dicky] writes the most cheery & understanding letter you know . . . he thinks the world of you.' It's a sentiment echoed by Ron's mother just eleven days later. She writes: '"Dickie" came to see me last night and sat and talked – & opened his heart to me – I feel I love that boy Ron – he is terribly fond of <u>you</u>.' The relationship is brought out well in Dicky's touching letter of 23 October 1942, shortly after Ron sailed from Liverpool:

> Thank you very much for your last letter, it was jolly decent of you to write in the circ[umstance]s. and believe me I appreciated it. I know how rotten you must have been feeling and how rushed you were. Connie said you received a telegram recalling you from leave in a deuce of a hurry.
>
> I have just been on a week's leave . . . I had a jolly wizard time too. Betty and I managed to spend every evening together very successfully although we didn't do much . . . We felt rather conscience-stricken every time we thought of you and Connie, it doesn't seem fair somehow that we should be able to spend lots of time together, enjoying ourselves (for 6 or 7 days together) when you two have to strike so many snags.
>
> Connie seems to be keeping herself pretty well in hand although she has taken a deuce of a knock over it Ron. She writes quite cheerfully, or at least as cheerfully as can be expected. Don't worry, I'll keep in touch with her, I wrote to her today as a matter of fact. Betty wrote to her as well earlier on this week so between the two of us we'll keep her as cheerful as we can Ron.
>
> If I get half a chance I'll pop into town and see your people from time to time.
>
> Cheerio and all the very best wherever you go
>
> yrs, Dicky

Given the integrity, the humanity so clearly evident here, it's no surprise that there are various photographs of Dicky amongst Ron's memorabilia, none sadder than the one fixed in his scrapbook. Indistinct and partially over-exposed, it shows a smiling, open-faced young man outside an RAF mess. Beneath it is a poignant caption: 'Dickie [sic] Huband. Killed July 1944. We were at ITW together, Aug - Oct 40.'

13 December 1943:

Darl – I had a marvellous weekend – I enjoyed every minute of it – you were everything I could ever wish for . . .

I've just been down to see the CO – he said I could come up to London this weekend if I like – but I said I'd rather have the following one after Christmas – so I can now stay on leave until Jan 3rd!!!!

14 December 1943:

Yesterday I went through the list of awards from Jan 43 – Sept 43 & I couldn't find George's anywhere. I still haven't heard from Owen about that either. I wrote to him about a fortnight ago . . .

16 December 1943:

I've had my Plaistow News Sheet – there's quite a lot about Lt & Mrs Hawkey – we'll have to try & get down to them one night later on. Fancy Ron Brooks being drowned – Plaistow is losing one or two people who used to come down to play polo & have a general mess about. No one ever hears of Mr & Mrs Lunn – I wonder what the position is there – whether they think much of the marriage? . . .

19 December 1943:

At last the week seems to be drawing to a close – I'll be with you tomorrow night – <u>Tonight</u>, to you . . .

I think I'll be leaving some time in the afternoon so I should be home at a fairly reasonable hour, so I get my first full day on 21st – then a fortnight with me wife . . .

Do you know what happened this time last year?

Ron's question appeared at the bottom of the final page, almost as an afterthought. Connie would have been only too aware, of course. On 20 December it would be exactly a year since he was shot down. In writing these words he had to pinch himself. It was hard to believe just how much things had changed during the intervening twelve months. They would be the last words he'd write until early in the new year.

4 January 1944:

First of all let me just thank you once again for a marvellous leave – I enjoyed it immensely, thanks to my little wife . . .

I've got your photo in front of me – everyone thinks it's very nice – especially me. Mr & Mrs T. thought it was excellent too . . .

They squashed my F/Lt by saying that the establishment was for one F/O [Flying Officer] *– so until they increase the establishment (which is under consideration) I'll remain an F/O – until May anyway – I'm due on time to be one then . . .*

Kibbler made a crack about my battledress – so I told him it reminded me of the days when I used to earn my living – he was middlin' quiet after that . . .

9 January 1944:

I went to the gliding site today – I didn't get back till after 2 pm. It was very windy & raining like mad but we managed to erect the glider – unfortunately there was a spot of bother with the cable & nothing much was done before I came away . . .

I'll bet old Ferdie's pleased with his promotion – give him my congratulations – it certainly calls for a celebration . . .

Previous letters have contained the odd reference to gliding but, as his latest letter suggests, Ron is becoming increasingly involved in this important ATC activity. It will eventually take up more and more of his time.

11 January 1944 (first of two letters):

We've just had instructions down as to who can wear which medal. Apparently the 39-43 Star takes precedence over the Africa medal – so that's what I have to wear. The way they work out this medal business would give Fred Karno a headache. Anyway – if you were with the 1st or 8th Army you get a clasp to go with the 39 star . . . I'll tell you more when I see you . . .

It's a shocking day here – it's been pouring with rain ever since I got up. I hope it eases up a bit before I go out tonight – although I've got a better pair of windscreen wipers than on the old car. I'm not too happy about the new car so far – the engine seems to make an awful noise – although I must say it goes OK.

11 January 1944 (second letter):

I remembered something at lunch so I thought I'd write to you before I forgot it again. Do you know what happened to that photo of George sitting on the side of his A/C in N. Africa? Did Vickie ever send us a copy – & also have you got my photo back from the photo people – the one of George, Mac & Chemi? . . .

The photo of George Malan mentioned here was amongst Ron's memorabilia. It appears in *Fighters in the Blood*,[108] where the caption identifies 'the one and only' George – a quote lifted from a different picture. The original, on the first page of Ron's scrapbook, shows George in the cockpit with another pilot standing beside him on the wing root. The caption in full reads: 'The one and only "George". George Malan and Macdonald. Taken at Ayr.'

The second of the pictures to which Ron refers is another from his scrapbook, captioned 'Mac, P/O Le Cheminant, George. Taken at Ayr 1942. Chem later got DFC in Tunisia.' Of the others mentioned here, Mac (Pilot Officer J.W. Macdonald) was killed early in 72 Squadron's time overseas,[109] while Le Cheminant was another to survive a crash-landing unhurt after he was shot down on 2 December 1942. His final tally was six confirmed 'kills'. Unusually – and all the more creditable – every one of these was an Me 109.

17 January 1944:

It's only just after 10 AM now – so I expect you're not even half way home yet. It's an awful anti-climax after I've left you in the morning – everything seems very dead . . .

It seems there was quite an accident at Ilford last night. I expect you'll hear all about it when you get to the office . . .

Well sweetheart, I love you and I had a really wonderful weekend – thanks to you. Now I'm just looking forward to when I'll be with you again.

This letter, number 246 in Connie's box, was the last to be numbered. The sequence thus far has been meticulously accurate with just a single anomaly: the unexplained repetition two months later of serials 125-129, from July 1942. From now on Connie simply files letters in date order without any further identifiers. As a consequence, a number of Ron's letters appear to be missing.

---

108. Air Marshal 'Black' Robertson, *Fighters in the Blood*, (Pen & Sword Books Ltd, Yorkshire - Philadelphia, 2020), pp.74-5.
109. See notes on Ron's letter of 5 December 1942, Chapter 28.

The Ilford accident to which he refers was indeed serious. In evening darkness and dense fog, two crowded trains collided. The driver of an express passed danger signals at speed and ran into the back of a stationary train, telescoping its rear carriage and derailing and damaging others. One of the nine fatalities was an RAF officer[110] and three more were US military personnel; of thirty-nine injuries, twelve were US Servicemen.

25 January 1944:

Just a note to tell you how things are – altho' I expect I'll be home almost as soon as you get this.

The train was about ten minutes late in starting but was only about 5 minutes late at Colwyn Bay. A chap met me at the station & said that a room had been booked for me at Conway – so I came along here [the Castle Hotel] *straight away.*

We had lunch with GB when we were up here before at the same hotel – it's very nice – the last breakfast is at 10 AM – which just suits me . . .

This morning I went for a walk – it's blowing a gale here . . . I had lunch with the DIO – then he took me through to Llandudno & I had tea with him – then brought me back about 6 pm. It's now about 6.30 & I'm due out at 7 . . .

1 February 1944:

I'm terribly busy – there's stacks of paperwork to get through . . .

I've had letters from Jack, Dicky – Owen – I'm due to get my 39 Star & clasp any week now . . .

I'm due to go to a semi-official cadets party tonight but I'll ring you before I go . . .

I had a very nice week end darl – as you say – being everything to each other we soon get over all sorts of odd problems . . .

2 February 1944:

I'm very nearly finished with all the work I had yesterday – I do hate to let things hang around for days . . .

---

110. Squadron Leader H. Allen; his name appears on the Emmanuel College, Cambridge, Roll of Honour.

That wound stripe business looks awfully odd – it's just as though a caterpillar were crawling up my sleeve – I'm fair decked out in ribbons etc. now. They haven't got any 39 Star & clasp in stores – so I'll have to wait until they get one from somewhere else.

The awarding of a brass 'Wound Stripe' mentioned here was re-introduced in 1944, only to be discontinued after 1946. It followed an Army practice first introduced in 1916.

3 February 1944:

Everything's a bit messed up this week owing to arrangements having to be made for a big 'do' on Monday. All sorts of big pots are coming down so even if I do get home Friday, I'll have to get back here on Sunday evening . . .

I've got some better news now – I managed to get our NAAFI ration today for January – 160 Players @ 1/6 [15p] for 20 & 4 bars of choc. & 2 Mars. I've given Steve 20 Players – so you & Ferdie & Else can have 140 @ 1/6 for 20. I rather fancy it will be 100 @ 1/6 and 40 @ 0d for young Tub! Still – you're very welcome to all I can give you – even tho' it's only cigarettes . . .

I must go now – I'm due 'up the valley' at 6 pm.

8 February 1944:

I was very sorry to hear that Grandma was dead – although we all knew that it was only a matter of time before she went. In some ways it is probably better for her – she'd been pretty bad for some time & was getting less & less able to look after herself. I expect Mum will be writing to me later on.

Well, darl, yesterday went off very well indeed. I went to both lunch & dinner, was introduced to various Air Marshals & Lord Harewood.[111] The latter, by the way, impressed me quite a lot. I expected a bit of a dodderer, but although he's 61 he was quite sprightly. He gave an excellent after-dinner speech – putting into few words what an ordinary speaker would have taken a week to tell you. I was speaking to a Wing/Co before dinner & he said that Lord Harewood was an excellent soldier in the last war – was put up for the VC twice & had DSO & Bar by 1915 – so he's not so slow

---

111. Henry Lascelles, 6th Earl of Harewood KG GCVO DSO* TD JP DL, was son-in-law to King George V and Queen Mary and brother-in-law to Edward VIII and George VI.

as some people make out. The great Taffy Jones was there – I sat opposite him at dinner & next to him at the boxing. He asked after Brian & we had quite a chat. The boxing itself was very good – the general feeling being that Wales would be beaten by N.E. Command but we won 8-5 . . .

I stuck that photo in my log book & also those taken at Biggin – so I hope I'll be able to keep a record for years to come.

Of the log book photos Ron mentions here, the first is relatively small; it's of his original Spitfire, RN-H, with 'Connie' in beautiful copperplate script. The others, all A5 size and taken in April 1942, comprise two of King George VI meeting 72 Squadron aircrew, one of King Haakon of Norway during a similar visit, and an informal grouping of pilots at dispersal. Every individual in these pictures is named, together with any decorations and, where relevant, his eventual fate. Many, of course, didn't survive the war – as was the case with six of the fourteen aircrew who appear in the dispersal group.

9 February 1944:

I heard from Mum today – but I'm going to write & tell her I can't get up for the funeral on Friday . . . I'd be very glad if you'd see about a wreath, Tub – but as far as going to the funeral – I'll leave that to you – I don't really think it's necessary for you to worry about it, I expect a few people will be unable to go anyway.

13 February 1944:

I had to go out & look at another boxing do last night – there wasn't a dinner or anything of that sort – and the show itself wasn't too good so I was glad when I got away. I was back here by 10.15. This morning I went to a local school to tell them how I won the war – it went off very well & the CO proposed a vote of thanks & that was that . . .

15 February 1944:

I didn't get here [the Castle Hotel, Neath] *till after 9 pm last night so I didn't start a letter then – I had a couple of beers & crawled off to bed. This is a very nice place, as I believe I told you last time I came here. I only wish you were able to come along with me. It would be so marvellous if you could . . .*

17 February 1944:

I couldn't write to you yesterday – I went off to an aerodrome & then on to visit an ATC unit (what an anticlimax!) – anyway I was supposed to stay in Swansea last night & come home here this morning, but as I got through all my work by 8 pm I drove back here – just in time for supper at 10 . . .

Well, darling – the week's gradually going – & you'll be here tomorrow so I'm in a very good mood . . .

Shortly after Connie's visit Ron managed to arrange a brief period of leave. It's nearly two weeks before his next letter.

1 March 1944:

I saw the CO yesterday & he wants me to go on this fortnight's tour with the A.M. S/Ldr – so I'll do my best to get up for a week end before the 16th . . .

I see that there was a raid last night – I do hope that everything is OK at home . . .

Most of my next letters will be very short, sweet – I've got a fair bit of organising to do . . .

There's one thing about this tour – It'll cost me about £10 but I should clear about £14 so that'll mean that we'll have £4 to the good. What with that and my expenses for Feb we can have quite a good week's holiday.

The raid to which Ron refers here was part of the 'Little' or 'Baby Blitz' – night bombing raids on London and the south of England that took place between January and May 1944. Operation STEINBOCK, as it was known in Germany, was launched primarily for propaganda purposes in retaliation for Allied raids. With no specific military objective, it was the Luftwaffe's final strategic bomber offensive of the war. The last week of February saw a series of raids on Westminster, the London docks and even Colchester to the east; the most intense were those on the nights of 22, 23 and 24 February. Vere Hodgson summed things up pithily: 'It has been hell's delight most of the week'[112] was her diary entry for Sunday 27 February.

---

112. Hodgson, op. cit., p.454.

222

2 March 1944:

Well, darl, I'm very happy that you can come down on the 11th. I've got to go to mid-Wales next week but I should be back on Friday . . . I really have been busy this week & I must say it's a change . . .

Old Ferdie's being very nice about your time off I think Tub – buy him a drink for me on the strength of it . . .

5 March 1944:

This morning I had to go with the CO to inspect a local sqdn. When I went to start the car the battery was flat so Mrs T. and I had to push it down the hill before it would go. Anyway – apart from that all went off well . . .

I'm going up to Presteigne tomorrow so I doubt whether I'll be able to write to you because I'll be driving most of the day and visiting a unit at night . . .

P.S. Do you remember this time last year?

According to time and date I was just getting to Liverpool St to phone you. I shall always remember you on the phone – you <u>did</u> seem pleased – which pleased me no end. Then I had to knock your hat off – I <u>have</u> been rough to you in my time haven't I?

6 March 1944:

It's just midnight, the witching hour – & I'm all tucked up in bed. There's an electric fire in my room on a 1d [.004p] meter & although I put 1d in a quarter of an hour ago the fire's still going strong . . .

I've stayed at this place [the Radnorshire Arms, Presteigne] *before & most of the people I met then are still here. One ancient Brigadier was very pally – but his wife was <u>very</u> 'county' & she could certainly talk!*

8 March 1944:

I've had fun and games with the car recently – 4 punctures in 2 days! This morning both the off front <u>&</u> spare tyres were flat so you can imagine how I felt. Anyway – I've just got the car back & I'm waiting for a phone call before I can go anywhere – so I've got time to write a short note to you . . .

I've been rushing around like a two year old lately – I'm fair busy! Anyway – all will be well on Friday – I'll be there!

9 March 1944:

Do you realise that it's two years on Friday that I first put your engagement ring on! Many happy returns . . .

13 March 1944:

I do hope you had a good trip back & managed to get a spot of breakfast. I phoned the 'Compleat Angler' this morning and the form is this: – We can only be put up in the Annexe (this has H & C) & we'll have to leave on Thursday because of Easter bookings. I said I'd confirm in a couple of days – I'll phone you tonight – but this is to give you the gen in case I can't get through . . .

14 March 1944:

I'm glad you got back OK. I wrote to Marlow today confirming our stay & asked them to reply to me at Woodford – so you can open the letter when it comes . . .

When I was home last Dad said he'd like to go to the ATC Boxing at the Albert Hall on May 8th (Monday) & as there are one or two wives going I thought you'd like to go as well – so I've bought three tickets. If you'd rather not go I can soon get rid of the ticket – so don't be afraid to say. Actually, it's quite good & I think you'd enjoy it . . .

15 March 1944:

I've been very busy today clearing up odd things so that everything will be OK when the S/Ldr arrives tomorrow . . .

From the 'Stop Press' in the Argus office[113] *it appears that there was a fair sized raid on London last night – although no details are given – I hope that everything's OK at home . . .*

Well, old darling girl – I'm glad our holiday is OK – I've put in for my leave, & you should get confirmation from Marlow soon . . .

---

113. The *South Wales Argus* was printed in Newport, near Ron's office.

It'll be grand going away together again, won't it – I'll bet I'm as excited as you! Maidenhead's only 5½ miles away so we can have a noggin with Arthur one day . . .

It's only another fortnight before I'll see you, Tubs – I'm getting really anxious about it – not actually <u>anxious</u> but pretty het up – I like the idea of going somewhere new with you . . .

The 'fair-sized raid' on the night of 14/15 March Ron mentions here was again part of the Baby Blitz. A hundred or so German bombers hit London with some 160 tons of high explosive and incendiary bombs. The main target was Whitehall and, specifically, Buckingham Palace. Although damage was relatively limited, nearly 400 fires were reported. Strangely, there's no mention of this in the indefatigable Vere Hodgson's diaries, although by this stage, more than four years into the war, they've understandably become less detailed.

16 March 1944:

At the moment I'm just waiting for that S/Ldr to arrive and then I start playing nursemaid. From the sound of things you're going to be a busy little girl from now on – what with swimming, cycling, hockey, netball & hiking! Still – at least you'll get out in the air a bit more.

If I'm not stooging tonight I'll give you a tinkle at about 5.30 – so if you don't hear from me by the time you get this you'll know I'm a busy little bee! . . .

18 March 1944:

We're kept very busy here [Hawarden] – first lecture at 9 am & the last at 8.20 pm . . .

Being here has brought back to me the fact that I had my first letter here saying that you loved me. It seems ages ago that I was here. I remember so many things that happened – my wallet came to the Sergeants' Mess here on my birthday in '41 – I had my first crash here – dozens of things seem to come to my mind. Funnily enough, the S/Ldr i/c gunnery here was my F/Cdr in 111 – a chap by the name of Brown. We've had quite a natter about the old times. He knew Hugo, Colli, & lots of others

*including Pete Durnford & the Czechs. He's called his young son after
old Hugo.*

*The AM S/Ldr I'm with is a very good type & we get on well together –
so that's a help. I'm supposed to be giving a lecture tomorrow on 'ops' –
I expect you'll be having a cup of tea by the fire. I feel much more like
writing to you about 'us' when I'm away – I seem to have a more settled
mind – there aren't any phone calls to distract me or people dropping into
my room to ask about this & that.*

*I am glad we're married, sweet – it gives me a great feeling of happiness
and contentment . . .*

There's a lot to explain here. First, the crash Ron mentions is that of 18 August
1941, where he departed the Hawarden runway. His aircraft ended up on its
nose and he ended up in front of Wing Commander Flying.[114]

Next, the 111 Squadron flight commander referred to is the same
Ronald Clifford Brown who appears almost a year earlier[115] – a chance
encounter at Mount Vernon Hospital. 'Colli' is Squadron Leader Count
Franz Ferdinand Colloredo-Mansfeld, who owed his name and title to his
Austrian parentage.[116] He took over from Timber Woods as Ron's flight
commander in June 1942 and went on to command 132 Squadron. Eighteen
months later, on 14 January 1944, flying at low level, he was shot down
and killed by enemy flak over France. Shortly afterwards, in March, came
the announcement of his second DFC, a development that casts doubt on
the earlier theory that George Malan may possibly have been debarred
from receiving a posthumous award. That said, it may be that different
rules applied to the award of a Bar to a DFC. Another possibility is that
at the time of Colli's death official approval had *already* been granted for
his award. This was clearly the case for the award to Jack Ranger's 'since
deceased' brother. In any event, and as with his own decoration, official
announcements – the gazetting – often came some weeks after unofficial
leaks. So Ron may simply be chasing a chimera. But none of this takes away
the disappointment he feels over the fruitless search for recognition for his
much admired friend.

---

114. See Chapter 12 above, the letter of 20 August 1941 and accompanying comments.
115. See the conclusion of Chapter 19.
116. It appears that he had at least dual citizenship. In 72 Squadron's operations record
'USA' appears after his name.

20 March 1944:

The course finished last night & we're not going till after lunch so I've got a chance of finishing this before I go. I'm glad I managed to get through to you so quickly the second time last night – I felt lots better once I'd finished. Everything's absolutely OK this morning, & as I said in my letter yesterday I feel so much more settled now I'm married.

It was funny to come back here – but it's no good dwelling on the past – no matter how good it may have been – the future is the thing to look to now, and I think that being married to you is as good a start as I could wish for . . .

24 March 1944:

I'm certainly earning my money this trip – take yesterday for instance – we had to see the District Inspecting Officer in the morning & then go from Denbigh to Llanelli by 6.30. Actually we reached here by 6.40 which wasn't too bad. Everything is going OK – only one puncture so far (touch wood!).

I'll be coming back to Cardiff on Saturday so I can phone you as usual on Sunday. The S/Ldr has to go to AM for the weekend so that gives me a bit of a rest . . .

26 March 1944:

As I believe I told you before, we managed to get back to Newport for the weekend and I can rest for a day . . . I can tell you I'm rather fed up with driving – I've scarcely been out of the car for more than an hour or two the whole week . . .

The weather's glorious here – I do hope it's just as good when we're at Marlow. I don't expect I'll have much chance to write to you on Monday or Wednesday. On Monday I'll be driving to Haverfordwest & I'll be coming back on Wednesday so time will be rather limited . . .

Ron's leave, and the couple's stay at The Compleat Angler, is the catalyst for a review of their domestic arrangements. Frustrated by lengthy periods of separation, uncertainties about time off, and the difficulties of travel to and from London, they decide to investigate the possibility of securing family

227

accommodation near Ron's place of work. The risks that Connie's running – living and working in areas still subject to German bombing – also figure in their calculations, although by this time the intensity of the Baby Blitz is gradually reducing. (Soon, however, there would be a new threat. The first V-1 attack on London would be launched on 13 June; V-2 attacks would follow from 8 September.) There's employment to consider too. Connie is very happy working with her father. Should she move to South Wales, what were her job prospects? This, then, is the context for Ron's next letter.

12 April 1944:

As you can imagine there's a fair bit of stuff on my desk at the moment & I'm in no mood to really get down to it. I put an advert in the local paper today . . . I've asked George Griffiths to ask some of his house agent friends – the girls here are asking all their local mothers & friends so I hope I'll have something in due course – although it's going to be a big job – as we imagined.

I had a grand leave sweet – but it will be much better when we're both together always . . .

I'll go in to the Min of Lab. soon and see what the form is there.

13 April 1944:

I've not been inundated with replies to my advert as yet so I'm going to start the round of all the estate agents . . .

Keep hoping, darl – I'll let you know the minute I get a place.

14 April 1944:

I'm sorry I had no better news for you when I phoned yesterday. However, I think the idea of getting our stuff stored down here until we want it is very good . . . As it is – all we're doing now really is paying for storage – we don't often use our flat. Could you ring Pickfords at your end and see what they can do . . . I think we'd feel a bit more settled then – having one thing off our minds . . .

I bought a book this morning called Triumph over Tunisia – all about the air fighting out there. It staggers me to read all about 111 – Jonsson, & all

*the blokes I knew, but only about two lines about us. We had a bigger score
than they did – too! Still – it's good to read about the others.*

*This won't catch the early post I'm afraid – I've been out most of the morning
to see the MO re my eye & I couldn't settle down to this again until 4 pm.*

*I may be able to go to Cardiff & get fixed up with an eye rather than have
it sent from Blackpool. The MO's going to let me know.*

Ron's frustration that 72 Squadron's efforts in Tunisia had been played down
in print is more than justified, as Jimmy Corbin would much later confirm:
'On 6 January 1943, word came through that 72 Squadron had been awarded
the mantle of highest scoring squadron in North Africa with 31 confirmed
"kills".'[117] After all, with four of these to his personal credit and a share in a
fifth, he'd been a major contributor to the squadron's success.

16 April 1944:

*Another no-news letter – I walked up to Christchurch on Saturday
afternoon but there's nothing doing up that way. Those flats you mention
farther up the road are all taken . . .*

*I'm sorry to keep giving you all this uninspiring news, but that's all there
is, so far. Still, darl, we'll get somewhere sooner or later . . .*

*Don't get too worried if we don't get a place for a while darl – after all –
they told us the same thing in London when we started off to get a place
there – & we managed it OK in the end . . .*

*I haven't been to the Labour Exchange about a job for you yet – I thought
it would be better to wait until nearer the time when you come down.*

17 April 1044

*I've just phoned Pickfords at Newport & they say it'll cost 5/- [25p] a week
to store our furniture so I think the sooner we get it down here the better . . .*

*I'll go & visit some more estate agents this afternoon & see what the
form is . . .*

*There's a boxing 'do' at Kidlington, of all places, on Saturday but the
CO's not going & so I managed to get out of it – so it'll be OK for you to
come down on Friday.*

---

117. Corbin, op. cit., p.193.

18 April 1944:

I'm still hearing bad news about getting anywhere but I still plod on . . .
These letters don't seem to abound with optimism lately but I hope I'll be able to give you some good news one of these days . . .
I didn't get a chance to go to an estate agent yesterday as I had to rush off & do a job at Cardiff, so I'm going as soon as I finish this.

20 April 1944:

By the time you get this you'll be just about ready to catch the train – hurry up, darl – it's ages since we were together!
I heard about that raid on Tuesday night – the Argus was full of it on Wednesday. I hope no damage was done locally – anyway, you can give me the gen when you see me . . .

The Tuesday night Ron mentions here is 18/19 April. The final raid of the Baby Blitz was a relative failure and again goes unremarked in Vere Hodgson's diary. Only fifty-three of the 125 bombers that crossed the English coast reached London, thanks to problems with target identification and aircraft losses en route (seventeen in all). Despite these difficulties, Leyton and Walthamstow, East London districts not far from both parents' homes, were particularly badly hit.

Sadly, this is the last letter in Connie's box until January 1945, by which time she's eight months pregnant and still living with her parents in Woodford. The imminent arrival of the couple's first child had earlier put paid to any idea of a permanent home in Wales – that plus the difficulties of finding suitable accommodation that so frustrated Ron. His long and fruitless search proved dispiriting. However, until it became too uncomfortable for her to travel, Connie continued to make the best of any opportunity for a weekend together in Wales. Meanwhile her husband, a flight lieutenant now,[118] adroitly engineered trips to London with reasonable regularity. Importantly, he was able to enjoy ten welcome days' leave over Christmas. It felt good to once again be part of what was literally a growing family.

---

118. His promotion, as of 1 July 1944, was announced in *The London Gazette* of 4 August 1944.

Chapter 28

22 November 1942, Souk-el-Arba, Tunisia

With groundcrew and equipment yet to arrive, it took a couple of weeks or so for 72 Squadron to establish itself at Souk-el-Arba. It's ten days before Ron once again puts pen to paper. His letter mentions some of the reasons for this delay, albeit in a somewhat cursory way so as not to alarm Connie unduly. The reality comes later.

22 November 1942:

I haven't been able to write a line for over a week. I hope you got the letters and cables I sent from Gib – at least they'll help to give you an idea of how I'm keeping. We've had quite a time since we left there. We got to our aerodrome which was as muddy as blazes – I've never seen mud like it. It just stuck like glue. We slept on the floor and cooked our own food, got soaked in the rain, & altogether behaved like very new boy-scouts.
24/11/42   Just as I wrote that last bit, we got bombed & shot up a little – still – we're OK.

We don't have any regular mail service from here but there's a plane going back to more or less civilisation in half an hour so if I catch that you may get this in a fortnight or so.

We don't get much chance to write in the daytime – and as we're in tents we're not allowed to use lights & therefore can't write at night.

We all go to bed at 6.30-7 pm merely because its dark & we may as well get some sleep while we can.

This isn't exactly a rest cure but we're not doing so very badly – North Africa is much darker than Northern France – it's rather difficult to spot planes.

Please don't think I'm dodging letter writing, dear – but it's really difficult – I can't go into great detail but it's hardly like writing in the restroom at Gib. I haven't taken my clothes off for three days & haven't washed for two – still – we manage to get along. 'Connie' is still going strong despite Jerry's efforts.

How's everything darl? – I don't expect I'll get any mail yet as they've not organised the post office, so if I write letters without answering your queries – it'll be because I've not had any letters yet. I can't get any airgraphs or cables anywhere near here but will try as soon as we get near civilisation.

I'm always thinking of you darling – I carry both your photos in my pocket now – the one of the family & the other. The other photos I keep in my jacket so no matter what happens I'm well supplied.

I must go now dearest – let Mum know how things are – I'll try & write a decent letter later on.

The 'decent letter' would have to wait. But there was time for the one of shortest letters he ever wrote – effectively a post script to the one he'd just sealed:

24 November 1942:

Just a short line to wish you a very happy birthday and Christmas.

I hope this reaches you in time – I forgot to wish you a happy birthday in the other letter today.

Those first few days at Souk-el-Arba proved a rude awakening for 72; 'as hectic as any I'd known during the Battle of Britain' according to Jimmy Corbin.[119] It would be much the same for the other squadrons soon to join them as part of 324 Wing. Group Captain Ronnie Lees had 'decided it was time to assemble his widely dispersed Spitfire squadrons into a cohesive unit' under his command.[120] Next to arrive were 93 and 152 Squadrons, followed by the reconnaissance Hurricanes of 225 Squadron.

In practical terms, the squadron's first requirements were food and water. Food came in the form of K-rations, individually boxed meals first introduced by the US Army. Water was more of a problem, though. It was in short supply. Ron and his colleagues had to walk into the village to fill their water bottles from a bowser, remembering to add the all-important pills they'd been issued to help prevent disease. Since there wasn't enough for

119. Corbin, op. cit., p.171.
120. Oxspring, op. cit., p.124.

everyone to wash, they simply became scruffier by the day. With nowhere to sleep either, they managed to acquire a couple of largish bell tents, courtesy of the French Foreign Legion, who also provided some rudimentary but welcome cooking equipment.

Then there was the weather. Pleasantly warm during the day, once the sun went down, not long after five, the base was enveloped in an inky blackness and it became extraordinarily cold – a problem accentuated by the fact that crews had only limited additional clothing and no bedding to speak of, just a few paper-thin blankets, again scrounged from the French. It meant that for the first fortnight or so Ron woke up regularly in a shivering fit; he wasn't alone – everyone else was suffering in the same way.

If there was a consolation, it was the high level of activity. The squadron was kept busy from the start. On 21 November, the day after they arrived, Ron flew four times: an aerodrome patrol and three sweeps – more than 5½ hours' flying. It wasn't until the last of these sweeps that he found any targets. But, as his formation peeled in to strafe a number of enemy lorries, they received an unexpectedly warm welcome. The moment they came under attack the Germans set up a machine gun and returned fire with gusto. So effective was their response that Bob Oxspring was hit and forced to crash-land his damaged aircraft near Beja en route back to base. It was to be the first of a number of similar incidents, wheels-up landings that said as much for the Spitfire's construction as they did for the enemy's military prowess.

As if to rub salt into the squadron's wounds, the very next day the airfield was subjected to a series of attacks. After landing from his second sortie, an airfield patrol, Ron sat down to begin his next letter home. He'd written just a few lines when he looked up to see what he took to be one of the units destined to reinforce Souk-el-Arba preparing to land: a dozen or so aircraft in rough line astern, diving towards the runway. Suddenly there was a shout: *109s!* With that, aircrew and groundcrew scattered to the four winds. But there was nowhere to hide. Knowing that parked aircraft nearby would be obvious targets, as would the ditches where equipment was stored, Ron sprinted in the opposite direction before flattening himself on the ground as the sound of gunfire erupted all around. Some of this came from American anti-aircraft installations, although their 0.5 inch machine-guns proved remarkably ineffective. Not so the Me 109s, who hit both ammunition and petrol storage areas. The latter exploded with a deafening thud. The resulting blast was such that to Ron, fully 150 yards away, it felt as if he was sitting close to a roaring fire – far too close in fact.

Once the sound of machine-gun and cannon fire finally ceased, he could scarcely believe his luck. Still lying prone, and as scared as he'd been in his life, he was somehow unharmed, as were the rest of 72's pilots. He nevertheless decided to take advantage of the temporary lull – a follow-up attack was inevitable, he thought – to distance himself yet further from any likely target. Just as he started to move away, a voice called out, 'Give me a hand, Robbie!' He turned to see Sergeant Roy Hussey trying to drag a severely injured airman to the comparative safety of a nearby lorry; he'd been hit in the stomach and was bleeding profusely. Against his better judgement – the lorry was an inviting target – Ron turned back and helped position the casualty beneath its chassis. There they remained until satisfied that the immediate threat had passed.

Once the two pilots emerged to take stock of the situation, they could see things were bad. The squadron had lost several groundcrew who'd taken to the ditches. Also killed were a couple of Arabs who'd unwisely sheltered behind the squadron's petrol supply. Their charred remains were revealed only once Ron joined those throwing mud and dust onto the small fires that still burned. It was a deeply unpleasant sight, one he never wanted to see again.

An hour or so later the base was subjected to a second attack, this time by Fw 190s. Luckily they did little damage to the squadron's aircraft and none whatsoever to either aircrew or groundcrew. However, both 93 and 152 Squadrons suffered considerable losses, both materiel and personnel; indeed, not long afterwards, 152 was withdrawn from the front line. Ronnie Lees' 'cohesive unit' was rapidly falling apart.

To compound the base's problems, a third raid soon followed, this time by Ju 87 Stuka dive-bombers with a fighter escort. But by now such was everyone's state of alert that the combined formation was spotted some way off. There still wasn't much protection so Ron, like many of his colleagues, elected to clamber into the bomb-craters from earlier raids. Somehow he emerged unharmed from a frightening new experience. It was the first time he'd heard the Stukas' 'Jericho trumpets', twin sirens designed to create panic on the ground during their dive attacks. As a psychological weapon they proved every bit as effective as the bombing that this time saw 72 Squadron, too, suffer significant losses.

That the American anti-aircraft gunners once again failed to inflict any damage was hardly a surprise. Fortunately, the same was true when they attacked an RAF Blenheim towards the end of that same afternoon. In an event that was to have parallels for Ron not long afterwards, they opened up on the 'friendly' even though it was in company with a pair of Spitfires. By convention, an aircraft subject to friendly fire lowered its wheels as a signal; this the Blenheim did several times – alas to no avail. Meanwhile, Ron and his colleagues set off in an equally vain attempt to persuade the US gunners to desist. But by now the Blenheim and its escorts were disappearing into the distance, apparently unscathed. Whether this incident had any bearing on replacement of the US gunners by a detachment of two or three Bofors guns shortly thereafter wasn't clear; it was, nevertheless, a welcome development.

Ron summed up the events of a difficult day succinctly in his log book: 'Aerodrome blitzed. Not very funny!! 3 times in one day.' The upshot of these attacks was that eight 72 Squadron aircraft were completely destroyed; never again would it be possible to put the whole squadron in the air at the same time. The remaining aircraft therefore joined with the rump of 93 Squadron to form a composite unit, with leadership alternating between Bob Oxspring and George Nelson-Edwards, his fellow CO. This wasn't at all what Ronnie Lees had envisaged.

The last word on these Luftwaffe attacks relates to the increasingly regular night bombing to which Souk-el-Arba was now subjected, and the advent of a new phenomenon: butterfly bombs. On hitting the ground they opened out like peeled oranges and scattered shrapnel in all directions. Lying flat in their tents, astonishingly, Ron and his colleagues were again untouched; however, the tents themselves soon began to resemble colanders. There was nothing else for it. They'd have to dig slit-trenches. Once this was accomplished, aircrew spent a good part of most nights in relative safety, not that they got much sleep.

27 November 1942:

I'm starting this letter but when I'll be able to finish it is a moot point. The last time I started a letter to you we got pretty well shot up – I hope that history doesn't repeat itself. How are you darling? I do hope everything is going OK at home. We haven't had any newspapers, wireless or letters since we've been away so we haven't the faintest idea of how the rest of the world is progressing . . . We're kept very busy here for all sorts of reasons. There's always cooking to be done – trenches to be dug, water to be fetched, and of course, the odd sweep and patrol. As I told Mum the other day – I managed to get a 109 – my first on this campaign. Pete shared in the destruction of another with another chap [Jimmy Corbin, on 26 November]. *So far we're doing rather well – I hope it's going to continue.*

George & co. should be arriving pretty soon. I'll be glad to see him and get all the news of the wedding. I expect you've already heard from Vickie, so that news will be stale to you. I managed to post both those letters I wrote to you the other day – I do hope they reach you by Christmas . . .

Hello Tubb – I love you – I wonder how long it'll be before I'm <u>actually</u> telling you that? I keep praying that I'll be back soon & we can get married. Just the thought of that keeps me going – otherwise I'd be right in the dumps with all this messing about.

28/11/42.   Just after writing the previous bit I had to take off on a patrol with Pete Fowler and another chap. It was my lucky day again – we saw a Ju 88 underneath us and I led the section down onto it. I started firing at about 400 yds & kept on until his port engine blew right off. I had to break away then as I nearly collided with it. Pete saw it spin into the ground & I saw it burning – so that's another confirmed I've got. We've heard that some mail has gone for a Burton – I do hope that none of it was yours or mine.

Last night I got as far as putting my pyjama trousers on but after sitting in a trench for an hour I decided that although it's probably unhygienic, it's a darn sight better & more comfortable to sleep fully dressed.

I've done my flying for the day so I can just sit & write to you – although I suspect I shall be rudely interrupted fairly soon.

Look, sweet – if any letter of mine ends rather abruptly it'll mean that someone is going near civilisation & I've had to finish the letter so that it can be sent off. Just in case that happens now, I must tell you that I love you & want to marry you as soon as I set foot in England again. I've only been away from you for six weeks and yet it seems like six years . . .

This particular letter reached Connie relatively quickly. On 5 December she writes in her diary, 'Marvellous letter from Ron. He has shot down ME 109 & JU 88.' These confirmed 'kills' appear in his log book in the usual way. On 25 November the entry reads: 'Sweep. Bizerte . . . Met lots of bombers & 109s. Got <u>109E confirmed</u>. [swastika]'. Then on 27 November comes his only confirmed bomber (all his other 'kills' were fighters): 'Sweep. Tunis . . . <u>Destroyed JU 88</u>. Confirmed by Pete Fowler. [swastika]'.

It's typical of the care Ron takes not to worry his fiancée unduly that there's no mention of the loss of Johnny Lowe. On 27 November, two days after he, too, had been credited with a confirmed Ju 88, he failed to return from a sweep. His aircraft was eventually found not far from the airfield, his body still in the cockpit. He'd been shot down and crash-landed. It was the end of another tragically short marriage; he'd tied the knot just a week before the squadron embarked for Gibraltar.

On 30 November the newly-married George Malan arrived, together with one or two colleagues. Delighted to see his close friend once again, Ron was even more pleased by the arrival of the first of the personal effects he'd left behind, plus – more important still in the circumstances – some decent tents and proper camp-beds. These small home comforts would make a world of difference.

Having learned to cope with cold nights, the squadron was now introduced to another weather problem. One minute the skies were bathed in blue, not a cloud to be seen, the next the heavens opened and the base was deluged in what felt like a tropical storm. What was once a concrete-hard, baked mud airfield turned rapidly into a quagmire. As aircraft wheels began to sink into the mud, crews attempted to lift the wings by crawling underneath and applying brute force to relocate the oleo, only for the very same thing to happen; the wheel simply disappeared again into a glutinous brown mass. Even taxiing proved hazardous. In order to avoid aircraft becoming bogged down and propellers impacting the ground, a couple of airmen would position themselves on the tailplane prior to take-off – a practice that led to a terrifying incident for one individual. Noticing an apparent control restriction as he lumbered airborne, the pilot concerned was surprised to see in his mirror an airman still clinging to his tail. An improvised circuit quickly returned his unauthorised passenger to the ground, where he finally parted company with the aircraft thanks to a less than smooth landing. Although he suffered nothing worse than a broken arm, the 152 Squadron airman was so unnerved by the experience that he was immediately evacuated back to the UK as a casualty.

The storms also played havoc with the squadron's efforts to support the British Army, its *raison d'être*. They similarly put at risk the airfield patrols that represented the base's only real defence against seemingly relentless Luftwaffe attacks – relentless because they were mounted from well-found bases in Tunisia that didn't suffer in the same way.

2 December 1942:

With luck this should reach you long before some of my others.
I had a wonderful surprise this morning – one of our chaps who brought up a replacement was given a pile of mail to bring up here – & when he

*looked through it – lo & behold there was a telegram from you saying
you'd received both my cables. I feel a thousand percent better now – gee
darling – I do love you . . .*

*George has arrived & we again fly together – much to our delight.
Everything is still OK – but I still haven't taken my clothes off for days.
Excuse the scrawl, dear, but this may have to go any minute.*

*I'm so happy at having heard from you I really don't know what to say –
that cable means more to me than you'll ever guess.*

*Just in case this reaches you before my others I'll wish you a Very Happy
Birthday & Christmas. If you see anything you'd like – do buy it – otherwise
I'll buy you everything I can think of when I come back.*

The cable Ron mentions here is the one Connie sent to Gibraltar on
16 November, just as he departed for Maison Blanche. It was the first and
only domestic communication the squadron had received since their arrival
at Souk-el-Arba.

5 December 1942:

*There's almost no news . . . I'll have lots to tell you when I come home – both
interesting & complaining but I'm sure it'd all be censored if I tried to write it.*

*I explained to Mum that the paper shortage here is going to be a bit
difficult when I've got through my two pads & envelopes – still maybe we'll
have got some supplies by then.*

*Hello sweet – how I miss you!! I'm still in the high heavens over your
cable – it's <u>almost</u> as good as seeing you once a week when I was at Biggin.*

*George & I and another chap [Owen Hardy] shared a FW 190 the other day.
My score's gradually coming up – counting France – I've got 4⅓ destroyed –
1 prob and 3 damaged so far. Don't worry too much about that though, darl –
I'm far more keen on coming back in one piece than of getting Huns.*

*Old George made me laugh about his wedding – apparently his uniform
didn't arrive until about half an hour before the wedding & he said 'If I'd have
known there was so much to be done to get married I'd have thought twice
before I asked Vickie' – Still – that hasn't put me off by a mile – I'm still mad
to get married to you as soon as I get back. By 'mad' – I mean <u>keen</u>!*

It's often what Ron doesn't say that makes the most interesting news. The
period leading up to this latest letter was amongst the worst the squadron

endured since arriving at their new base. On 3 December, only four days after he arrived in North Africa and just after sharing the 'kill' Ron mentions, George Malan was himself shot down by an Fw 190. However, after the now familiar crash-landing he returned to Souk-el-Arba almost immediately, miraculously unscathed. It was a huge relief to Ron, who was convinced at the time that he'd lost his closest friend.

The engagement mentioned here resulted from the boss, who was leading a large formation, despatching Ron's three-man section to investigate possible ground targets; they were promptly bounced by enemy fighters. Meanwhile the remainder of the formation was set upon by American P-38 Lightnings – a blue-on-blue engagement that thankfully ended in a no-score draw. It wasn't the only time that the squadron would fall foul of their supposed allies. Oxspring would later produce a damning verdict on these Americans,

> pilots of the twin-engined, twin-tailed P-38s . . . experiencing their first war combats. Their aircraft recognition was suspect and . . . they just assumed that *any* single-engined, single-tailed fighter was hostile. Anxious to blood themselves, they homed in on friendly and enemy fighters alike, and we spent some anxious moments dodging their headlong attacks.[121]

Ron flew two sweeps on 5 December. The first proved uneventful but he had to return from the second with a rough-running engine. The formation he left behind was badly bounced and lost three pilots: Pilot Officer Macdonald, an Australian who'd joined the squadron at Biggin Hill, and two relatively inexperienced sergeants, Mottram and Browne. As so often happened in combat, no-one saw their demise. Another Pilot Officer, 'Lew' Lewis, was wounded in the same fracas. There's no mention of this in Ron's next letter, although it opens with a reference to the airfield being 'shot up again'. This was on 7 December, when he flew two sorties as 'Escort for 6 Bisleys'.[122] His log book entry for the first of these notes that he was 'Scared by 109G', while the second reads: 'Base shot up by 109s on our return!!' Two more narrow escapes!

---

121. Oxspring, op. cit., p.135.
122. An early armoured ground attack version of the Blenheim; production aircraft were renamed Blenheim Mk V.

9 December 1942:

I do miss you, Tubby dear – having just reminded you of that I'll give you all the latest news from the battlefront. We got shot up again but having learnt our lesson the first time we had our trenches to dive into & so escaped scatheless – even so my uniform again came off second best.

'The rains came' yesterday & I've never seen anything like it – the water just soaked everything – luckily I managed to get a battledress & gum boots & so my uniform has been saved at last. You'd never credit that so much mud could accumulate in so short a space of time. The only thing I can think of to compare it with is Passchendaele in the last war.

Yesterday I fell off the wing of a Spit & cut three fingers – so please excuse the writing as they are bandaged up pretty well now.

The rest of my kit arrived today so I rapidly got into my brown battledress. Ever since I've been thinking of the evening you sat and sewed all my buttons and wings on. The most common everyday things I do seem to bring back memories of you.

My diary has arrived with the rest of my kit so I can start keeping an account of my doings from now on. Actually my log book is pretty full of things that happened to us so I'll be able to give you a faithful record of our doings when I come back.

My 'Connie' has been nearly worked to death – it had to have an overhaul two days ago – with luck it will be OK tomorrow.

I don't know whether I've already told you but we think Tommy Wright has 'bought' it – I hope our information is incorrect because he was such a nice kid.[123]

As my camp kit is here I'll sleep in a bed tonight – the first time since I left England – bar once. It's nice having all our gear but it's a job to know what to do with it & I'd drop the lot for just one letter from you – the mail still hasn't caught up with us – I hope my letters are getting to you alright.

You remember I told you I met Dicky – well – it appears that he was shot down the other day & some Arab types came up to him – so, nothing daunted he brandished his revolver at them and said 'Pour les Anglais ou pour les Allemandes?' – Naturally they said 'Pour les Anglais' – they started to take him back to our side when some French types arrived & so Dicky went through the same procedure again – in the end he got back OK . . .

---

123. The rumour was true; P/O R.A. 'Tommy' Wright was killed in a Malta flying accident, 1 November 1942.

22 NOVEMBER 1942, SOUK-EL-ARBA, TUNISIA

For once the individual referred to here isn't Dicky Huband; it's Dicky Sharman, an ex-Bedford College schoolboy with whom Ron had become friendly during the early stages of training. At Brough he proved 'completely hopeless at some things'. Matters came to a head when he failed a navigation test and was sent to the CFI for a farewell interview prior to suspension. However, he somehow persuaded his interlocutor he was such 'a keen type' that he was worth another chance. After a lengthy interlude his colleagues were amazed to see Dicky return to their midst and, eventually, complete the Tiger Moth course successfully. Running into him again in Gibraltar, Ron was delighted to see that he was 'just the same slap-happy character' he'd been during their earlier friendship. He'd been flying reconnaissance Hurricanes when he was shot down and was later awarded the DFC.

13 December 1942:

I haven't been able to post the last letter I wrote you – it's still in my pocket – but I had to start another today – you see, I had a wonderful surprise this morning – some mail arrived and in it was a letter from you! It's marked 'No 8 letter' – so seven more are due to arrive at some time or other. I keep reading it over & over again.

Honestly, darl, it does really make all this messing about seem worthwhile. We're not having exactly a rest cure here and the conditions are far from being Biggin Hill-ish, but a letter from you saying you love me & are waiting for me to come back makes everything seem miles better & gives me much more heart to carry on.

Pete has joined George & I in our tent now – we argue & bind away to all hours of the night. We swipe tins of tea & sardines & sausages from odd people & then sit outside our tent and cook away at tea time – tonight we had quite a feed – the only snag being that we have to finish cooking by dusk as the light shows for a terrific way & we're not very keen on advertising our presence more than necessary.

We get lots of eggs & oranges here – Arab types bring them round & we haggle with them. The more or less stable price is 2½ francs per egg – but they'll try & get you to pay exorbitant prices if you're not careful. It's quite funny at times because if we don't want anything we tell them to '------ off' – or 'Go to Hell' – then a day or so later the same Arab will arrive and instead of saying 'B'jour monsieur' they just say '------ off' & smile sweetly – it makes us cackle no end . . .

241

I'm glad old Dicky's written to me, I won't write to him until I receive his letter – I've already written to him c/o you as I don't know his address . . .

I hope this letter goes off soon & gets to you in a hurry – then you'll know that your letters are reaching me. All I've put in my other letters is that 'No mail has reached us yet' – I hope that it hasn't disheartened you, dear. There's bound to be a delay at first. Even RAF officers back at civilisation ask us where "- - - - - -' is when we send back for replacements.

The other day the General[124] in charge of the army types who are doing the fighting in this region came to see us & say that the army appreciates all we're doing for them & 'would appreciate it a thousand times more if they were aware of the conditions under which you/we are operating'. At least it's a change for someone to say that we are actually some use. Quite a number of people are under the impression that we just fly when we feel like it – still – what's it matter. I've got your love – I don't give a damn for anything else . . .

It's now 7.50 pm – the three other types are all in bed asleep so I'd better not keep the old Hurricane lamp burning much longer . . .

16 December 1942:

We've reorganised our tent and now have a table as well as a lamp – so I can write in more or less comfort now.

On Monday [14 December] *I had to fly back to civilisation with a u/s a/c so I took two letters I'd written to you & one to Mum & got them sent off from there.*

I arrived fairly late in the afternoon & went to the officers' mess for lunch-cum-tea – I met a cook there who lives in Hornchurch & we had quite a yarn together about Ilford & Forest Gate – it was quite fun. He advised me not to sleep at this place – (we'll call it 'A' for short[125]) and so he took me to a little village about seven miles away to some French friends of his.

I had supper with the family – the old man was a great fat chap with a little wisp of a wife & two children (rather fat) of 13 & 14 – both girls. Everyone spoke at the same time to no one in particular – there was a terrific din at all times – I found my rusty French wasn't as bad as I thought – I could make myself understood most of the time although I expect my grammar was shocking.

---

124. Lieutenant General Kenneth Anderson CB MC, Commander British First Army during Operation TORCH.
125. Maison Blanche airfield, Algiers.

22 NOVEMBER 1942, SOUK-EL-ARBA, TUNISIA

By the way – the old chap owned a sort of cafe-hotel place. At night I slept in a wizard bed with <u>sheets</u>! That's a great luxury to anyone here.

In the morning M'sieur said he'd take us back to 'A' in his van at 6.30.

At 6 am I got up & had a black coffee & a roll – no one appears to eat breakfast at this place – & then waited to get into this van. However – before that could be organised I had to watch him fill innumerable bottles with wine, cut up half a pig – decide matters for the day with the family & at last he made a move for the van. This, however, was a false start. All the old boy did was to go & get a pig.

I swear it was the grandfather of all pigs – it was large, hairy and ferocious. When offering us a lift this French type forgot to tell us we'd be accompanied by this pig – all its feet were tied together & yet when we started off – this was at <u>8.15</u> am, the darn thing started ripping up the floorboards & behaving in a most awkward manner.

Three of us in the back wedged boxes of bottles & yet still the pig grunted & pushed about. At one time it pushed its snout over the front & the driver looked round & we nearly ended up in the ditch.

Honestly, darl – I've never had a ride like it – in the end we had to get up & leave the van & get a hitch hike to the aerodrome.

This might sound very trivial to you sweet – but I've made a lot of it because it's not the ordinary run of things with me. Actually I wasn't keen on flying to get the replacement but I found that it made quite a change & that, I'm told, is as good as a rest.

We're all het up at the moment – apparently someone heard Churchill's speech on the wireless recently in which he said there'd be no British troops in North Africa after March '43 – I hope he means we're all coming home then – although I fear that's wishful thinking . . .

Do you remember I had some photos taken at Ayr of myself – my crew & Jack Hilton standing on Connie's wing? Well, the chap who took them has discovered them. They're only small but they'll enlarge quite well. I'm sending you the above photo & also one of myself – Jack & Tommie – (in this letter) so will you let me know whether you receive them OK[126] . . .

By the way – George is very worried over what I might write to you – he thinks that you might tell Vickie & she'll worry like Hell – apparently he doesn't tell her anything at all – I know you'd rather I told you as much as possible because you'd worry twice as much if you were completely in the

---

126. These photographs, from Ron's scrapbook, are reproduced in *Fighters in the Blood*, op, cit., pp.74-5.

*dark. Anyway – darl – be careful what you tell Vickie – I think George is
making a mountain out of molehills but I said I'd let you know.*

*I've been posted to B Flight since yesterday – I bound a bit about it so
they let me take my aircraft (A/C) with me. I had to alter the 'H' to 'X' but
it's still got 'Connie' on it. It's the same A/C I flew from Gib – it's rather nice
on the controls and I hate to fly any other.*

*I had my scarf washed yesterday – it certainly needed it – I've not taken
it off – except to sleep sometimes – & wash – since I got to Gib. Even so, it's
as clean as ever it was – although we can't do any ironing out here.*

*I hear there's some mail arrived but it hasn't been sorted yet. I'll leave
this now & continue tonight – I may have more gen then.*
<u>*1 pm. 17th.*</u>

*Some wizard news, sweet. I've had a letter from you (the 7th) so I'm only 6
short now, one from Mum (her 4th) & one from Dicky. I'll write to Dicky later
on but in the meantime – do thank him for it. I feel as happy as a king with
all this mail – especially as I have two from you now. There's only one thing
I can't understand from your letter. You say you had a letter from <u>Betty</u> & she
sends her regards. The snag is the only Betty I can call to mind is Dicky's
friend and she doesn't know me. Will you give me further gen later on.*

*This morning as I was writing to you we had a wizard skylark overhead.
If you shut your eyes you could just imagine yourself lying in an English
field on a hot summer's day. He's started off again now – I think they've got
a grand whistle.*

Gee, Tubs – your letters are the nicest pick-me-up . . .

*Once again I'll have to leave this epistle as my efforts are required
elsewhere.*

*There's not much else of any import, things are much the same here –
we've got a news system organised though & a bulletin is posted outside the
adj's office every now & again & there's always a great queue of types to read
it. You've no idea how the little things tend to make life easier . . .*

The 'Betty' query towards the end here shows just how long mail took to
arrive. Dicky Huband's letter of 23 October, which would have confirmed
her identity, had yet to arrive.

While his own letter includes a great deal, once again there's a lot that Ron
omits – the reason for his move to B Flight and the story of his brief return 'to
civilisation' to mention but two newsworthy items. Why doesn't he say more?
The need to avoid adding to Connie's concerns is one possible reason. Another
is the letter's sheer length; it's already at eight pages. Then there's the high
level of squadron activity. It could well be that he simply didn't have the time.

His change of flights was a consequence of the previously mentioned departure of a flight commander and his replacement by David Cox – an internal adjustment to balance experience levels across the two flights. It's easy to understand why Ron omitted the machinations associated with what Jimmy Corbin described as a 'funny do'.

And it would have taken a number of pages to tell the full story of the delivery of a battle-damaged aircraft to Maison Blanche. All armament was removed to reduce weight and it had to be handled with considerable care. Some way into the transit to Algiers Ron spotted two US P-38s. As it happened he was on the same radio channel and became concerned when he heard an American say that he'd seen an Me 109. Defenceless and with a damaged main spar he was in no shape to engage the enemy, so he began weaving gently from side to side in an effort to identify the potential threat. As the P-38s continued to chat it became clear that their '109' was in fact his own slowly turning aircraft. He called them up and explained that what they'd identified as an enemy aircraft was actually a Spitfire; in fact he went further, showing the distinctive elliptical wings that should have been familiar to them. Eventually they acknowledged their mistake and left him to continue on his way. However, just before he arrived at Algiers the same two Lightnings reported another Me 109. Alert to the danger, Ron checked behind, only to see the pair closing on him. He immediately circled, revealing once again the unique Spitfire planform, pressed the transmit button and said: 'It's the same bloody Spitfire that you nearly shot down some miles back. Now bugger off!' They did, leaving him to carry out one of his more careful landings at Maison Blanche.

After his night in 'a wizard bed' (in reality a mass of straw in a loft, accessed by a rickety ladder) and abortive porcine commute, once he arrived back at the airfield next morning Ron set about arranging a replacement for his damaged aircraft. It proved more difficult than anticipated. After a lengthy wait he eventually managed to see the station adjutant and explain his mission. He was immediately whisked into the office of Group Captain Humphrey Edwardes-Jones,[127] OC No. 323 Wing, where he received notably short shrift. The Group Captain flatly refused to authorise him to take another aircraft back to Souk-el-Arba where, like so many others, it would 'only get shot up on the ground'. Somewhat incensed, and undaunted by the considerable rank gradient across the CO's desk, Ron made an impassioned

---

127. As a flight lieutenant test pilot serving with the Aircraft & Armament Establishment, Martlesham Heath, Edwardes-Jones was responsible for assessing the Spitfire prototype, K5054. His positive report led to an immediate order for 310 aircraft on 3 June 1935. Air Marshal Sir Humphrey Edwardes-Jones KCB CBE DFC AFC eventually retired in 1961.

plea: if only the squadrons there had more aircraft they'd stand less chance of being caught on the ground. But it was to no avail. He was ushered out with a curt dismissal: 'Now go away and be a good boy.'

What on earth do I do now? Distinctly 'brassed off', he naturally gravitated to the dispersal area. En route there he ran into a couple of Australian pilots who seemed equally displeased with their lot. They'd been marooned in Algiers for what seemed ages. No one knew what to do with them. There was no operational flying – in fact, they weren't getting any flying at all. As a result they were in a state of high Aussie dudgeon. This chance encounter gave Ron the glimmer of an idea. Taking his new-found friends with him, he ambled into the dispersal office and began chatting to the duty sergeant. Conveniently omitting to mention his earlier encounter with the station commander, he explained that he and his colleagues had come to pick up three aircraft for 72 Squadron. In no time at all the sergeant produced the required Spitfires. At this the threesome piled what little gear they had behind their seats and promptly departed for Souk-el-Arba. Knowing how badly the squadron needed the aircraft – pilots too for that matter – Ron had no qualms whatsoever about the deceit involved in their acquisition. Needless to say, his boss was delighted to receive such an unexpected bonus: three for the price of one!

Finally, the 'news system' Ron mentions towards the end of his lengthy missive was thanks mainly to the efforts of a young clerk destined for greater things. It all began when the CO first saw the bulletin in production. After 'listening to a full ten-minute radio broadcast of the overseas BBC news [the] airman turned round to a loaded typewriter and without a single error hammered out news sheets for distribution to various elements of the unit.'[128] So impressed was Oxspring by this demonstration of initiative and memory that he promptly redeployed the airman onto intelligence duties; here he completely transformed the production of operational records and combat reports. His abilities were such that he quickly earned the nickname, 'Reuter'. Eventually commissioned in the intelligence branch, Michael McCaul would go on to enjoy a long and distinguished career in the security and intelligence world, culminating in 1975 when he became a CMG (Companion of the Order of St Michael and St George).

That night, after sealing his latest letter ready for the censor's scrutiny, Ron slept fitfully. The base was bombed once again; this time it was 'too close for comfort'.

---

128. Oxspring, op. cit., p.150.

Chapter 29

31 January 1945, Newport, Monmouthshire

With Connie soon to produce her first child Ron takes every possible opportunity to escape from 'Bloody Newport', where doing 'nothing all day' has become a regular comment in his diary. An exception is the entry for 17 January, one that reveals the true extent of his frustrations: 'Tons of work on sport. Don't feel like it! Oh for a bowler!'

Most weekends are spent supervising gliding, while on weekdays he continues to journey far and wide, more often than not on gliding-related business. Towards the end of the month one such task provides an excuse, courtesy of devious routing, for a night at home with Connie – albeit at considerable risk, given the atrocious weather conditions: 'snow and ice!!' After this, and the weekend leave that follows, Ron's letters resume.

24 January 1945:

It's nearly 4 o'clock & this is the only chance I've had of writing to you. We managed to get back last night at 11.15 but I must say I wasn't too keen on the ride. We were about the only things moving – everything else had packed up for the day – still – we got back OK – so all's well.

I haven't had time to write much, darl, but I was terribly glad to get home & see you again . . .

31 January 1945:

At the present time it's thawing like mad here & also raining just for good measure. The roads are now little rivers. However – it's clearing the snow away – which is a blessing . . .

I'm sorry I had to rush off as I did on Monday but I really didn't have a lot of time. Actually I got to Paddington with five minutes to spare &

*managed to get a seat. We were an hour late but the train was quite warm &
so I slept most of the time . . .*

*We've got a meeting on here tonight so I've got to gen up on 'my part' so
I can't stay too long on this.*

*I had a grand time with you over the weekend, darl – the only snag is that
you made me want to stay at home the whole time . . .*

The new month begins with a plethora of sports meetings involving travel
backwards and forwards across much of South Wales. One particular visit,
on Sunday 11 February to RAF Fairwood Common, just west of Swansea,
brings an unexpected encounter that delights Ron. He hasn't seen Jimmy
Corbin, who regarded him as a 'great friend', since their time together at
Souk-el-Arba. It turns out that Corbin left the squadron in June 1943 on
posting to RAF Eshott in Northumberland. His dismay at another instructor
posting was tempered by serving on the gunnery flight as Squadron Leader
Bob Doe's second in command. [129] Indeed, it was 'a privilege . . . He was one
of the highest scoring aces of the Battle of Britain and a superb pilot.' [130] It's
just as well the job was to Corbin's liking because he was destined to remain
there until the end of the war.

As Connie's due date approaches, Ron contrives a few more days' leave;
first there's a long weekend, 15-18 February. Then he's back at Woodford again
on Thursday 22nd, just in time to see Connie give birth. At 10.30 that night, at
Kings Lea nursing home, just a few hundred yards along Kings Avenue from
Ferdie and Else's home, their first child weighs in at a healthy 7 lb 14 oz.

After staying with his parents until the Sunday, Ron returns to Wales and
'Nothing but ruddy sports – !!!! Feeling fed up!!' However, he returns almost
immediately for a couple of days, delighted to see Connie go from being
'not too fit' to 'looking better' before he has to return. The following week is
notable only for one of his regular appointments with an eye specialist; then
he's home once again for a long weekend. By now Connie is 'out of nursing
home – looking very well' and happily accompanying Ron on their first few
walks together as a family, the new addition well wrapped up in his pram.
Then, inevitably, it's 'Back to bloody Wales!'

During the next few months Ron's correspondence becomes increasingly
intermittent. Connie has her hands full, of course. Compensation comes by

---

129. Wing Commander R.F.T. Doe DSO DFC* retired with more than 14 confirmed 'kills' to
his credit.
130. Corbin, op. cit., p 218.

way of regular telephone calls and occasional brief visits. But these fleeting days with his family leave Ron more and more frustrated. His diary records numerous episodes of 'Feeling fed up' after going 'Back to ruddy N'port'. It doesn't help his demeanour that he also has to make time for regular appointments with a specialist about the fitting of his new eye.

19 March 1945:

I'm so glad I caught you all at home on Sunday – Mum & Dad certainly seemed pretty pleased with your effort. I can imagine old Father fussing round you . . .

The coat seems a great success, too – I'm anxious to see it & see just what I've bought you for a belated 21st birthday present . . .

I won't be able to write much today, sweet – as there's quite a bit to do. Re my putting my foot in it!

We had a sports meeting at 10.30 on Sat. at Wrexham, Soccer finals in the afternoon & Boxing Finals at night.

Owing to a spot of bother getting one of the armoured cars going we didn't arrive till 12.45 – to be greeted on the steps of the hotel with 'Bad show – should have been here' – This was repeated some six or seven times in public by some ATC S/Ldr – consequently, Harry as the senior Command Staff Officer, took umbrage. However – we saw some preliminaries of the boxing in the afternoon & then watched the soccer match – after which we started to go – having to get as far as possible before dark. As we left, this S/Ldr rushed up to me & <u>demanded</u> that I stay or else he'd put in an adverse report to Groupie. Consequently, I got a little peeved & told him what he could do with his report. He thereupon saw Harry & told him that I must stay. Harry more or less repeated what I said (only much neater – pukka barrister style) & we left.

However – the Control Board apparently told this S/Ldr to pipe down & not do anything – so there the matter rests at present. Harry is actually quite peeved at being treated like a little boy who's stolen the jam & is breathing fire. I think it will be as well for the S/Ldr if he just lies low.

As his regular visits to local as well as far flung ATC units continue, so does Ron's involvement in sports events, mainly boxing and soccer. When the weather allows, there's gliding too, of course. He flies the odd sortie himself, although not without incident. On Sunday 25 March the winch cable snapped shortly after launch. With the aircraft at only 200 feet, his instructor grabbed the controls and made a successful emergency landing. It was a mildly uncomfortable experience, certainly not the sort of thing he's prepared to mention to a wife who still tends to worry a great deal, particularly about his flying. Nor is it mentioned when he sees her next day, the first of two overnight stays fitted in around a meeting at the Air Ministry – a trip that concludes with the now familiar diary entry: 'Back to bloody Wales'. The following weekend he begins a period of ten days' leave that concludes with the inevitable entry, emphasised this time by an exclamation mark!

19 April 1945:

I'm a bit easier at work today – things have slacked off a shade. Hence the fact that I've got time to write to you. We've got a meeting on Saturday so things are rather hanging fire till then. I wrote to Mum this morning & thanked her for putting us up . . .

I wondered whether you'd notice that Tuck had got away – he almost messed up my day off at Gravesend the day he got shot down over Boulogne . . .

The reference here to Wing Commander Bob Stanford Tuck, one of the RAF's most respected and successful fighter pilots, warrants further explanation.

While based at Gravesend the 72 Squadron routine was for pilots to be given one day off a week, from 1 o'clock on one day until the same time the next. At 12.30 on 28 January 1942, Ron's scheduled day off, Tuck unexpectedly decided to carry out a sweep. Although he 'thought an awful lot of him', Ron was more than a little irritated to find himself part of his formation; it would delay his planned departure for London. They eventually 'took off and tore up and down the Channel, Bob Tuck demanding information from base as to what was happening.' Frustratingly, not least for Tuck himself, there was no sign whatsoever of any enemy activity. Wasting no time after landing, Ron headed straight for London to see Connie. On his return the next day he 'was staggered to hear that Bob Tuck, having got fed up with nothing happening on the sweep, had decided to do a rhubarb with another chap from Biggin Hill and he'd been shot down by flak over France.'

Like so many others, Tuck was forced to crash-land his damaged aircraft, in his case near Boulogne. He spent the next couple of years in Stalag Luft III where he was involved in planning the mass escape; however, he

250

was moved to a satellite camp before the breakout took place. Involved in escape planning once again at his new camp at Belaria, he finally absconded in company with a Polish airman on 1 February 1945. He then made his way through Poland until he met the advancing Soviet Army and eventually found his way to the British Embassy in Moscow. The story of his escape and arrival by ship at Southampton is the news to which Ron refers here.

25 April 1945:

I'll be leaving on Friday & won't be back till Sunday. I'll try & phone you later.

Kiss the wee fat man for me . . .

All my love to you, dear . . .–

Sorry I'm in such haste but I've got a lot to do today to prepare for the weekend.

The following day Ron notes in his diary: '2 years ago George killed in Tunisia.' The loss of his great friend is still fresh in his mind, the date permanently etched there. This entry represents a rare departure from the norm of 'sports meeting', 'gliding', 'boxing', 'played cards', played darts', 'to flicks' and the inevitable disparaging comment about Wales.

There's another welcome departure from the norm on 4 July. He returns home to take Connie and their young son to visit his parents at Broadstairs where they've acquired a boarding house. There they enjoy a short holiday with the odd 'beautiful day on the beach' and the family having a 'grand time'. In the middle of their time away, Ron's diary entry for Tuesday 8 May announces: 'VE DAY!! European War over!' Good news though it is, his comment merely serves to exacerbate the frustration he feels with RAF life. Increasingly, he longs to return to the civilian world and the job in London that awaits his return.

Up until this point the difficulties Ron encounters with depth perception have been limited to passing mention of the problems of driving in blackout and bad weather, problems that drivers with two good eyes had to confront too, of course. The first and only indication that he's making progress in this respect comes on 30 May, when he writes, 'Played darts. Getting much better.' One can only marvel at how he maintained an unblemished driving record over the years. That said, he'd be happy to admit that close-proximity parking was never his forte.

A relatively lengthy period of leave in early June, including another few days at Broadstairs, concludes with a predictable comment on 14 June:

'Return to Wales!! I <u>still</u> dislike it.' Concessions that life there could occasionally be tolerable are few and far between, and most often associated with gliding, notably on 27 June when he 'Did good circuit'. Then he's back on his travels – soon to receive some welcome news.

10 July 1945:

We had a very good time in Edinburgh. The North British Hotel is very nice indeed . . .

The Wing/Co is in all the afternoon & keeps popping in & out – so this may be a short letter.

I'm glad the wee man is still OK after his vaccination – I'll bet he's quite a size when I see him next. I'm longing to see you both again – it seems ages since I was last home.

I felt very homesick over the weekend – even though I had a grand time looking round Edinboro' – the match[131] was very good and ended in a draw 2-2.

11 July 1945:

It was very good of you to phone me last night – although I rather feel that you <u>had</u> to phone me or burst with excitement! Still – as long as I get the news I don't mind. It's pretty staggering really isn't it! It's almost too good to be true. I do hope that everything comes out OK because I know how much you must be banking on it (& <u>me</u>).

It sounds a lovely house – I'm very anxious to see it – but in any case you can carry on with any arrangements you like . . . I suppose you've already decided just where every piece of furniture's going – good old Tubby – I wish I could see your face – I'll bet it's all excited. Actually, I won't feel happy till I'm really in the place – once we've got a couple of things in it it's going to take a hell of a lot of moving to get us out!

Well – re Edinburgh – we left on Friday morning & arrived at Edinburgh at 10.10 at night. It was a long run but we had a carriage organised and played cards – slept – so the time went fairly quickly. The North British Hotel is a smashing place – I only wish you could have been there. I wandered round Princes St early Saturday morning – then we all met the Lord Provost

---

131. An 'ATC International Football Match', Scotland v Wales at Tynecastle Park, Saturday 7 July 1945.

who made an excellent speech, entertained us to a light lunch & then had us shown over the City Chambers – where we were given the book I've sent you. You'll notice the Lord Provost has autographed the front page of the book. It was a grand game of soccer in the afternoon . . . before a crowd of 14,000. The Scottish papers had lots about the match the following day. At night we went to see Harry Gordon[132] (I've sent the programme). On Sunday we went to Edinburgh Castle, the Forth Bridge – then the Zoo in the afternoon, by which time it was nearly 4 pm; so we had tea & left at 5.40 on Sunday night arriving here at 6.30 Monday morning. I was in bed again by 7 am & came into the office at 3 pm.

We're still gliding every night – although I'm off tonight as I'm due at a cocktail party in Cardiff with Wing/Co Devitt. It's a sort of farewell party for him as GB's back now & Devitt's going to AM again next week . . .

I'm longing to see the wee fat man again – I bet I'll notice a difference in him. Is he having any trouble with his arm, darl?

16 July 1945:

I reckon I've proved that saying 'Absence makes the heart grow fonder'! – I'm just longing for the time when I can come home and see you again.

This month is going terribly slowly, darl – it's a good job I'm kept busy. We really are working hard at the gliding site – every night from 6 pm - 10 – Saturday from 3 pm - 9 – Sunday 10 - 9 pm – so far the weather's been good to us but the weekend was dreadful – rain by the gallon!

I've just written to Peach telling her the furniture is being moved on Wednesday & asking her to have the furniture covered whilst being moved & also at the new address. I told her you'd tell her the new address – I don't know it.[133]

By the way, have you any idea how much Pickfords are charging for the removal? I haven't much odd cash in my account . . .

I'll bet I'll notice a terrific difference in our wee fat man when I see him again. I hope you don't get much bother with him when his arm begins to heal. I'm sorry I can't be with you while all this is going on – still – you're a pretty capable little wife, I reckon – I'm terribly proud of you sweet . . .

---

132. A popular Scottish comedian and impressionist.
133. 'Normanhurst', 20 Falmouth Avenue, Highams Park, London E4.

24 July 1945:

I love you. The time's gradually drawing to an end, when even the longest month must end & I'll be able to see you again. The RAF seem to be hurrying up with their demobbing according to the papers but Harry's still here although he's Group 7. He's had his medical though – so it won't be long. I expect things will get organised later & demobbing will become quicker. I'm longing for the time when I'm out the RAF for good. I think it'll be rather nice living with you & wee fat man forever.

There's no news – as usual – although the gliding is going very well so far. Percy & I are after a record number of launches for the month. We took 1,000 as our target & so far have done 884 – so we stand a good chance of doing more than the 1,000. We've managed to pass 6 cadets already as proficient in gliding. Old Harry's very pleased although he doesn't show it. If we do get the record there'll be a write up in the Argus & the ATC Gazette – so I'll send you copies on.

They did indeed set a Welsh ATC record: 1,123 launches. It was acknowledged, with an accompanying picture, in the *ATC Gazette*, October 1945, found amongst Ron's memorabilia.

This is the last substantive letter Connie retained. Piecing together subsequent events as the war eases to a close, for Ron it's more of the same: sports organisation (including athletics now, too), gliding, numerous related meetings and then, in the long evenings away from home, beer, darts, snooker and the cinema. He nevertheless takes every opportunity to get home and visit the couple's new flat. He sees it for the first time on 3 August, just two days before Graeme is christened. Then comes frustration. With decorators yet to finish the necessary refurbishment, a month later they still haven't moved in.

Thursday 20 September marks a major step in Ron's medical rehabilitation. His regular appointments with eye specialists have paved the way for the fitting of a new plastic eye at Uxbridge. He spends two days there undergoing a 'very tiring' procedure before being allowed home for the Sunday; consultations then continue for another two days before he eventually returns to Wales. No sooner does he arrive than he has to return to London, this time for a full medical examination.

On 3 October Ron receives the news he's long awaited, and indeed angled for: he can 'apply for posting' at last. Wasting no time whatsoever, he arranges to start work at London Command at the end of the month. His initial reactions to the move, recorded in his diary, say it all. On Monday 29 October, 'So far – so good'; then a day later, 'Little work – Home every night – Very nice'. Happiness is complete when, on 1 November, the couple finally move into their new home in Highams Park, not far from Ferdie and Else.

Ron's new job is remarkably similar to the one he's just left. It involves visiting ATC units, lecturing and attending events; but the difference in lifestyle is palpable. It feels as though he's at last living as a family man, becoming even closer to Connie – if that were possible – and watching their young son grow up. Life couldn't get much better. And with the end of the war, marked by the formal Japanese surrender on 2 September, he looks forward confidently to a return to civilian life, a return to the Ocean, early the following year.

Chapter 30

19 December 1942, Souk-el-Arba, Tunisia

19 December 1942:

I've had a wizard day today. I've again received letters from you & Mum. Yours was your ninth so up to now I've had 7, 8 & 9 from you, & the others have either gone for a burton or else they're on their way.

This won't be a very long letter because I've only just posted the 14th & 15th to you but I was so cheered up by getting some more mail that I just had to sit down and write to you again . . .

Your letters are such a tonic, sweet – I keep reading them over & over again.

By the way – I've got another Hun – an ME 109 – destroyed <u>definitely</u> – after a bit of a 'do' we both finished up at 0' & he ended up on the hillside. I'm as pleased as Punch over the affair & have duly recorded it for you in my diary. Don't worry about me, darl, – I'm honestly not taking any unnecessary risks.

The whole complement of our tent is at present answering letters like mad. We can send them off every day now but I don't know how long they'll be in reaching you – I hope that you've got at least half my letters by now . . .

A gramophone has arrived for us & believe it or not, they've also sent, among others, two Bings – 'Shepherd Serenade' & 'Do you care?' – needless to say they're both nearly worn out. Gee – the memories they bring back! . . .

P.S. George & Pete send their love.

Connie's diary reveals that she wrote that very same day, adding presciently 'I haven't heard lately & it worries me.' Ron's own letter, ironically one of the most upbeat he ever wrote, is to be his last for almost four weeks. Consistent with his efforts to avoid worrying his fiancée, his reference to 'a bit of a 'do'' vastly underplays the trauma of the previous day's events.

Ron and Chas Charnock were on the left side of a large formation turning right down-sun when they caught sight of more than twenty Me 109s and Fw 190s diving down to attack. Despite frantic calls as they broke up and left into the sun to negate their attackers' advantage, the remainder of the formation continued their turn, unaware of the threat. Meanwhile, they had to look after themselves. He saw Chas destroy a 190 (his seventh and penultimate success)[134] before suddenly finding himself in a spin. He'd mishandled the aircraft as it spiralled upwards and simply run out of airspeed. Realising that there was no point in trying to pull out and climb up again, *I'd be a dead duck on my own*, he continued spinning until as close to the ground as he dared. Then he set off for home as fast as he could manage.

Unfortunately, he'd been seen and found himself in company with three 109s. They were uncomfortably close behind, 'taking odd pot shots . . . every now and again' as he flew 'right down onto the deck . . . weaving in and out of valleys, frightening the life out of camels and odd bodies'. Not only was Ron in deep trouble, he was hampered by a misfiring engine (the cause later identified as a clogged fuel filter). He couldn't outrun the enemy fighters but he could still outturn them; each time one came within range and opened fire he simply turned hard into his pursuer. His tactics worked to the extent that he eventually managed to shoot down one of his attackers. At this another turned for home. The third, however, was 'a bit of a keen type' and continued to harass him until, some five miles from the airfield boundary, the arrival of another Spitfire finally persuaded him to give up the chase.

When Ron finally landed at Souk-el-Arba he was out of ammunition, had very little fuel remaining and was drenched in perspiration. Small wonder. The outcome of this exercise, the ultimate in terms of self-preservation, is summarised with admirable brevity, and indeed honesty. In his diary he wrote 'Felt rather scared!', while his log book entry for a 1 hour 40 minute sortie on 18 December reads: 'Sweep. Mateur . . . Bounced by 109Fs. Destroyed one 109F. 7 bullet holes in "Connie".' As usual, the underlining is in red and the entry concludes with the customary thickly-drawn swastika. It was his fifth confirmed 'kill'. But things might so easily have turned out differently. Just how close he'd come to being shot down himself can be

---

134. It's possible that this was in fact Charnock's eighth 'kill'. The citation for his DFM in April 1941 cites four 'kills' at a time when only three are recorded in Christopher Shores' and Clive Williams' seminal *Aces High* (Grub Street, London, 1994), p.172. It's notable that all Charnock's recorded successes are against enemy fighters.

judged by the fact that, after he climbed shakily from the cockpit, he found the aforementioned bullet holes neatly grouped in the fuselage, just behind the armour plating protecting his seat.

This sortie would also prove to be Chas Charnock's last with 72, although no one was aware at the time.[135] He'd simply failed to return. A hugely popular member of the squadron, there was unbounded delight when a message eventually arrived from the hospital at Bône that the squadron's 'lovable rogue' was safe.

With 'Connie' being repaired, Ron didn't fly the following day; nor was he scheduled to fly on 20 December either. Towards the end of that Sunday afternoon he was relaxing with others around their newly acquired gramophone. Listening, half dozing, to Vera Lynn singing 'Do I love you?' it felt almost like home. He'd rarely felt so relaxed or, if he were honest with himself, so homesick. Hearing such melodies once again reminded him not just of his fiancée, but of all the other things about England that he missed so much: family, friends and a way of life – albeit a way of life much changed from pre-war days.

He was jolted out of his reverie by his new flight commander, Derek Forde.[136] *Would he mind flying the evening airfield patrol for him? He didn't really feel in the mood.* With little else to occupy him, Ron welcomed the opportunity, although it was a regret that he couldn't take 'Connie'; his own aircraft was still being repaired after all the excitement of a couple of days ago. Without further ado he climbed into the allotted aircraft, 'RN-B', and took off with Sergeant Hussey to begin their patrol.

It wasn't long before his aircraft began acting strangely, as if it wanted 'to fly itself. [He'd] hold the stick steady only for the aircraft to fair bump up and down, like going on a roller-coaster. There was obviously something funny somewhere.' There was little option but to return to base, where he landed safely after some forty minutes. Reflecting on these events many years later he opined that, if he'd 'had any sense he'd have stayed down'. He didn't though. He took another aircraft, 'RN-R', and rejoined Hussey in the air. It would prove a fateful decision.

Some thirty-five minutes into this next sortie he received a report that a raid of more than twenty aircraft was inbound from Medjez-el-Bab, some forty miles due east. To Ron this was welcome news. It wasn't just the prospect of more action, he felt they had the advantage: high enough to

135. See introduction to Chapter 13 above.
136. See also Chapter 15 above.

deal with any enemy top cover and well positioned to effect a bounce on anything coming in lower. *Lo and behold, here they come!*

As the pair prepared to dive on the enemy formation, which was by now only about a dozen miles from Souk-el-Arba, Ron had an uncomfortable feeling. It all seemed far too easy. He was more than familiar with the Luftwaffe tactic of fighting in layers, the lower element acting as bait to lure unsuspecting attackers into the sights of those flying high above them. But try as he might, he could see no sign of any aircraft above them. Then, just as he and Hussey closed almost to within range of the enemy formation, Ron suddenly saw what he took to be an Me 109, but was in fact an Fw 190, at ground level; it was coming up underneath his number two, almost close enough to open fire. Immediately he called Hussey to break. Nothing happened. Despite another 'Break!' call, his number two continued straight ahead, focused entirely on his own attack.

At the time Ron could conclude only that Hussey didn't hear him. *Perhaps his R/T is U/S?* While this wasn't uncommon – it had happened to him a week earlier, prematurely curtailing a sweep – evidence that came to light many years after the event suggests that there may have been another factor. [137] It seems entirely possible that his companion was so intent on adding to his own score that he ignored Ron's call.[138] At the time, though, the reason mattered not. The 190 had opened fire; there were tell-tale flashes from his gun ports. Ron's only option was to pull across, meeting Hussey's attacker almost head on and giving him a quick burst of gunfire. He didn't rate his chances of downing him but it ought be enough to negate his attack, or so he thought. He'd no idea at the time, but he succeeded in distracting one of Germany's most celebrated aces,[139] inflicting minor damage on his aircraft too, because the next thing he knew . . . a crashing sound filled the cockpit. It was accompanied by an enormous thump. He'd no idea what happened. All he knew was pain. There was blood everywhere and he could see nothing out of his right eye . . .

---

137. See Owen Hardy and Jim Norton correspondence quoted towards the end of Chapter 7 above.
138. At the time it was one confirmed and one probable.
139. Oberleutnant (later Major) Erich Rudorffer, who was credited with at least 219 victories.

Chapter 31

30 May 1985, Frinton-on-Sea

It was one of those mornings that reminded him why he'd moved to the Essex coast on retirement: bright sunshine, a brilliant blue sky and the odd puffy white cloud scudding by in the breeze. But something was nagging at Ron's conscience, disturbing the equilibrium of his settled routine. Never one to rush into things – 'There's all tomorrow untouched yet' could have been the family motto – he knew that this particular task was one he couldn't put off much longer. And what better time to start than on his grandson's second birthday?

Shortly after my brother's son James was born, he mentioned that he'd like him to know more about his grandfather's wartime experiences. More than once he'd suggested that perhaps Father might put something down on paper, for the record as it were? Sitting in his favourite armchair, sipping the tea delivered by his devoted wife – still touchingly true to the promise in her letter of 11 October 1942, 'to wait on you & look after you & just make you the happiest person on earth' – Ron felt he could probably do better than that. Why not put something on tape? It would be much more personal.

The first step was to gather together all his memorabilia: his flying log book, the scrap book he'd manufactured from stiffened paper inside an old RAF binder, and plastic bags full of various other links with the past: photographs, letters, magazines, newspaper cuttings, and any number of documents. But this methodical preparation simply became a distraction and threatened to introduce further delay. Memories came flooding back – not least when he opened his log book to find a piece of folded white silk. It was from a parachute. Then there was more silk, this time in the shape of detailed maps of France and North Africa. He soon realised that if he weren't careful he'd end up wallowing in nostalgia, further delaying the task he'd now set himself. But where to start?

Sitting amidst this cornucopia of memories, he decided on a simple, chronological approach, guided mainly by the entries in his log book. First, though, he needed some form of script. It didn't have to be word for word – just a few points on which he could extemporise. With that, he found a pad of lined A4 paper and began making the odd note. Smiles regularly creased his tanned face, the by-product of a relaxed, seaside way of life, as his mind went back more than forty years: to people and places, music and memories long since forgotten. It soon dawned on him that the task he'd set himself was more difficult than he'd imagined. Perhaps, subconsciously, he'd had an inkling of this earlier; maybe that was why he'd procrastinated so long?

Leafing through his log book, Ron paused on the final entry. He sighed wistfully, a faraway look in his eye as he read the remarks against his forty-five-minute 'aerodrome patrol' on 20 December 1942: 'Shot down by 109G[140] (with Sgt Hussey – "Dolt!"). Credited with 109 – later. Here endeth my 'Ops' career!!!' As the comment in parentheses suggests and, as his colleagues would later learn, 'when he got shot down he blamed Hussey for it'.[141]

Turning the page, he came to where he'd summarised his brief flying life:

TOTAL HOURS (ALL AIRCRAFT)	541.50	
TOTAL HOURS SPITFIRE	393.05	
TOTAL HOURS OPERATIONAL	192.55	
TOTAL NO. OF SWEEPS	99	
RHUBARBS, SCRAMBLES, PATROLS, CONVOYS ETC	58	

TOTAL E/A	DESTROYED	$5\frac{1}{3}$ ($6\frac{1}{3}$ according to AM)[142]
	PROBABLES	1
	DAMAGED	3

---

140. It was actually an Fw 190 (see Chapter 30 above), a fact that came to light during the author's further research.
141. Corbin, op. cit., p.153.
142. There's no evidence of this additional Me 109 'kill' other than a log book note: 'Dec 20. Me 109F Destroyed. (I didn't make a claim but was credited by sqdn.)'. Luftwaffe records show the loss of only a single 109 that day, allegedly to anti-aircraft fire. It's the aircraft Sgt Hussey claims as his second victory. (Ron only damaged Rudorffer's Fw 190.) Since earlier German records suggest that Ron's first 'probable' was actually a 'kill' justice was arguably done in the end – if only in numerical terms.

How did it all begin? Checking that he had a fresh tape in his small Sony Walkman, he pressed the 'record' button. It locked into place and he began to speak:

> Hello John, this is about the longest letter or dictation that I shall make to you or to young James. It's something we've discussed on various occasions, and it's not supposed to be a line-shoot, but merely to give you and young James, in future years, some idea of what it was like in the early part of the war. This won't be full of exciting doings; there were long periods of complete boredom and you may find it boring to listen to half the time. But for what it's worth, here goes . . .

Although John listened to these tapes soon after they arrived, it wasn't until more than twenty years later that he finally began to transcribe them. As he did so he couldn't help but smile, marvelling at the easy fluency and droll sense of humour of the man he knew so well. Having finally completed a task that brought almost a shared sense of intimacy, he was left with a couple of regrets: first, that he'd waited so long before starting. And second, that his mother, the woman with whom Ron had shared his life, would never hear these tapes or read the transcript. A copy, comprising some sixty odd pages, is held by the Imperial War Museum and elements have since found their way into more than one book: *Fighters in the Blood,*[143] of course, and *Spitfire: A Very British Love Story.*[144] If the former sold Father a little short, the latter was too long on artistic licence for a son whose hope is that this volume provides a more fitting epitaph.

---

143. Robertson, op. cit.
144. John Nichol, *Spitfire: A Very British Love Story* (Simon & Schuster UK, 2018).

Epilogue

In a book that reveals fresh perspectives on Ron 'Robbie' Robertson's brief RAF career, inevitably there's much that will remain forever hidden. No matter that I now have a closer, more intimate understanding of my father than before, fleshing out his story has required an occasional element of informed conjecture.

Little is known of his early life, the late teens and early twenties that would have done so much to mould his character. That said, he seems to have enjoyed his first foray into the business world – enough, indeed, to return to it for the rest of his working life. The contrast with his wartime exploits, however, is stark. These were two entirely different environments, worlds apart.

There's no evidence either as to the roots of his sporting interests, although there may be a clue in what little is known of his own father, James Fair Robertson. An Edinburgh Scot born in 1875, he was said to have played football for Heart of Midlothian. The club's records suggest two possibilities: either he made a single appearance as a goalkeeper in 1906, or he was on the club's books in 1902 as a left back with no first team experience. Family folklore also has it that he was a Powderhall sprinter, but again it proved impossible to verify this.[145]

With nothing more known of Ron's heritage, it's often the insights revealed in letters from friends that make possible a more nuanced, more considered retrospective. But in a sense it's a picture that lacks clarity. The dearth of information from the final months of the war and immediately following his discharge is frustrating. It's impossible to know how it felt to cast off his uniform and adapt once again to the relatively mundane world of business.

---

145. A professional handicap, the format of the Powderhall Sprint, now known as the New Year Sprint, has remained unchanged since its first running in 1870.

So what more can be said about the father I thought I knew? If overcoming fear is the essence of courage, then he was unquestionably a brave man. He was undeniably fortunate, too, and seems to have entered into a pact with Lady Luck. If little of this comes as a surprise, the same is true of his appreciation of the arts – music, theatre, opera and ballet. But what is new is the intriguing possibility that this latter sensitivity might possibly be related to an early appetite for the ladies, something he blithely exposes in his initial correspondence. But again, it's impossible to know.

Another revelation is the nature of Ron's latter day emotional struggles. Initially he juggles priorities with ease, pursuing his flying ambitions while at the same time nurturing affection for a much younger girl. However, as their mutual attraction grows, he finds it difficult to strike the right balance. The key factor here is the wartime environment, captured perfectly by Brian Kingcome's recollections of the Battle of Britain:

> I remember a frenetic social life after we were stood down at dusk. All that youth and energy and adrenalin, so much living to do and so little time to do it in. When each night could be our last, we couldn't afford to waste it in sleep.[146]

Such sentiments help explain why Ron is prepared to sacrifice almost anything for the chance to spend just a few brief moments with Connie.

That he relishes the exhilaration, the romance, the sheer beauty of flying is also no surprise. Nor is the fact that he enjoys the thrill of combat, although 'enjoyed' may not be the right word to describe the sense of stimulation it provided. There is also the satisfaction of being able to measure progress, and indeed personal success – primarily in terms of day-to-day survival, but also evidenced in the swastikas inked into his log book. There are satisfying intangibles too: close personal friendships and the professional respect that is its own reward.

Such considerations bear on Ron's struggle to resolve the competing demands of duty and emotion. By the time the problem of reconciling his RAF responsibilities with his love for Connie comes to a head, it has already led to the odd incident that appears out of character until seen in context. Then, when he's finally forced to confront the prospect of lengthy enforced separation, his life comes perilously close to tilting out of balance.

---

146. Robertson, op. cit., p.16.

EPILOGUE

Ironically, deployment to North Africa restores a sense of equilibrium. Spartan living conditions and the constant threat of enemy attack – on the ground as well as in the air – leave little time for much else, even his hitherto prolific letter-writing. That all of this effectively comes to an end inside two months with his accident, is in many ways a blessing in disguise. It allows him to focus his one remaining eye entirely on his fiancée and bring forward their marriage on his return.

Destined to spend the rest of the war grounded, it's understandable that his enthusiasm for the RAF begins to wane. Separated from his new wife for much of the time, his frustration is compounded by a job that's tedious in the extreme. It's certainly not one he can throw his heart and soul into. His heart is with his wife in London, while soulless South Wales is his surrogate home. In such circumstances, the very occasional fractious moment during the early years of their marriage, hinted at in his letters, is no more than to be expected.

As to how he copes with his final days in the RAF and the transition back to civilian life, there's just the barest hint: through devotion to family life with his wife and young son it seems. He remained close to his parents too, the more so after his own father died in the early 1950s. While it's impossible to know whether his wartime experiences left a lasting legacy, what can be said with absolute certainty is that this extraordinarily relaxed individual ambled gently through the rest of his life letting absolutely nothing bother him.

Like all the best stories, this one has a happy ending. Although there was a great deal about Ron's time in the RAF that he loved, never for one moment did he regret leaving. Nor did he ever complain about the legacy of his time as a Spitfire pilot. He was philosophical about it, as his retrospective diary entry for 20 December 1942 suggests: 'Got shot down by 109G. Crash landed near Souk el Khemis. Bags of 109s about – lucky to come off as easily as I did.'

Happy in his own skin, he was more than content with his lot in life. After all, he'd survived experiences that sadly took the lives of all too many close friends and colleagues. Most of all, though, he was happily married to the woman he loved. The fifty-six years that he and Connie spent together, never again to be parted, were extraordinarily contented ones. Their loss was felt deeply by two sons who owed them so much. There's a sense of this in the tribute fixed to a wooden bench on the cliffs above the site of their Frinton beach hut. It reads: 'In memory of our beloved parents, Ron DFC & Con Robertson. To live in hearts we leave behind is not to die.'

Appendix

Logbook Extracts – R.J.H. Robertson

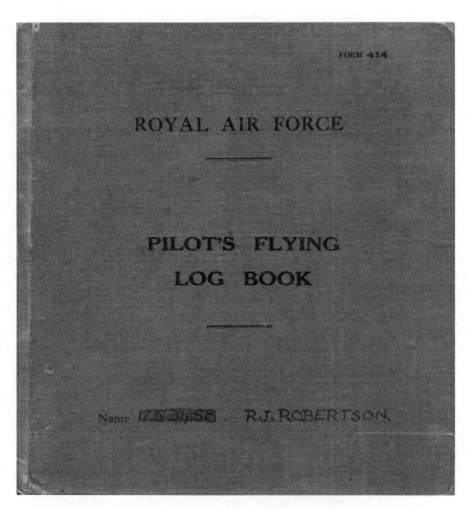

Robbie's flying logbook. He blacked out his original RAF number when it changed with his commissioning.

The award of Robbie's RAF flying badge came on 11 July 1941, when he'd flown just over 139 hours (see Chapter 10).

Robbie's logbook assessment on posting from 111 Sqn, November 1941 (see Chapters 14 and 22).

Pages recording Robbie's bale out on 14 March 1942 (see Chapters 16 and 18).

YEAR 1942		AIRCRAFT		PILOT, OR 1st PILOT	2ND PILOT, PUPIL OR PASSENGER	DUTY (INCLUDING RESULTS AND REMARKS)
Month	Date	Type	No			
						BIGGIN HILL (from 28.2.42)
						TOTALS BROUGHT FORWARD
MARCH	3	SPITFIRE	RN-I	SELF	—	To BIGGIN HILL
MARCH	3	SPITFIRE	RN-I	SELF	—	SWEEP GOSGOGNE
MARCH	6	SPITFIRE	RN-H	SELF	—	AEROBATICS
MARCH	8	SPITFIRE	RN-H	SELF	—	To BIGGIN HILL
MARCH	8	SPITFIRE	RN-H	SELF	—	SWEEP. ABBEVILLE
MARCH	9	SPITFIRE	RN-H	SELF	—	CONVOY. THAMES ESTUARY
MARCH	9	SPITFIRE	RN-H	SELF	—	To BIGGIN HILL
MARCH	13	SPITFIRE	RN-H	SELF	—	SWEEP. TARGET SUPPORT WING.
MARCH	14	SPITFIRE	RN-H	SELF	—	AIR TEST
MARCH	14	SPITFIRE	RN-H	SELF	—	To BIGGIN HILL
MARCH	14	SPITFIRE	RN-H	SELF	—	SWEEP LE HAVRE.
MARCH	23	SPITFIRE	RN-H	SELF	—	SWEEP
MARCH	24	SPITFIRE	RN-H	SELF	—	SWEEP. ESCORT COVER.
MARCH	26	SPITFIRE	RN-H	SELF	—	FORMATION
MARCH	27	SPITFIRE	RN-H	SELF	—	A/C TEST + AEROBATICS
MARCH	27	SPITFIRE	RN-H	SELF	—	PATROL. TENTERDEN
MARCH	28	SPITFIRE	RN-L	SELF	—	SWEEP.
MARCH	28	SPITFIRE	RN-H	SELF	—	SECTOR RECCO + WARNING.
MARCH	29	SPITFIRE	RN-R	SELF	—	SWEEP
MARCH	29	SPITFIRE	RN-H	SELF	—	SWEEP
MARCH	30	SPITFIRE	RN-H	SELF	—	FORMATION
					SUMMARY	MARCH 1942 SPITFIRE
					UNIT	72 SQDN.
					DATE	1.4.42
					SIGNATURE	R.J. Robertson

GRAND TOTAL [Cols. (1) to (10)] 317 Hrs. 45 Mins.

F/Lt. O.C. 'A' FLIGHT. O.C. 'A' FLIGHT. TOTALS CARRIED FORWARD

	SINGLE-ENGINE AIRCRAFT				MULTI-ENGINE AIRCRAFT						PASS-ENGER	INSTR/CLOUD FLYING [incl. in cols. (1) to (10)]	
	DAY		NIGHT		DAY		NIGHT						
	DUAL (1)	PILOT (2)	DUAL (3)	PILOT (4)	DUAL (5)	1st PILOT (6)	2nd PILOT (7)	DUAL (8)	1st PILOT (9)	2nd PILOT (10)	(11)	DUAL (1)	PILOT (2)
TOTALS BROUGHT FORWARD	55.55	179.10		1.45	37.25	45.30		3.05	5.10		10.05	7.55	1.30
		.15											
		1.10					Took off, other engine wouldn't start. Packed it up off Beachy Hd.				Same flak from Boulogne – well below us.	
		1.10											
		.20											
		1.15					Took 6 Bostons to bomb Abbeville. Saw no bomb drop, light flak, no e/a					
		1.10											
		1.40											
		1.20					To MAIDENHEAD – No e/a or FLAK.					
		.15											
		.15											
		1.25					Took 6 Bostons. Ger. Glycol 1433 on my back caught fire. Baled out.					
		1.35					Dunkirk – St. Omer – Hardelot. Nothing happened. Saw lots of e/a					
		1.25					6 Bostons to Abbeville. Saw many e/a – none attacked.					
		1.15					Whole squadron formation. London humming river.					
		1.05											
		.50					e/a reported in area.					
		1.35					Ostend. Saw e/a – not near enough to report.					
		1.35					Stooge for no e/a.					
		1.30					Dunkirk + Cadsand. Nothing seen.					
		1.40					St. Omer. Nothing seen.					
		1.00											
						MONTHLY TOTAL					22.45		
						OPS.					14.55		
						NON					7.50		
						TOTAL OPS HRS.					41.50		

OC 72 SQDN.

YEAR 1942		AIRCRAFT		PILOT, OR 1ST PILOT	2ND PILOT, PUPIL OR PASSENGER	DUTY (INCLUDING RESULTS AND REMARKS)														
MONTH	DATE	Type	No.																	
				—	—	TOTALS BROUGHT FORWARD														
APRIL	1	SPITFIRE	RN·G	SELF	—	DOG FIGHTING.														
APRIL	10	SPITFIRE	RN·I	SELF	"	To Southend.														
APRIL	10	SPITFIRE	RN·I	SELF	"	AIR FIRING. RETURN to BIGGIN														
APRIL	10	SPITFIRE	RN·I	SELF	"	SWEEP. ST.OMER. FLAK from GRAVELINES - TOO CLOSE!														
APRIL	11	SPITFIRE	RN·I	SELF	"	CONVOY - CANCELLED.														
APRIL	11	SPITFIRE	RN·I	SELF	"	SCRAMBLE. CHASED ALL OVER CHANNEL. SAW PLYMOUTH														
APRIL	12	SPITFIRE	RN·I	SELF	"	MACHINE GUN TEST. AIMED AT BOULOGNE. MORE I HIT IT.														
APRIL	12	SPITFIRE	RN·I	SELF	"	CONVOY PATROL off HARWICH														
APRIL	12	SPITFIRE	RN·I	SELF	"	SEARCH PATROL. LANDING FOR SOME CHAP IN CHANNEL.														
APRIL	13	SPITFIRE	RN·I	SELF	"	AIR TO GROUND FIRING.														
APRIL	13	SPITFIRE	RN·I	SELF	"	SWEEP. under Doting GRAVELINES - ARDRES - DUNKERQUE. NOTHING DOING.														
APRIL	14	SPITFIRE	RN·I	SELF	"	SWEEP? Boulogne - Gravelines. Got jumped near Dieppe. Squirted at FW 190 in Channel. My first squirt at a Hun!														
APRIL	14	SPITFIRE	RN·I	SELF	"	DETUNE - Biggin Hill.														
APRIL	16	SPITFIRE	RN·I	SELF	"	SWEEP Escort Cover to Hurribombers. MISSED HARROWBEATS - ST. NAZAIRE.														
APRIL	17	SPITFIRE	RN·I	SELF	"	SWEEP. LE TOUQUET - DUNKIRK. NOTHING DOING. SAW 109's. WASN'T PLAY.														
APRIL	17	SPITFIRE	RN·I	SELF	"	SWEEP. ESCORTED 6 BOSTONS TO CALAIS. FLAK BUT NO E/A														
APRIL	18	SPITFIRE	RN·I	SELF	"	SWEEP. ST. VALERY - CALAIS. VERY QUIET APART FROM FLAK.														
APRIL	19	SPITFIRE	RN·I	SELF	"	SWEEP. TO DIEPPE. NOTHING DOING.														
APRIL	22	SPITFIRE	RN·I	SELF	"	CINE GUN. BOULOGNE - CALAIS. NOTHING DOING.														
APRIL	24	SPITFIRE	RN·I	SELF	"	CONVOY . DOVER														
APRIL	24	SPITFIRE	RN·I	SELF	"	SWEEP. ST. OMER - DUNKIRK. GOT A FW 190													PROBABLE !! DELETED	
APRIL	26	SPITFIRE	RN·I	SELF	"	SWEEP. ESCORT 6 BOSTONS ST. OMER . SAW E/A - NOT ATTACKED														
APRIL	26	SPITFIRE	RN·E	SELF	"	SWEEP? ESCORT HURRIBOMBERS CALAIS. FAIRLY QUIET.														

GRAND TOTAL [Cols. (1) to (10)]   345 Hrs.   55 Mins.

TOTALS CARRIED FORWARD

The record of Robbie's first claim: a Fw 190 on 24 April 1942; the 'Confirmed' was later downgraded to a 'Probable' (see Chapter 18).

LOGBOOK EXTRACTS – R.J.H. ROBERTSON

Year 1942 Month / Date	Aircraft Type	No.	Pilot or 1st Pilot	2nd Pilot, Pupil or Passenger	Duty (Including Results and Remarks)
					TOTALS BROUGHT FORWARD
MAY 20	SPITFIRE	R.N.H	SELF	—	SCRAMBLE - DOG FIGHT
MAY 22	SPITFIRE	R.N.H	SELF	—	FORMATION
MAY 22	SPITFIRE	R.N.F	SELF	—	A/C TEST
MAY 23	SPITFIRE	R.N.H	SELF	—	SWEEP
MAY 24	SPITFIRE	R.N.H	SELF	—	CINE GUN
MAY 25	SPITFIRE	R.N.H	SELF	—	FORMATION
MAY 25	SPITFIRE	R.N.I	SELF	—	ANTI- RHUBARB
MAY 26	SPITFIRE	R.N.I	SELF	—	A/C TEST
MAY 27	SPITFIRE	R.N.H	SELF	—	SWEEP
MAY 30	SPITFIRE	R.N.H	SELF	—	LOCAL
MAY 30	SPITFIRE	R.N.H	SELF	—	SWEEP
MAY 30	SPITFIRE	R.N.H	SELF	—	SWEEP
MAY 31	SP/FIRE	R.N.H	SELF	—	SCRAMBLE
MAY 31	SPITFIRE	R.N.H	SELF	—	SWEEP. (5) TO DATE)

SUMMARY: MAY 1942
UNIT: 72 SQDN
DATE: 1. 6. 42.
SIGNATURE: R.J. Robertson

GRAND TOTAL (Cols. (1) to (10)) Hrs. 391. Mins. 50

31 May 1942 was a good day for Robbie: a 'Confirmed' Fw 190 and another 'Damaged' (see Chapter 20).

YEAR 1943 Month/Date	AIRCRAFT Type	No.	PILOT, OR 1st PILOT	2nd PILOT, PUPIL OR PASSENGER	DUTY (INCLUDING RESULTS AND REMARKS)	Single-Engine Day Dual	Pilot	Multi-Engine Day Remarks	1st Pilot	Pass Enger	Instr/Cloud Flying
					TOTALS BROUGHT FORWARD	25.55	34.45	45.37.25	45.30	10.05	7.35	1.30
JUNE 17	SPITFIRE	RN.H	SELF	—	SWEEP.		1.30	LE TOUQUET - CHANNEL - NOTHING DOING.	3.05	3.10	10.05	7.35	1.30
JUNE 18	SPITFIRE	RN.H	SELF	—	CINE GUN.		.40				
JUNE 19	SPITFIRE	RN.H	SELF	—	SWEEP		1.10	WITH TIMBER - "BREAK OPEN THEIR DOORS!"			
JUNE 19	SPITFIRE	RN.H	SELF	—	CHANNEL RECCO.		1.30	DIEPPE - LE TREPORT. DAMAGED TWO SMALL BOATS.			
JUNE 20	SPITFIRE	RN.H	SELF	—	CHANNEL PATROL		1.30	LE HAVRE. DAMAGED COASTER.			
JUNE 20	SPITFIRE	RN.H	SELF	—	SWEEP		1.20	CALAIS- OSTEND. DMGD + VERY ACCURATE FLAK. 0500 HRS!!			
JUNE 21	SPITFIRE	RN.H	SELF	—	CINE GUN		1.10	HARDELOT - ST. OMER. DAMAGED FW 190			
JUNE 21	SPITFIRE	RN.H	SELF	—	ANTI-RHUBARB		1.15	HASTINGS - DUNGENESS.			
JUNE 22	SPITFIRE	RN.H	SELF	—	TO MARTLESHAM		.25	FOR SQUADRON GUNNERY COURSE.			
JUNE 23	SPITFIRE	RN.H	SELF	—	AIR FIRING.		.25				
JUNE 23	SPITFIRE	RN.H	SELF	—	TO BRADWELL.		.35				
JUNE 24	SPITFIRE	RN.H	SELF	—	FROM BIGGIN		.35				
JUNE 25	SPITFIRE	RN.H	SELF	—	AIR FIRING		.25				
JUNE 25	SPITFIRE	RN.H	SELF	—	TO NORTH WEALD		.25				
JUNE 26	SPITFIRE	RN.H	SELF	—	FROM NORTH WEALD		.45				
JUNE 27	SPITFIRE	RN.H	SELF	—	TO NORTH WEALD		.20	WITH 'GEORGE' MALAN.			
JUNE 28	SPITFIRE	RN.H	SELF	—	FROM NORTH WEALD		.40	BEAT UP NORTH WEALD. LOST GUN PANEL - OUTER STBD.			
JUNE 29	SPITFIRE	RN.H	SELF	—	MARTLESHAM - BIGGIN		.30				
JUNE 29	SPITFIRE	RN.H	SELF	—	CONVOY.		.45	REMOVED - ROUGH ENGINE. NEARLY SHAKEN TO PIECES.			
JUNE 30	SPITFIRE	RN.H	SELF	—	TO LYMPNE.		.30				
JUNE 30	SPITFIRE	RN.H	SELF	—	PATROL. DUNGENESS.		.35				
	SUMMARY:- JUNIOR		SPITFIRE.					MONTHLY TOTAL	40.10	3.05	3.10	
					O.C. 'A' FLIGHT						
	GRAND TOTAL [Cols. (1) to (10)] 422 Hrs. 00 Mins.				TOTALS CARRIED FORWARD	25.65	36.10	45 37.25	45.30	10.05	7.35	1.30
								O.C. 72 Sqdn.	3.05	3.10		

'Timber' Woods would have been amused signing off this monthly summary. It included the attack on small boats that attracted the attention of the station commander, Gp Capt 'Dickie' Barwell (see Chapter 22).

Robbie's busy first few days in theatre included two 'kills': an Me 109 and a Ju 88 (see Chapter 28).

December 1942 proved a fateful month: a Fw 190 and Me 109 'Confirmed', then Robbie's final sortie. He was shot down by Oberleutnant Erich Rudorffer, a Luftwaffe *Experte* who went on to claim 224 aerial victories. Robbie did, however, manage to put a few bullet holes in the German's Fw 190 (see Chapter 30).

Abbreviations

AA	Ack-Ack, or anti-aircraft
A/C	Aircraft
AC2	Aircraftsman 2nd Class
ADC	Aide de Camp
AE	Air Efficiency Award
AFC	Air Force Cross
aka	also known as
AM	Air Ministry
AOC	Air Officer Commanding
APO	Army Post Office
ATC	Air Training Corps
ATS	Auxiliary Territorial Service
AVM	Air Vice-Marshal
BFW	Bayerische Flugzeugwerke
CBE	Commander of the Order of the British Empire
CCS	Casualty Clearing Station
CFI	Chief Flying Instructor
CinC	Commander-in-Chief
CMG	Commander of the Order of St Michael and St George
CO	Commanding Officer
c/o	Care of
CWT	Hundredweight (112 lbs or 8 stones)
DE	*Daily Express*

DFC	Distinguished Flying Cross
DFM	Distinguished Flying Medal
DIO	District Inspecting Officer
DL	Deputy Lieutenant
DSO	Distinguished Service Order
E/A	Enemy Aircraft
EFTS	Elementary Flying Training School
ENSA	Entertainments National Service Association
F/Cdr	Flight Commander
F/Lt	Flight Lieutenant
F/O	Flying Officer
F/Sgt	Flight Sergeant
Fw	Focke-Wulf
GC	Group Captain
GCB	Knight Grand Cross of the Order of the Bath
GCVO	Knight Grand Cross of the Royal Victorian Order
HMHS	His Majesty's Hospital Ship
HMS	His Majesty's Ship
HMT	Hired Military Transport
i/c	In charge of
IF	Instrument Flying
ITW	Initial Training Wing
JP	Justice of the Peace
Ju	Junkers
KG	Knight of the Garter
kia	Killed in action
LAC	Leading Aircraftsman
MC	Military Cross
Me	Messerschmitt
MM	Military Medal
MO	Medical Officer

ABBREVIATIONS

NBG	No Bloody Good
NCO	Non-Commissioned Officer
OC	Officer Commanding
OTU	Operational Training Unit
P/O	Pilot Officer
PR	Public Relations
PT	Physical Training
PUSC	Plaistow United Swimming Club
RAFVR	Royal Air Force Volunteer Reserve
RE	Corps of Royal Engineers
RMS	Royal Mail Ship
RNVR	Royal Navy Volunteer Reserve
R/T	Receive(r)/Transmit(ter)
SC	Swimming Club
SFTS	Service Flying Training School
Sgt	Sergeant
S/L	Squadron Leader
S/Ldr	Squadron Leader
Sub-Lt	Sub-Lieutenant
TD	Territorial Decoration
U/S	Unserviceable
U/T	Under Training
VC	Victoria Cross
VR	Volunteer Reserve
WAAF	Women's Auxiliary Air Force
W/Co	Wing Commander
WEF	With Effect From

Index